▶ Dedication

To Anne Wanja, my friend, companion, and wife of many years; and to our children, Nathan Mburu, Edi Mue, and Beti Wanjiru, for having put up with me all these years as I pursued my scholar's dream.

The Legal Advisor for Librarians, Educators, & Information Professionals

The Digital Librarian's Legal Handbook

John N. Gathegi

Neal-Schuman Publishers, Inc.
New York   London

> **The Legal Advisor for Librarians, Educators,
> & Information Professionals**
>
> No. 1—*The Complete Copyright Liability Handbook for Librarians and Educators*, by Tomas A. Lipinski
> No. 2—*Professional Liability Issues for Librarians and Information Professionals*, by Paul D. Healey
> No. 3—*The Digital Librarian's Legal Handbook*, by John N. Gathegi

Published by Neal-Schuman Publishers, Inc.
100 William St., Suite 2004
New York, NY 10038
http://www.neal-schuman.com

Copyright © 2012 Neal-Schuman Publishers, Inc.

All rights reserved. Reproduction of this book, in whole or in part, without written permission of the publisher, is prohibited.

Printed and bound in the United States of America.

The paper used in this publication meets the minimum requirements of American National Standard for Information Sciences—Permanence of Paper for Printed Library Materials, ANSI Z39.48-1992.

PLEASE READ THIS
This publication is designed to provide accurate and authoritative information in regard to the subject matter covered. It is sold with the understanding that the publisher is not engaged in rendering legal, accounting, or other professional service. If legal advice or other expert assistance is required, the services of a competent professional person should be sought." *From a Declaration of Principles adopted jointly by a Committee of the American Bar Association and a Committee of Publishers*

Library of Congress Cataloging-in-Publication Data

Gathegi, John Ng'ang'a.
  The digital librarian's legal handbook / John N. Gathegi.
    p. cm. — (The legal advisor for librarians, educators & information professionals ; no. 3)
  Includes bibliographical references and index.
  ISBN 978-1-55570-649-4 (alk. paper)
  1. Copyright—United States. 2. Digital libraries—United States. 3. Librarians—United States—Handbooks, manuals, etc. I. Title.

KF2995.G38 2012
346.7304'82—dc23

2011039126

Contents

Series Editor's Foreword   xi
   Tomas A. Lipinski
Preface   xiii

1 INTRODUCTION TO LEGAL ISSUES IN DIGITAL LIBRARIES   1

Introduction   1
Copyright   2
   How Do You Determine Whether Something Is Subject
      to Copyright Law?   2
   How Do You Determine Who Owns a Copyright?   3
   Can Copyright Ownership Be Transferred?   4
   What Are the Rights in Copyright?   4
   What Are the Limitations on These Rights?   5
Trademarks and Trademark Protection   6
Patents   8
Trade Secrets   9
Rights of Publicity and Privacy   9
Endnotes   10

2 WHAT ARE THE SPECIAL FEATURES OF DIGITAL LIBRARIES AND WHAT ARE SOME OF THE LEGAL IMPACTS OF THOSE FEATURES?   13

Dynamism and the Problem of Nonpermanence   13
The Complexity of Multimedia Content   15
   E-books   15
   Document Icons and Page Thumbnails   16
The Legal Complexities of Multiple, Heterogeneous Collections   18
   Internet   18
   Commercial Databases and Data Sets   19
   Collective Works and Compilations   20
   Different Goals   21
Legal Issues in Open Access/Closed Access   22
   Open Access Initiatives: Issues   22

Creative Commons	23
Closed Access	24
Endnotes	24

3 WHO ARE CONTENT OWNERS? 27

Initial Ownership	28
Single Author	28
Joint Authors	28
Work for Hire	30
Collective Works	31
Ownership in Derivative Works	31
Government Works	32
Other Claimants	33
Copyright Transfers	34
Recovering Damages and Profits	34
Endnotes	36

4 WHAT RIGHTS DO CONTENT OWNERS HAVE AND WHAT ARE THE LIMITATIONS TO THOSE RIGHTS? 39

Right of Reproduction	39
Right to Make Derivative Works	41
Right of Distribution	42
Right of Performance	43
Right to Display	44
Visual Art	44
Limitations on Rights	46
First-Sale Doctrine	46
Fair Use	48
Section 108	49
Endnotes	54

5 HOW LONG DO THE RIGHTS LAST? 57

Post-1978 Works	57
Preexisting Works	59
Termination of Transfers and Licenses for Pre-1978 Works	61

Effect of Termination ... 62
Formalities and Their Effect on Duration of Copyright ... 63
    Restoration of Lost Rights Due to Formalities ... 64
Expiration of Copyrights ... 66
Endnotes ... 67

6 HOW ARE RIGHTS ACQUIRED FROM OWNERS? ... 69

Transfer of Copyright ... 69
Termination of Rights in Transfers and Licenses Granted after January 1, 1978 ... 72
Reacquisition of Rights and Licenses by Reversion ... 74
Endnotes ... 75

7 WHAT SHOULD YOU KNOW ABOUT DIGITAL MEDIA LICENSES? ... 79

Introduction ... 79
Need to Interact with Multiple Parties ... 80
Examining the License ... 81
    New Uses and Geographical Considerations ... 82
    Alteration or Modification of Content ... 83
Compulsory Licenses for Copyrighted Music ... 84
Endnotes ... 86

8 WHAT IS INFRINGEMENT AND WHAT ARE THE RESULTS OF INFRINGEMENT? ... 87

Infringement ... 87
    Contributory Infringement ... 89
    Vicarious Infringement ... 89
Not Infringement ... 90
    Fair Use ... 90
    Library and Archives Reproduction ... 92
    Performance and Display for Teaching and Instruction ... 93
    Computer Programs ... 95
Other Noninfringing Activities ... 96
Action for Infringement ... 96
Remedies for Infringement ... 96
    Injunctions ... 96
    Impound and Disposition ... 97

Damages for Infringement	97
Civil	97
Criminal	98
Endnotes	100

9 WHAT SHOULD YOU BE AWARE OF IN DIGITAL RIGHTS MANAGEMENT SYSTEMS? — 103

Introduction	103
Violations of the DMCA	104
Exemptions for Libraries and Similar Institutions	105
Reverse Engineering Exemptions	105
Encryption Research Exemption	106
Privacy Exemption	107
Security Testing Exemption	107
Analog Devices Compliance	107
DMCA Challenges	109
Fair Use and the DMCA	110
Endnotes	111

10 WHAT ARE SERVICE PROVIDERS AND WHAT IS THE SERVICE PROVIDER SAFE HARBOR? — 113

Introduction	113
Service Providers	114
Designated Agent Requirement	114
Transitory Transmissions	115
Intermediate Storage	116
Preaccess Conditions and Removal of Infringing Material	117
Innocent Service Provider	118
Linking Exemption	118
Nonprofit Educational Institutions	119
Takedown or Disable Liability and Counternotifications	120
Identifying Infringers	121
Injunctions to Service Providers	122
Conclusion	122
Endnotes	123

11 WHAT ARE COPYRIGHT ROYALTIES? — 125

Introduction — 125
Compulsory License Royalties and Copyright Royalty Judges — 126
Former Copyright Arbitration Panels — 129
Copyright Clearance Center — 131
Conclusion — 132
Endnotes — 132

12 WHAT IS PROPRIETARY AND PRIVATE INFORMATION? — 135

Proprietary Information — 135
    Trade Secrets versus Proprietary Information — 135
Proprietary Search Engines — 137
    Meta Tags — 138
Privacy — 138
Evaluating Data Providers — 141
Endnotes — 142

13 INTERNATIONAL ASPECTS OF COPYRIGHT — 145

Introduction — 145
The Berne Convention — 146
WIPO Copyright Treaty — 150
Universal Copyright Convention — 152
Agreement on Trade-Related Aspects of Intellectual Property Rights (TRIPS) — 153
Conclusion — 155
Endnotes — 155

APPENDIXES

Appendix 1: Notices of Termination of Transfers and Licenses (Code of Federal Regulations) — 161
Appendix 2: Exemption to Prohibition Against Circumvention (Code of Federal Regulations) — 167
Appendix 3: Quick-Reference Compilation of Notable Points from Each Chapter — 169
Appendix 4: Quick-Reference Compilation of Compliance Checklists — 191

Appendix 5: Resources for Finding Copyright Owners and Clearances   195
Appendix 6: Suggested Analyses for Hypothetical Questions
            from Each Chapter   197

Index   207
About the Author   223

Series Editor's Foreword

I recall first meeting John N. Gathegi at an American Society for Information Science and Technology (ASIS&T) conference a number of years ago. We had been e-mailing for some time before the annual meeting but had never spoken face-to-face and so decided to meet one evening in the hotel lobby with the thought of going out for dinner that or another night. We had a vague idea of what each other looked like (as photographs available on the web are often limiting). We were both in the atrium of the conference hotel talking with other people, standing about three or four feet away from each other. We turned toward each other, realizing that we had actually been standing next to each other for some time and, lo and behold, we finally met. The circumstances of our meeting are an appropriate analogy through which to introduce to the reader this, the third book in our series on legal issues confronting libraries, because legal issues involving digital content in libraries are a bit like that. One can prepare for the issues—just as we had prepared for our meeting—but often not recognize the variety of problems until one is standing next to the matter or in the midst of a project.

The intersection of media-rich collections and accessible content in libraries has increased much over the past decade. Libraries increasingly acquire digital content as well as convert existing content to that format. Legal issues related to digital library collections and services are likely to persist not only in the library school classroom as a topic of discussion but in the field as an issue of practice. This book serves then as a preparatory as well as a preemptory work. John Gathegi has done a fine job surveying the legal issues, primarily copyright, related to digital content in libraries. The work produced is a sound overview and easy-to-read introduction to the issues, including recent and relevant case law. Some discussion of the intricacies of copyright ownership, transfer, termination, and restoration are included as well throughout several chapters. An introduction to licensing is included in Chapter 7. Lingering issues regarding the Digital Millennium Copyright Act (DMCA) are covered in Chapters 9 and 10. An overview of international issues concludes the discussion. Several useful appendixes are included. Chapters contain useful summary points and application examples.

This book is the third in a series on a range of legal topics in libraries: *The Legal Advisor for Librarians, Educators, & Information Professionals*. (The first book in the series is Tomas Lipinski's *Complete Copyright Liability Handbook for Librarians and Educators* and the second is Paul Healey's *Professional Liability Issues for Librarians and Information Professionals*.) While the number of legal titles published in the library and information science (LIS) area is proliferating, numerous areas are still underdeveloped, resulting in an imbalance among topics. In addition, the titles are somewhat discordant in style. Furthermore, some still lack the sound legal scholarship that is desired by the series editor and publisher and, in this way, the series serves to push the discussion of legal issues in LIS into the next level or generation of not only scholarly but, it is hoped, practitioner inquiry.

Practitioners in the library or information center in both the private and public sectors and including those serving schools, archives, manuscript and special collections, and, to a lesser extent, museum collections as well should find this monograph and others in the series useful. This book, like others in the series, can be viewed as a "what" and as a "how" book: *what* is the law and *how* does it affect us and *how* do we comply with it and use the law where we can to our advantage? Other administrators within the organization will also find this book and others in the series useful, from chief information officers to network and computing managers to distance and other education coordinators and even general counsels. Like others in the series, this could also be used in support of library school and related curriculums such as collection development or management, for example, as well as serving as a textbook in library law or possibly information policy and ethics-related courses.

Each monograph in the series follows a similar pattern: presentation of the law and its application through discussion of the law and examples specific to library (in its varied iterations), archive, or educational circumstances; case studies (question-and-answer or other format) and bullet-point summaries conclude each substantive chapter; appendixes include compliance or practice tools such as checklists, audits, model policy, or other sample language, such as signage or notices where appropriate, etc. The goal of the series is to provide practical, readable information drawn from sound legal analysis on a variety of specific legal topics. Each title is based on sound legal scholarship written by leading experts in the field and offers practitioners a useful tool for compliance. As a result, this monograph accomplishes two additional goals: it serves as a tool for creating a compliant environment within your library and its broader institutional context and, as a result, can help create a "law-aware" environment within your organization—and thus it also functions as a risk-management device.

Future topics in the series include licensing, use of public library spaces, gifts, privacy, and confidentiality. The series editor and publisher are committed to including only the highest quality contributions to the series from authors who have strong research foundations as well as experience in both law and libraries or related information settings. We hope you enjoy and, moreover, find useful our efforts. We welcome your feedback as well as your ideas for new additions to the series.

Tomas A. Lipinski, JD, LLM, PhD
Professor and Executive Associate Dean
Indiana University, School of Library and Information Science
Indiana University–Purdue University, Indianapolis

Preface

Digital libraries and intellectual property issues are intrinsically intertwined. Indeed, it would not be an overstatement to say that copyright, a branch of intellectual property law, is one of the most important challenges facing digital libraries. Understanding the intricacies involved is perhaps even more complex than the technical construction and maintenance of digital content. *The Digital Librarian's Legal Handbook* explores the intellectual property challenges in digital content, with a focus on copyright law issues. It is designed to provide the digital librarian with a clear understanding of copyright law and how it affects the management of digital content, providing a guide for avoiding many of the legal pitfalls that abound in this area and providing answers to the most frequently encountered legal questions in digital libraries.

The Digital Librarian's Legal Handbook discusses the various characteristics of digital libraries and collections, such as dynamism and multimedia content, as it weaves intellectual property issues through those concepts. It discusses the importance of determining content ownership, demonstrating that this is often quite a complicated process, especially where copyrights have been transferred. Even though copyright formalities such as registration, notice, and renewals are no longer required, the book discusses why these are still relevant when managing digital content. Termination of rights in copyright transfers and licenses and the effect of that termination on copyright ownership are also described.

Among the surprises the reader will encounter in this book is a little-known fact about the power of the Librarian of Congress to appoint copyright royalty judges, including the chief copyright royalty judge.

ORGANIZATION

The content of *The Digital Librarian's Legal Handbook* is arranged so that, after the first chapter, one need not read it sequentially but may refer to parts of interest under any of the other chapters. Chapter 1 begins with a general review of intellectual property issues, including the main intellectual property tools: copyright, patents, trademarks, trade secrets, and right of publicity. It discusses the specific tools applicable to digital collections and why they are applicable.

Chapter 2 introduces the specific features of digital collections that impact, or are impacted by, various intellectual property issues, such as the dynamism of digital content and the complexity of multimedia content. The chapter also discusses preservation and access issues in digital collections, as well as the legal issues involved in open and closed access.

Chapter 3 examines the details of content legal ownership, providing the reader with a road map on how to determine the ownership of content for various purposes, including seeking permission to use copyright-protected works. It is emphasized here that authorship is not synonymous with copyright ownership, and that copyright ownership can sometimes change hands many times by transfer, making the task of seeking copyright permission difficult. As well, there may be other copyright ownership claimants created by operation of law, such as a divorced spouse claiming a partial interest in a copyright.

The specific rights granted by copyright are analyzed in Chapter 4, which also discusses the legal limitations to copyright designed to provide the incentive–creativity balance. In this chapter, the reader finds that while the "First Sale" doctrine seems increasingly irrelevant in the digital world, debate has started to rage on whether there is, or should be, a "Digital First Sale" doctrine. Fair use and the library and archives exception to the copyright exclusive rights are also discussed in this chapter.

Chapter 5 is an analysis of the duration of the rights provided by copyright, including a discussion of the restoration of rights that had been lost due to compliance with the formalities previously required.

Chapter 6 discusses the acquisition of rights, including those rights acquired by copyright transfers. It is important to remember that copyrights are divisible, and that the copyright owner may transfer all or just some of the exclusive rights. The chapter also discusses the termination of copyright transfers and licenses and the reversion of those rights to the grantor or lawful successors.

Chapter 7 takes a closer look at digital media licenses, continuing the discussion about the need for interaction with multiple parties that began in Chapter 2 and looking at some of the clauses likely to be included in licenses that could have an impact on how digital media is used and exploited. The chapter also discusses the need to interact with multiple parties when seeking a license, especially for multimedia content.

Chapter 8 takes the reader into the infringement arena, an area that is the background of concern throughout the book. Here, the chapter examines what infringement is, including the various exemptions from infringement claims that copyright law provides. This chapter also discusses actions for infringement, including remedies and damages provided by law.

Chapter 9 examines digital rights management within the context of the Digital Millennium Copyright Act (1998) and discusses the various exemptions for violation claims provided for under the act. In the digital world, Internet service providers can include many institutions, including libraries.

Chapter 10 discusses the safe harbor provided for service providers whose systems are used by third parties in infringing activities. The chapter examines the various requirements for eligibility of protection under this safe harbor and discusses notifications and takedown requirements for infringing material.

Because digital content managers may find themselves involved in paying royalties to content owners, Chapter 11 discusses the royalty system under the Copyright Act and demonstrates the extraordinary powers provided the Librarian of Congress in the royalty litigation system.

Chapter 12 briefly looks at other proprietary information, including proprietary search engines and trademarks. Also examined here is the notion of privacy in the digital context.

The handbook concludes with Chapter 13's examination of the international aspects of copyright, and discussing the various international treaties to which the United States is a party, including the Berne Convention for the Protection of Literary and Artistic Works, the World Intellectual Property Organization (WIPO) Copyright Treaty, and the Agreement on Trade-Related Aspects of Intellectual Property Rights (TRIPS).

NOTABLE POINTS AND CHECKLISTS

Throughout the book, Notable Points and Checklists sidebars are provided to enhance the reader's understanding of the material. Notable Points and Checklists are numbered and pulled together as appendixes at the end of the book, so that the reader has one ready-reference place to locate them without going through each page in the book. A hypothetical question appears at the end of each chapter that pulls some of the most salient points from that chapter into a real-world example. Suggested responses to the hypothetical questions are provided at the end of the book in Appendix 6.

RESULTS

The reader should come out with a very detailed understanding of how copyright law maps onto the management of digital content. A good digital librarian has no choice but to be conversant with intellectual property aspects of digital content. Failure to do this will lead to the possibility of legal exposure for infringement actions. The goal of *The Digital Librarian's Legal Handbook* is to help the digital librarian gain awareness of potential problems and thus avoid such exposure.

1
INTRODUCTION TO LEGAL ISSUES IN DIGITAL LIBRARIES

IN THIS CHAPTER

We begin with a general review of intellectual property issues and the main intellectual property tools applicable to digital collections:
- Copyright
- Trademarks and trademark protection
- Patents
- Trade secrets
- Rights of publicity and privacy

INTRODUCTION

Digital libraries are essentially collections of organized informational items in digital format that can be accessed utilizing a computer.[1] Digital libraries and collections are ubiquitous in our current information age. With growing computing power and expanding storage technology, it was only a matter of time before digital libraries took center stage in our professional and social lives. All manner of collections have had to deal with intellectual property issues, especially the issue of copyright. Digital collections, because of their special characteristics, raise even more challenges when it comes to intellectual property considerations.

We begin this introduction with a brief review of intellectual property, assuming the reader has had some preliminary exposure to this subject. Intellectual property covers a wide range of branches that include copyright, trademarks, trade secrets, and patents. Other areas covered that may or may not be relevant to the present discussion include the right of publicity. However, because of the complexity of digital collections, one or more branches of intellectual property may apply. We examine the details of some of these intellectual property applications in the chapters that follow.

COPYRIGHT

Copyright is anchored in two major theories: the economic right or economic protection theory and the moral rights argument. The *economic right theory* argues that creativity in society is a good thing. But to stimulate that creativity, the creators need incentives. Such incentives may include providing limited monopolies with an economic value, such that the author may sell or otherwise dispose of his or her creation for monetary or other value. The *moral rights argument* is more prevalent in Europe than it is in the United States. This theory asserts there is an intangible relationship between an author and that author's creation. This relationship remains even after the sale of the physical embodiment of the creation.

In the United States, copyright is derived from the constitutional clause that grants U.S. Congress the power to "promote the progress of science and other useful arts."[2] In exchange for authors sharing their genius with society, Congress is authorized to reward such persons (including legal entities) with a limited monopoly. Congress implemented this power through the passage of the Copyright Act. Among the exclusive rights granted to authors are the rights to reproduce their work, to prepare derivative works, to distribute copies of their copyrighted works, to perform and display works publicly, and to digitally transmit sound recordings.[3] These exclusive rights are tempered by limitations that allow others to lawfully trample on those rights, as long as they do so within the confines of fair use. Whether others have adhered to fair use is a case-by-case determination that takes into account the nature of the use, the amount of material used, and purpose of the reuse.[4] Copyright law thus differentiates lawful appropriation of information from unlawful misappropriation.

This book focuses primarily on the copyright aspect of intellectual property rights in digital collections, yet other aspects such as trademarks and trade secrets are also important in digital collections. Although some of the following topics are considered in much more detail in subsequent chapters, we briefly consider here some of the more frequently encountered questions in copyright.

How Do You Determine Whether Something Is Subject to Copyright Law?

The first question a digital librarian will probably ask is whether a work is subject to copyright law. At first blush this might appear to be a straightforward question, but it is not. While section 101 of Title 17 of the U.S. Code defines what matters are subject to copyright,[5] one would need to reference other sections to determine whether a work subject to copyright is indeed still protected by copyright and, if so, when this protection might expire. Publication dates, for example, are essential.

Generally speaking, pre-1923 works are likely to be out of copyright. From 1923 to 1963, works received copyright protection of 28 years duration, renewable for 47 years (now 67 years). If not renewed, the work passed into the public domain. After 1976, works were automatically covered on creation, and no renewal of copyright is required. Given these dates, Lavoie, Connaway, and Dempsey have calculated that approximately between 72 and 90 percent of the combined Google 5 collection would be subject to copyright protection.[6] However, digital library experts have acknowledged that it really is difficult to know how much is under copyright (and how much of that is orphan) versus how much is in the public domain.[7] However, that has not stopped efforts at trying.[8] Regardless of the dates issue, some libraries might have a privilege under section 108 to digitize copyrighted works.[9] We discuss copyright duration in more detail in Chapter 5.

Notable Points 1: Material Not Subject to Copyright[10]

Following are examples of works not subject to copyright; applications for registration of such works cannot be entertained:

(a) Words and short phrases such as names, titles, and slogans; familiar symbols or designs; mere variations of typographic ornamentation, lettering, or coloring; mere listing of ingredients or contents;

(b) Ideas, plans, methods, systems, or devices, as distinguished from the particular manner in which they are expressed or described in a writing;

(c) Blank forms, such as time cards, graph paper, account books, diaries, bank checks, scorecards, address books, report forms, order forms, and the like, which are designed for recording information and do not in themselves convey information;

(d) Works consisting entirely of information that is common property containing no original authorship, such as, for example, standard calendars, height and weight charts, tape measures and rulers, schedules of sporting events, and lists or tables taken from public documents or other common sources;

(e) Typeface as typeface.

How Do You Determine Who Owns a Copyright?

If there is no section 108 privilege, the digital librarian might want to know the owner of a copyright for the purpose of seeking permission or licensing the work for inclusion in a digital library.

Initial ownership of the copyright in a work is conferred to the author.[11] If there is more than one author of a work, the authors co-own the copyright of the joint work.[12]

Where an employer or someone else has contracted someone to prepare a work, however, the employer or this other person would be considered the author under section 201, subsection (b) of the code, and would own all the rights in the copyright, absent a written and signed agreement to the contrary.[13]

Collective works present a special situation, because in addition to the copyright of the work as a whole, which may be owned by another entity, each individual contribution to the work has its own copyright protection that initially is vested to the author of that contribution.[14] The copyright owner in the collective work has reproduction and distribution rights only as part of that particular collective work, or its revisions, as well as other collective works in the same series that may come later.[15] We discuss copyright ownership in more detail in Chapter 3.

Can Copyright Ownership Be Transferred?

Knowing who had the initial ownership of copyright is only half the quest. Like other property, copyright ownership may be transferred in whole or in part by conveyance, operation of law, or by intestate succession, and the new owner of an exclusive right has the same protections and remedies as did the original copyright owner.[16] Copyright ownership is not subject to involuntary transfer by government action except as provided under Title 11.[17] We discuss copyright transfers and acquisitions in more detail in Chapters 5 and 6. We also discuss licensing in Chapter 7.

What Are the Rights in Copyright?

As we indicated, copyright provides the owner of a work with a bundle of rights that are exclusive to the owner: the right of reproduction of the copyrighted work; the right of preparing derivate works; the right of distribution of the copyrighted work; the right of public performance in the case of literary, musical, dramatic, sound recordings (including by means of digital audio transmission), and choreographed works; and the right of public display of such works.[18] In addition, under the Visual Artists Rights Act and subject to the fair use per the discussion that follows, authors of works of visual art have the so-called rights of attribution and integrity.[19] These include the right to claim authorship of a work, to prevent the use of their names as authors of a work they did not create, and to prevent the use of their names on a work that has been so modified or mutilated such that it would be prejudicial to their reputations. This does not include mutilation or distortion that is merely the result of the passage of time or nature of the material.

The rights of attribution and integrity are not transferable and can be waived in a written instrument that specifies the identity of the work and the use to which the waiver applies. A waiver by one author of a jointly authored work waives the right for all authors.[20] Rights of attribution and integrity are distinct from copyright ownership, and transfer of copyright does not extinguish the rights, absent a written agreement.[21] Likewise, waiver of the rights does not constitute transfer of ownership of a copy of the work, or copyright ownership in the work. In Chapter 8, we discuss what constitutes infringement of copyright.

What Are the Limitations on These Rights?

These rights are limited in very important ways. Section 107, for instance, codifies the judicial doctrine of fair use defense to copyright infringement.[22] Use of a copyrighted work, including reproduction for such purposes as research, scholarship, criticism, teaching, comment, or news reporting, is not considered infringement. Fair use is determined by consideration of four factors: the purpose or character of use, especially whether the use is for nonprofit, educational purposes or is of a commercial nature; the nature of the copyrighted work; how much and how substantial the portion used in relation to the work as a whole; and the effect of this use on the potential market value of the copyrighted work. The fair use defense applies regardless of whether a work is unpublished.[23]

Notable Points 2: Copyright Protection

- Copyright protects original expression that has been fixed in a tangible medium.
- Copyright is covered under federal law, but some states also have copyright laws. State laws are preempted by federal law in this area.
- Copyright protection is automatic; no registration is required.
- Copyright protection has limited duration.
- Copyright does not protect ideas or facts.
- Copyright can be transferred.
- There are some limitations on copyright, such as fair use.
- Duration:
  - Individual author: Life of author plus 70 years
  - Joint authors: Life of the surviving author plus 70 years
  - Corporate work: The earlier of 95 years after publication or 120 years since creation

Also, libraries and archives and their employees working within the scope of their employment may, under section 108, reproduce and distribute a copy of a work, provided (1) this is not done for commercial purposes, (2) the library's collections are open to the public or researchers, and (3) a notice that the work is or may be copyrighted is included in the reproduced or distributed work.[24] Rights under this section are more fully discussed in Chapter 9.

Owners of a particular copy may also sell or otherwise dispose of their lawfully made copy without the copyright owner's permission, but in the case of works subject to restored copyright can only do so within a 12-month window.[25] This right does not extend to the rental, lease, or loan of a computer program for purposes of direct or indirect commercial advantage.[26]

> **☑ Checklist 1: Baseline Questions**
>
> ❑ Is the digital work subject to copyright law?
> ❑ Who "owns" the copyright?
> ❑ What are the available rights?
> ❑ What, if any, are the limitations on these rights?

Certain performances and displays are also exempt from copyright infringement if they occur as teaching activities of a nonprofit educational institution. This exemption does not apply to works that are "produced or marketed primarily for performance or display as part of mediated instructional activities transmitted via digital networks" or to copies that are not legally made.[27]

We now move to a different but related area of intellectual property protection in digital collections and content. We discuss rights of content owners and the limitations to those rights in Chapter 4.

TRADEMARKS AND TRADEMARK PROTECTION

Trademarks originated in the need to identify makers of goods.[28] A trademark identifies the source of goods and builds goodwill for that maker. Over time, users of those particular goods may come to associate that particular mark with a certain quality and may come to rely on that mark as an indicator of such quality. Owners of digital collections may want to have the collection associated with them for the purposes of advertising or a statement of quality. The trademark reduces costs of information by making it easy for consumers to identify both the source and quality of a product. Trademarks in the United States are protected by the Lanham Act of 1946[29] as well as by state and common law. The Lanham Act defines trademarks to include words, names, symbols, or devices that serve to identify goods or products in commerce.[30] One good reason why trademarks are important in digital collections is that, unlike in copyright, there is no requirement for originality for protection.[31] A content owner can have a trademark in the collection, even though other aspects of intellectual property belong to another party.

Not all trademarks can be legally protected, and not all to the same degree. Protection and degree of protection will depend on the mark's "strength." An arbitrary name or phrase is strongest, while those names or phrases suggestive of a product, descriptive of a product, or simply generic are successively weaker.[32] Trademarks, however, can move from being arbitrary to being generic by their very success (e.g., Kleenex) and would be subject to cancellation if it is determined that the mark has become generic for the class of goods or services for which it is registered; likewise, it could be canceled if it is found to have been abandoned or to comprise any matter that, as a whole, is functional.[33]

Not all words or phrases are initially protectable or registrable as trademarks. The courts have traditionally recognized four categories for potential trademarks: (1) generic, (2) descriptive, (3) suggestive, or (4) arbitrary or fanciful.[34]

The generic category refers to "the name of a particular genus or class of which an individual article or service is but a member"[35] or connotes the "basic nature of articles or services."[36] Trademark protection is not available for generic terms.[37]

The descriptive category, on the other hand, "identifies a characteristic or quality of an article or service."[38] The Lanham Act does not ordinarily provide trademarks to descriptive terms, although they may acquire secondary meaning in the consuming public's mind and thereby gain protection.[39] One court has observed that generic and descriptive terms are distinguishable only in terms of degree.[40] A descriptive term can achieve the status of a protected mark; a generic term cannot.[41] Descriptive terms are also subject to a fair use defense, where the term is used in its descriptive sense rather than its trademark sense,[42] to prevent trademark registrants from exclusively appropriating a descriptive term. This is not the same "fair use" found in copyright.

The court in Soweco defined a trademark in the suggestive category as suggesting, rather than describing, "some particular characteristic of the goods or services to which it applies and requires the consumer to exercise the imagination in order to draw a conclusion as to the nature of the goods and services."[43] An example of a suggestive trademark is Coppertone, a brand of tanning and sunscreen products. Arbitrary or fanciful marks, on the other hand, "bear no relationship to the products or services to which they are applied."[44]

In digital collections, the reader is more likely to encounter *service marks*, which under the Lanham Act are defined similarly to trademarks and are afforded similar protections.[45] A less commonly used term in discussions of intellectual property is *trade names*, which are not protected by the Lanham Act but may be protected under common law.[46]

The digital librarian may also encounter *certification marks*, which essentially offer a guarantee of authenticity and "may be registered without proof of secondary meaning, but must be made available in a nondiscriminatory fashion to anyone who complies with the terms of the certification."[47]

> **Notable Points 3: Trademark Protection**
>
> - No originality requirement is needed for trademark protection.
> - Trademarks are protected by federal, state, and common law.
> - A digital content owner can have a trademark in collection even when another party has intellectual property rights in other aspects of the collection.
> - Degree of trademark protection will depend on the mark's strength, with arbitrary and fanciful marks receiving the strongest protection.
> - Over time, marks can move from arbitrary to generic.
> - Check your digital content or system does not violate others' trademark.
> - Duration: Not limited. A trademark is valid as long as it is commercially used and as long as the mark does not become generic.

PATENTS

Most intellectual property discussions concerning information content do not include the issues of patents. In this book, we try to point out, whenever we can, patent implications of digital collections and libraries (e.g., patents in search engines). In summary, a patent is a government-granted monopoly given to an inventor for a limited period in exchange for sharing knowledge about his or her invention with society. To be protected by a patent, the invention, discovery, or process must be new, useful, and nonobvious. A patent is issued under federal law and gives the inventor the right to exclude others from the use of that invention. If the patent has joint owners, each owner can independently license the invention. Like copyright, patents are rooted in article I of the U.S.

> **Notable Points 4: Patent Protection**
>
> - Patents protect novel, useful, and nonobvious inventions.
> - Patents exclude others from using the invention without the patent holder's authorization.
> - Patents are issued under federal law.
> - Duration:
>   - Utility: 20 years from the date of filing
>   - Design: 14 years from the date of issue

Constitution and are anchored in the same theory of incentives to creators by the use of a limited monopoly, after which the creations are supposed to pass on to the public domain. A cautionary note in relation to trademarks: just because a patent has expired does not mean trademark protection is automatically ended.

TRADE SECRETS

Although not generally considered one of the "big three" in the intellectual property arena, *trade secrets* are an essential part of digital collections and, as we shall see, may increasingly assume an important role when discussing "digital markings" and authentication of digital collections. Trade secrets are valuable because they are kept secret; they have no value once they are generally known. Unlike copyright and patents, trade secrets are a creature of state law. Also, unlike copyrights and patents, the period of protection is not limited. As long as a trade secret is kept secret, it will be protected. However, information that can be reverse engineered to reveal a trade secret is not protected. None of the other intellectual property regimes requires of the right owner an effort to maintain secrecy. Thus, a trade secret and a patent cannot both protect the same invention, because the former demands secrecy while the latter demands disclosure.[48] Trade secrets are further discussed in Chapter 12.

> **Notable Points 5: Trade Secret Protection**
> - Trade secrets are valuable because they are not generally known.
> - Trade secrets are protected under state law.
> - Trade secrets derived from reverse engineering are not protected.
> - Duration: Not limited. Protection may be perpetual, as long as the trade secret remains a secret.

RIGHTS OF PUBLICITY AND PRIVACY

Generally, the use of a person's identity, either by photo, voice, or name for commercial benefit (e.g., in advertising) requires written consent. These so-called rights of publicity originate from state and common law. For digital content managers, it is important to realize that the identity of deceased persons is protected in some states and may be enforced by the individual's estate. Privacy in the context of digital content is an issue that we take up in Chapter 12.

> **HYPOTHETICAL #1**
>
> Mr. Digital Librarian has just signed a license to embed the Super Intelligent Search Engine (SISE) into the library website. It is touted as so intelligent that it anticipates the direction of the research as the user types in a search. Mr. Librarian is so excited about his new toy that he makes a presentation before 500 of his colleagues at a conference and invites them to check it out for one week, providing a password that will allow them to look at the technical insides of the search engine as well as make copies of the technical specifications and user-guide documents. What issues should Mr. Digital Librarian have taken into account?
>
> *A suggested response to this hypothetical question can be found in Appendix 6.*

ENDNOTES

1. Oren Bracha, *Standing Copyright Law on Its Head? The Googlization of Everything and the Many Faces of Property*, 85 TEXAS LAW REVIEW, 1799–1869 (2007).
2. U.S. Const., art. I § 1, cl. 8.
3. 17 U.S.C. § 106 (2006).
4. 17 U.S.C. § 107 (2006).
5. *Id.*
6. Brian Lavoie, Lynn S. Connaway, and Lorcan Dempsey, *Anatomy of Aggregate Collections: The Example of Google Print for Libraries*, 11(9) D-LIB MAGAZINE (2005), http://www.dlib.org/dlib/september05/lavoie/09lavoie.html.
7. John P. Wilkin, *Bibliographic Indeterminancy and the Scale of Problems and Opportunities of "Rights" in Digital Collection Building* (February 2011), http://www.diglib.org/publications/reports/ruminations_1/.
8. Brian Lavoie and Lorcan Dempsey, *Beyond 1923: Characteristics of Potentially In-Copyright Print Books in Library Collections*, 15(11/12) D-LIB MAGAZINE (2009), http://www.dlib.org/dlib/november09/lavoie/11lavoie.html; Lorcan Dempsey, *Libraries and the Long Tail*, 12(4) D-LIB MAGAZINE (2006), http://www.dlib.org/dlib/april06/dempsey/04dempsey.html; Michael Cairns, *580,388 Orphan Works—Give or Take* (September 9, 2009), http://personanondata.blogspot.com/2009/09/580388-orphan-works-give-or-take.html; CONSTANCE MALPAS, CLOUD-SOURCING RESEARCH COLLECTIONS: MANAGING PRINT IN MASS-DIGITIZED LIBRARY ENVIRONMENT (Dublin, OH: OCLC, 2011), available at http://section108.gov/.
9. 17 U.S.C. § 108 (2006).
10. 37 C.F.R. 202.1.
11. 17 U.S.C. § 201 (2006).
12. 17 U.S.C. § 201 (a) (2006).
13. 17 U.S.C. § 201 (b) (2006).

14. 17 U.S.C. § 201 (c) (2006).
15. 17 U.S.C. § 201 (d) (2006).
16. *Id.*
17. 11 U.S.C. § 101 (2006).
18. 17 U.S.C. § 106 (2006).
19. 17 U.S.C. § 106A (2006).
20. 17 U.S.C. § 106A (e)(1) (2006).
21. 17 U.S.C. § 106A (e)(2) (2006).
22. 17 U.S.C. § 107 (2006).
23. *Id.*
24. 17 U.S.C. § 108 (2006).
25. 17 U.S.C. § 109 (a) (2006).
26. 17 U.S.C. § 109 (2006).
27. 17 U.S.C. § 110 (2006).
28. WILLIAM BROWNE, A TREATISE ON THE LAW OF TRADEMARKS, 1–14 (Boston: Little, Brown, 1885).
29. 15 U.S.C. § 1051 et seq. (2006).
30. 15 U.S.C. § 1127 (2006).
31. Trade Mark Cases, 100 U.S. 82, 94 (1879).
32. Vision Center v. Opticks, Inc., 596 F.2d 111 (5th Cir. 1980).
33. 15 U.S.C. § 1064 (3) (2006).
34. *Vision Center*, 596 F.2d 111.
35. *Id.* at 115.
36. American Heritage Life Insurance Co. v. Heritage Life Insurance Co., 494 F.2d 3, 10–11 (5th Cir. 1974).
37. William R. Warner & Co. v. Eli Lilly & Co., 265 U.S. 526, 528 (1924).
38. *Vision Center*, 596 F.2d, at 115.
39. 15 U.S.C. § 1052 (e-f).
40. Soweco, Inc. v. Shell Oil Co., 617 F.2d 1178, 1184 (5th Cir. 1980).
41. Vision Center, 596 F.2d, at 115 n.11.
42. *Soweco, Inc.*, 617 F.2d, at 1185.
43. *Id.* at 1184.
44. Abercrombie & Fitch Co. v. Hunting World, Inc., 537 F.2d 4, 9 (2d Cir. 1976).
45. Murphy v. Provident Mutual Life Ins. Co., 923 F.2d. 923, 927 (2d Cir. 1990).
46. Anti-Defamation League of B'nai B'rith v. National Mexican American Anti-Defamation Comm., Inc., 510 F.2d 1246, 1247 (D.C. Cir. 1975).
47. Community of Roquefort v. William Faehndrich, Inc., 303 F.2d 494 (2d Cir. 1962).
48. ROGER D. BLAIR and THOMAS F. COTTER, INTELLECTUAL PROPERTY: ECONOMIC AND LEGAL DIMENSIONS OF RIGHTS AND REMEDIES (Cambridge: Cambridge Univ. Pr., 2005).

2

WHAT ARE THE SPECIAL FEATURES OF DIGITAL LIBRARIES AND WHAT ARE SOME OF THE LEGAL IMPACTS OF THOSE FEATURES?

IN THIS CHAPTER

We examine the specific features of digital collections that impact, or are impacted by, various intellectual property issues as well as preservation, access, and associated legal issues:
- Dynamism and nonpermanence of digital content
- Complexity of multimedia content
- Legal complexities of multiple, heterogeneous collections
- Legal issues in open and closed access

DYNAMISM AND THE PROBLEM OF NONPERMANENCE

Unlike their print counterparts, digital libraries have some unique features that present challenges in both development and management, especially from a legal perspective. In this chapter, we examine three such features. Digital libraries and collections (1) are dynamic, (2) may suffer issues of nonpermanence, and (3) may have more than one media format.

Early ancestors of digital libraries were simply text material converted into a digital format but still contained in a physical container, such as magnetic tapes, CDs, and DVDs. With the development of digital networks and the concomitant transcending of space, digital libraries have come a long way.[1] Digital libraries and collections are dynamic. Items are constantly being added, and corrections and modifications are made to specific files and databases as the need arises. This means a file accessed today may not be identical to the file with the same name that was accessed yesterday. A pressing question then has been how to preserve digital collections and how to vouch for their integrity.

> **Notable Points 6: Dynamism of Digital Content**
> - Digital content is dynamic.
> - Technology changes in format, data definition, and metadata content can threaten the accessibility of digital content.
> - Migration of data may infringe on the exclusive right of reproduction.
> - Structural and data elements rearrangement may infringe on the exclusive right to make derivative copies.

Preservation efforts are fraught with legal problems. Chief among these is how to ensure copyright noninfringement, not just by unauthorized exercise of the authors' exclusive rights but also by determining which parts of the content are protected by copyright, especially where availability to content is provided and agreement with copyright holders is desired. A persistent question is whether the digital librarian still has the necessary rights in the collection. Also, issues of privacy and confidentiality may be raised by the dynamism and nonpermanence of digital collections, as may ethical issues in health and personal data.[2]

Despite perceptions to the contrary, "Digital information is in fact fragile and at risk."[3] Changes in technology can render some digital files corrupt and unreadable. The longer the time frame required for future access, the more the uncertainty with information preservation. Challenges include changes in format, data definitions, and metadata content.[4] The format problem is exacerbated by the fact that many formats are proprietary and continue to evolve into more complex versions with newer features and functions, sometimes "orphaning" earlier versions.[5] Legal access problems can occur when a proprietary owner contractually limits access or goes out of business.[6]

One way of handling format changes in digital preservation is migration of data, both in terms of software and hardware. This will sometimes involve rearranging structural and data elements sequence.[7] Two copyright problems arise. First, the act of migration usually will involve copying the information, which may be an infringement of the author's exclusive reproduction right. Also, the rearrangement of the structural and data elements may trigger the trampling of another right: the author's exclusive right to make derivative copies. Unless the privilege afforded to libraries and archives by section 108 (discussed in Chapter 4) applies, permission to migrate may have to be sought from the copyright holder. Other issues include whether a file conversion would be a violation of

> **Checklist 2: Follow-Up Baseline Questions**
> - ☐ What content is protected by copyright?
> - ☐ Does the digital librarian have all the necessary rights?
> - ☐ Are there privacy and confidentiality issues?

the Digital Millennium Copyright Act (discussed later in this chapter) and whether, for evidentiary purposes, a migrated file is the same as the original file.

THE COMPLEXITY OF MULTIMEDIA CONTENT

As well as being dynamic and raising the problem of nonpermanency, digital collections also may contain a mixture of different media formats, including text, sound, graphics, video, and a variety of other file formats.

E-books

Good examples of multimedia digital collections are electronic books, or e-books. An e-book could have, for example, an article about a country, a video about parts of the country, and a sound file of examples of music from the country.

Although e-books are usually found in proprietary devices, some may also be accessible through a central server. An owner of an e-book collection has many of the same concerns that a publisher of any other digital content has in terms of the susceptibility of the content to be easily copied. Digital rights management technology (discussed in more detail in Chapter 9) is used to control access to e-book content that is copyright-protected, to preserve the copyright owner's exclusive rights. There are, however, e-books available free of copyright protection that a digital collection librarian can link to from the digital library.[8] Aggregators of e-books, such as NetLibrary (a division of OCLC), provide access to a digital library's e-content on a 24/7 basis by negotiating intellectual property rights with publishers to provide access to content hosted on their servers. Aggregators usually provide their own digital rights management technology, thus easing legal issues for the digital librarian.[9]

"Stocking" e-books in a digital library requires that the digital librarian understand the access limitations that come with the digital rights management as well as the different pricing models. These models can range from outright purchases (much like print versions) to limited time and number of persons per access; they may also come with use restrictions that define practices such as printing, downloads, and amount of content that can be accessed. The models are constantly being tweaked. In early 2011, HarperCollins, a major e-book publisher, instituted a limit on e-book circulations for libraries. It imposed a requirement that new titles would circulate only 26 times, after which the license would expire.[10] This led to protests and boycotts by libraries, consumers, and authors; an ongoing petition, which can be found at Change.org, requests that HarperCollins reverse this decision.[11]

Legal issues in this area are complicated by the fact that some media formats are covered by rules specific to the media (e.g., sound files). Also, conversion of media from one format to another may cause copyright infringement (e.g., conversion of text into audio formats). More so than text works, dates on which a sound recording was first fixed determine the nature of the legal protection available. No federal copyright protection was available for sound recordings prior to February 15, 1972, but Public Law 92-140, the Sound Recording Amendment Act of 1971, rectified the situation by providing federal copyright protection to works recorded or fixed after that date.[12] Pre-1972 works, however, may be protected by state criminal law statutes or common law until February 15, 2067, against unfair competition or misappropriation.[13] June M. Besek provides an exhaustive guide on dealing with copyright issues for pre-1972 sound recordings for the purposes of digital preservation and dissemination.[14]

> **Notable Points 7: E-books as Example of Multimedia Collection**
>
> ▶ E-books are a good example of multimedia digital collections.
> ▶ Publishers use digital rights management (DRM) technology to control access to e-book content.
> ▶ Some non-copyright-protected e-books are available to digital libraries.
> ▶ E-book aggregators provide access to digital library content on their servers by negotiating rights with publishers.
> ▶ Access to digital content is subject to DRM technology and different pricing models.

Document Icons and Page Thumbnails

Other newer versions of familiar formats, such as document icons and page thumbnails, present new legal issues.

Document icons are small visual representations of documents.[15] Icons can include information about a document format or genre (e.g., PDF document, webpage, or folder). Page thumbnails, on the other hand, are small images of a page, usually displayed in reduced resolution, that can be enlarged by a reader for viewing.

In discussing thumbnails, two rights that are exclusive to the copyright holder are implicated. Because they make copies of the images that they crawl, search engines may violate the author's exclusive right to make reproductions of a work.[16] Also, because the thumbnails are shown to the users, search engines may also violate the author's exclusive right to public display.[17] However, the use of thumbnails may rely, as noted in the following discussion of the *Kelly v. Arriba* and *Perfect 10 v. Google* cases, on one of the exemptions to the author's exclusive rights: fair use, discussed in this chapter and in Chapter 9.

In *Kelly v. Arriba Soft Corp.*, a photographer, whose copyrighted images were displayed by a visual search engine operator on the operator's website and those that it had licensed, sued the search engine operator.[18] The operator had built its database by copying images from websites and reducing these images to thumbnails that could be enlarged by clicking on the thumbnail. The lower court ruled the operator's use of the thumbnails fair use, as the character and purpose of its use was "significantly transformative and the use did not harm the market for or value of [the photographer's] works."[19] The 9th Circuit affirmed the lower court's ruling that the display of thumbnails was fair use.

In *Perfect 10 v. Google*, it was a website operator's turn to sue Internet search engines.[20] Perfect 10 published adult photographs in both a magazine and on a website, and it had expended considerable resources to the development of the brand name for the magazine and website. Google and Amazon.com, search engine operators, have an image search function that retrieves thumbnail images in response to a textual search string query. Some of the images so retrieved came from Perfect 10's website, and it sued both Google and Amazon. The district judge, when considering plaintiff Perfect 10's motion for an injunction against Google, put the issue in perfect context:

> The principal two-part issue in this case arises out of the increasingly recurring conflict between intellectual property rights on the one hand and the dazzling capacity of internet technology to assemble, organize, store, access, and display intellectual property "content" on the other hand. That issue, in a nutshell, is: does a search engine infringe copyrighted images when it displays them on an "image search" function in the form of "thumbnails"?[21]

The district court was of the view that Perfect 10 was likely to succeed in its claim that the display of thumbnails was a direct infringement by Google of its copyrighted images, and issued a preliminary injunction from creating and displaying Perfect 10's images. The district court distinguished Arriba's use of thumbnails in Kelly, in that Perfect 10's market for downloading reduced-size adult thumbnails into cell phones was superseded by Google's use of Perfect 10's thumbnails. However, the 9th Circuit later ruled that the thumbnails were fair use because they did not detract from the economic value of the images, and thus Google could continue displaying Perfect 10 thumbnails that came up following a search.[22]

The next frontier for legal issues in the digital world is already being framed by the emergence of many social networking spaces, such as Facebook and YouTube, and tools such as blogs, wikis, RSS feeds, podcasting, mashups, social bookmarking, photo sharing, such as Flickr and Delicious, and mobile applications. Liability concerns here include copyright infringement, defamation and false information, and trademark issues. These concerns are exacerbated because the terms of use of these tools are ultimately controlled by a third party.[23]

> **Notable Points 8: New Challenges in Digital Content**
>
> ▶ Digital versions of familiar formats present new legal challenges.
>
> ▶ Because search engines show thumbnails to users, they may be in violation of the author's exclusive right of display.
>
> ▶ Court cases have, however, found most uses of thumbnails to fall under the fair use exemption.
>
> ▶ The next frontier in legal issues will probably be presented by social networking tools and spaces.

THE LEGAL COMPLEXITIES OF MULTIPLE, HETEROGENEOUS COLLECTIONS

A feature related to the complexity of media content just discussed is the multiple, heterogeneous nature of digital collections. This feature can usefully be analyzed in two parts: the different types of digital collections and the different goals of digital collections. Digital libraries often have collections of different types designed to meet a variety of goals.

Internet

The Internet can be viewed as one giant digital collection—a sort of a metacollection. Individuals, libraries, and other organizations often take subsets of the Internet to form specific collections. This is generally done through bookmarking and linking. While there have been few legal challenges to bookmarking, linking has generated some legal issues, more so in some European countries than in the United States. The earliest linking litigation in the United States was the case of *Ticketmaster Corp. v. Microsoft Corp.*[24] In that case, Ticketmaster accused Microsoft of using hyperlinks to its Seattle city guide without permission and of violating Ticketmaster's trademarks. The case was settled without resolving the legal issues. In 1998, claims of copyright infringement arising from linking were dismissed in a case filed in a federal district court in California, but the court suggested that when the linking website is aware of infringing material and facilitates access to such material, then multiple linking claims might be entertained.[25] Indeed, a case one year later suggested websites that actively direct users to infringing websites could be held liable for contributory infringement.[26] In 2000, *Universal City Studios v. Reimerdes* took up the linking question in the context of the anticircumvention prohibitions of the Digital Millennium Copyright Act (DMCA) and declared that linking liability would arise only where the party responsible for linking knows that the infringing material is on the linked-to site, knows that circumvention technology residing in the linked-to site may not be lawfully offered, and creates or disseminates the link for the purpose of disseminating the technology.[27] As we shall see later, under certain conditions spelled out in the DMCA, the law does provide a safe harbor for service providers who merely provide links to web content. Nevertheless, the digital content manager who provides web linking should be aware, as Sableman points out, that linking can implicate trademark infringement, false advertising, copyright infringement, and even misappropriation.[28]

Framing is another issue that has been litigated. The Washington Post sued Total News for providing links that would display content from other publishers on its website framed on a Total News webpage.[29] Not only did Total News use Washington Post's logo, the link had the effect of republishing content that Total News had not created. Again, this case was settled without the opportunity for fully exploring the legal issues. Lisby argues persuasively that framing is copyright infringement, because it creates a derivative work by putting original content in a new context.[30]

The courts have also found unauthorized web posting of copyrighted material to be an infringement of copyright. A photographer who took photos of photos at an event and posted them on a website was found to have violated copyright in *Scanlon v. Kessler.*[31] Similarly, a defendant who scanned copyrighted photographs and put them on his website had engaged in unauthorized reproduction.[32]

We only briefly mention here the other whole area of republishing news reports by noting the doctrine of Hot News Misappropriation developed through litigation originating from the print world and resurrected in the digital world.[33] This doctrine allows parties to bring a misappropriation claim instead of a copyright infringement claim where a publisher has expended resources to create news material and another entity has reproduced and republished the material.

Notable Points 9: The Internet and Digital Content

▶ Digital collections come in multiple types; they are heterogeneous.

▶ The Internet can be said to be the biggest digital collection of all.

▶ Legal issues on the Internet have included linking and framing.

▶ Courts have found the unauthorized posting of copyrighted material on the web to be copyright infringement.

Commercial Databases and Data Sets

Libraries and other organizations may have, as part of their digital collections, commercial databases. The major issues here involve copyright protection and licensing. Sometimes patent law may be involved, especially with regard to built-in search engines. However, as Osenga notes, databases do not easily fit into the enumerated statutory categories for patents.[34] It is now recognized that databases satisfying Feist's requirement for originality are protected. Data sets may be viewed in the same category as commercial databases, with less emphasis on copyright and more emphasis on licensing issues.

Collective Works and Compilations

What Is a Compilation?

Section 101 of the copyright code defines a compilation as "a work formed by the collection and assembling of preexisting materials or of data that are selected, coordinated, or arranged in such a way that the resulting work as a whole constitutes an original work of authorship. The term 'compilation' includes collective works."[35]

Are Collective Works and Compilations Subject Matters of Copyright Protection?

Just to make sure it is understood that compilations fall under the subject matter of copyright specified in section 102, section 103 explicitly declares that compilations are indeed included but points out that protection extends only to what the author has contributed and not to the underlying or preexisting material. Nor does it extend to preexisting material that has been used unlawfully.[36]

Collective works and compilations may or may not have common characteristics. In a collective work, individual components are generally independent copyrightable works, while compilations may include material that is not necessarily copyrightable.[37] Separate contributions to a collective work can have copyright protection that is distinct from copyright in the collective work as a whole. Owning a copyright in a collective work entitles the copyright owner to "only the privilege of reproducing and distributing the contribution as part of that particular collective work, any revision of that collective work, and any later collective work in the same series."[38] The court in *New York Times Co., Inc. v. Tasini* explored the question of whether a copyright owner in a collective work who republished all or a part of the compilation in an electronic database could prevail against an assertion of copyright infringement from the author of a contribution in the compilation.[39] The case involved freelance writers who had sued a newspaper publisher for making their articles available in electronic databases. The newspaper asserted a privilege offered by section 201(c) of Title 17:

> Copyright in each separate contribution to a collective work is distinct from copyright in the collective work as a whole, and vests initially in the author of the contribution. In the absence of an express transfer of the copyright or of any rights under it, the owner

of copyright in the collective work is presumed to have acquired only the privilege of reproducing and distributing the contribution as part of that particular collective work, any revision of that collective work, and any later collective work in the same series.[40]

The Supreme Court focused on the perception of a user of the articles as presented in the database and rejected the newspaper's reliance on the section 201(c) privilege. The privilege, however, continues to be available given the right circumstances. A second circuit court, for example, affirmed the granting of summary judgment to the *National Geographic* publisher who had made a searchable digital collection of past issues of the magazine (dubbing it the Complete National Geographic), against freelance authors and photographers who had sued the magazine for the use of their work in this new medium.[41] The court relied on its holding the fact that the original context of the magazine was present in the new Complete National Geographic and that the digital work was a new version of the *National Geographic* magazine. The database at issue in Tasini, on the other hand, did not allow users to view the underlying works in their original context.

> **Notable Points 10: Compilations and Collective Works**
>
> ▶ Databases that meet Feist's requirement for originality are protected.
> ▶ Compilations are also protected, but underlying preexisting material is not protected.
> ▶ Compilations and collective works are not necessarily the same.
>   • Individual components in a collective work are generally independent copyrighted works.
>   • Compilations may include material that is not copyrightable.
> ▶ Separate contributions to a collective work have copyright protection that is distinct from the copyright in the work as a whole.
> ▶ Copyright in a collective work entitles its owner to reproduce and distribute the contribution as part of that particular collective work and its revisions.

Different Goals

As well as being heterogeneous and having multiple formats, digital collections also have different goals.

Preservation

One of the goals of digitization, as mentioned, is preservation. Some institutions have a legal privilege to preserve. Section 108, for example, addresses the need for preservation and conservation.[42] Legal issues that are likely to arise here include not only copyright but also evidence. We discuss section 108 more comprehensively in Chapter 9.

The previously discussed issue of nonpermanence acquires critical importance when it comes to maintaining documents for legal evidentiary purposes. In December 2006, changes were put into effect in the U.S. Federal Rules of Civil Procedure (FRP) that institute a new category of evidence: Electronically Stored Information (ESI), which is designed to work within the existing rules of production of "documents."[43] Under the rules, a party must provide to other parties "a copy—or a description by category and location—of all documents, electronically stored information, and tangible things that the disclosing party has in its possession, custody, or control and may use to support its claims or defenses."[44] While the rule does not specify the version of the electronically stored information that should be produced, Rule 26(f) does oblige the parties to conference and "discuss any issues about preserving discoverable information" as well as "any issues about disclosure or discovery of electronically stored information, including the form or forms in which it should be produced."[45]

A closely related issue to nonpermanence for evidence is authenticity. Digital information can be vulnerable to tampering or corruption. Depending on the nature of the collection, authentication methods such as digital signatures, version control, and encryption may be necessary.[46]

Access

Access and preservation or conservation are very much intertwined. There could be any number of reasons for seeking access, including for entertainment, research, or safeguarding culture. Copyright is always an issue, as, for example, not all copyrightable works have the same protection duration. Different publications are covered under different copyright protection terms, depending on when they were created or published. However, the issues most likely to rise are those of licensing for access. By access, we are also referring to use.

As cultural preservation institutions, museums are dealing more and more often with the world of copyright and copyright issues as they move to digitize their collections.[47] Especially in an international context, museums additionally find themselves with the special problems of creators' moral rights of integrity and attribution. We revisit these issues later in the book at appropriate junctures.

LEGAL ISSUES IN OPEN ACCESS/CLOSED ACCESS

Open Access Initiatives: Issues

In response to the escalating prices of electronic and print publications, individuals and institutions have begun to explore alternative ways of accessing and providing access to this material—a movement toward open access that has been gathering momentum. The most common response has been to seek alternative forms of publication. Some institutions have also experimented with ways to acquire copyright permissions for the purpose of digitizing books accessible through open access.[48] In this chapter, we focus on two major efforts: creative commons and self-archiving.

Creative Commons

Under modern copyright law, copyright attaches to a work the moment it is affixed onto a tangible medium. Thus, an author, upon creating a work, receives copyright as a default, with the attendant exclusive rights. To exercise any of these rights, the user would have to obtain permission from the copyright holder. Open access, however, denotes the provision of scholarly and other publications without the constraints of copyright. In some cases, the author may retain the copyright but give a general license for use with nothing more required than attribution.[49] The author may also assign copyright to an entity that will then make the work freely available and not assign such copyright to an entity, such as a commercial journal, that will assert the exclusive rights. There are many such open-access journals.[50]

Creative Commons, as espoused by Lawrence Lessig, envisions a world where exclusive copyright is not the default—that is, where an author takes only as many sticks from the copyright bundle as he wishes and indicates to users which of those sticks in the copyright bundle they can use without trespassing on the author's selectively retained rights.[51] Lessig and his colleagues developed a series of contract templates to allow authors to identify the particular rights they wish to retain and those they wish to give away; these templates can be obtained at CreativeCommons.com. For example, an author may assert only the right to commercially exploit the work but allow any other use of the work. Or the author may allow all use of the work, including commercial exploitation, requiring only attribution of authorship.[52]

Works are typically submitted to an electronic repository such as the Social Science Research Network. They can also be submitted to servers in the author's institution or may be self-published on the author's own website. Indeed, many academic institutions are now establishing institutional repositories in which affiliates can submit work to be publicly accessible, and many journals are allowing authors of copyrighted articles to post the final postacceptance manuscripts to these repositories. Unfortunately, the "404 File Not Found" error that appears when a search leads to a nonfunctional website is still a problem. This is being addressed by web archiving efforts both at the macro (whole World Wide Web archiving) and at the micro (institutional and individual web archiving) level.

Closed Access

Closed access essentially means that access to material is restricted to the members of the licensing community. The members of this community may be individual institutions or coalitions of institutions. Unlike open-access content, which can be uncovered by a search engine query, closed-access material is inaccessible except through a licensing arrangement, and the license need not provide accommodation to fair use.[53]

One of the biggest misconceptions with open access is the idea that all rights for the author are extinguished on opening up the work to free access. Digitization projects will still need to look closely at what, if any, residual rights remain.

In the next three chapters, we examine the important question of content owners, as this is a threshold topic in the digital content world. We also analyze the rights these content owners have, the limitation of those rights, and the duration of the rights.

HYPOTHETICAL #2

The New Age Library has just acquired the digital collection of the *Twilight* series, newly reformatted into 3D video. The collection also includes scholarly commentary in different digital media, some of it from Europe. New Age Library patrons are able to electronically access all of the digital collection, including the *Twilight* series, and can friend the commentators on Facebook. What are the issues to consider?

A suggested response to this hypothetical question can be found in Appendix 6.

ENDNOTES

1. Oren Bracha, *Standing Copyright Law on Its Head? The Googlization of Everything and the Many Faces of Property*, 85 TEXAS LAW REVIEW, 1799–1869 (2007).
2. W. L. Anderson, *Some Challenges and Issues in Managing, and Preserving Access to, Long-Lived Collections of Digital Scientific and Technical Data*, 3 DATA SCIENCE JOURNAL 191 (2004), http://www.jstage.jst.go.jp/article/dsj/3/0/191/_pdf.
3. Geoffrey Adams, *Partners Go Dutch to Preserve the Minutes of Science*, September/October RESEARCH INFORMATION (2004), http://www.researchinformation.info/risepoct04archiving.html.
4. Anderson, *supra*, note 2, at 7.
5. Caroline R. Arms, *Keeping Memory Alive: Practices for Preserving Digital Content at the National Digital Library Program of the Library of Congress*, 4(3) RLG DIGINEWS (2000), http://worldcat.org/arcviewer/1/OCC/2007/08/08/0000070511/viewer/file1442.html#feature1.

6. IAN BARNES, PRESERVATION OF WORD PROCESSING DOCUMENTS (Canberra: Australian Partnership for Sustainable Repositories, 2006), http://www.apsr.edu.au/publications/word_processing_preservation.pdf.
7. Arms, *supra*, at note 5.
8. Project Gutenberg, *Free eBooks by Project Gutenberg* (2011), http://www.gutenberg.org/wiki/Main_Page.
9. Sue Polanka, *Off the Shelf: E-book Aggregators*, Booklist (May 15, 2008), http://www.booklistonline.com/ProductInfo.aspx?pid=2710528.
10. Josh Hadro, *HarperCollins Puts 26 Loan Cap on Ebook Circulations* (February 26, 2011), http://www.libraryjournal.com/lj/home/889452-264/harpercollins_puts_26_loan_cap.html.csp.
11. Andy Woodworth, *Tell HarperCollins: Limited Checkouts on eBooks Is Wrong for Libraries* (2011), http://www.change.org/petitions/tell-harpercollins-limited-checkouts-on-ebooks-is-wrong-for-libraries.
12. JUNE M. BESEK, COPYRIGHT ISSUES RELEVANT TO DIGITAL PRESERVATION AND DISSEMINATION OF PRE-1972 COMMERCIAL SOUND RECORDINGS (Washington, DC: Council on Library and Information Resources and Library of Congress, 2005), 16–17.
13. 17 U.S.C. § 301 (c) (2006).
14. Besek, supra, note 12.
15. William C. Janssen, Document Icons and Page Thumbnails: Issues in Construction of Document Thumbnails for Page-Image Digital Libraries (Palo Alto, CA: Palo Alto Research Center, 2004).
16. 17 U.S.C. § 107 (2006).
17. *Id.*
18. Kelly v. Arriba Soft Corporation, 280 F.3d 934 (9th Cir. 2002).
19. *Id.* at 939.
20. Perfect 10 v. Google, Inc., 416 F. Supp. 2d 828 (C.D. Cal. 2006).
21. *Id.* at 831.
22. Perfect 10, Inc. v. Amazon.com, Inc., 508 F.3d 1146 (9th Cir. 2007).
23. John F. Delaney, *Poking and Tweeting: Social Media Overview, 1034 Practising Law Institute* (February–March 2011), PLI/Pat 43.
24. Ticketmaster Corp. v. Microsoft Corp., No. 97-3055 (C.D. Cal. 1997).
25. Bernstein v. JC Penney Inc., 50 U.S.P.Q.2d 1063 (C.D. Cal 1998).
26. Intellectual Reserve Inc. v. Utah Lighthouse Ministry Inc., 75 F.Supp.2d 1290 (D. Utah 1999).
27. Universal City Studios Inc. v. Reimerdes, 111 F.Supp.2d 294 (S.D.N.Y. 2000), 341.
28. Mark Sableman, *Link Law Revisited: Internet Linking Law at Five Years*, 16 BERKELEY TECHNOLOGY LAW JOURNAL (2001), 1273–1343.
29. Washington Post Co. v. Total News, Inc., No. 97 civ. 1190 (S.D.N.Y. 1997).
30. Gregory C. Lisby, *Web Site Framing: Copyright Infringement Through the Creation of an Unauthorized Derivate Work*, 6 COMMUNICATION LAW AND POLICY (2001), 541–556.

31. Scanlon v. Kessler, 11 F.Supp2d 44 (S.D.N.Y. 1998).
32. Tiffany Design Inc. v. Reno-Tahoe Specialty Inc., 55 F.Supp.2d 1113 (D. Nev. 1999).
33. International News Service v. Associated Press, 248 U.S. 215 (1918); Barclays Capital Inc. v. Theflyonthewall.com, 700 F.Supp.2d 310 (S.D.N.Y. 2010).
34. Kristen Osenga, *Information May Want to Be Free, but Information Products Do Not: Protecting and Facilitating Transactions in Information Products*, 30 CARDOZO LAW REVIEW (2009), 2099–2145.
35. 17 U.S.C. § 101 (2006).
36. 17 U.S.C. § 102, 103 (2006).
37. Roy Export Co. Establishment of Vaduz, Liechtenstein, Black Inc., A. G. v. Columbia Broadcasting System, Inc., 503 F.Supp. 1137 (S.D.N.Y. 1980), judgment aff'd, 672 F.2d 1095 (2d Cir. 1982).
38. 17 U.S.C. § 201 (c) (2006).
39. New York Times Co., Inc. v. Tasini, 533 U.S. 483 (2001).
40. 17 U.S.C. § 201 (c) (2006).
41. Faulkner v. National Geographic Enterprises Inc., 409 F.3d 26 (2d Cir. 2005).
42. 17 U.S.C. § 108 (2006).
43. F.R.P. 26.
44. F.R.P. 26 (a) (1) (A) (ii).
45. F.R.P. 26 (f).
46. Claire M. Germain, *Legal Information Management in a Global and Digital Age: Revolution and Tradition*, 35 INTERNATIONAL JOURNAL OF LEGAL INFORMATION (2007), 134–163.
47. Guy Pessach, *Museums, Digitization and Copyright Law: Taking Stock and Looking Ahead*, 1 JOURNAL OF INTERNATIONAL MEDIA AND ENTERTAINMENT LAW (2007), 253–281.
48. Denise T. Covey, Acquiring Copyright Permission to Digitize and Provide Open Access to Books (Washington, DC: Digital Library Federation and Council on Library and Information Resources, 2005).
49. Germain, *supra*, note 45.
50. See Directory of Open Access Journals (2011), http://www.doaj.org/.
51. Lawrence Lessig, CC in Review: Lawrence Lessig on Supporting the Creative Commons (October 6, 2005), http://creativecommons.org/weblog/entry/5661.
52. Creative Commons, *About the Licenses* (2011), http://creativecommons.org/licenses/.
53. Covey, *supra*, note 47.

▶3
WHO ARE CONTENT OWNERS?

IN THIS CHAPTER

We examine the types of legal content ownership and discuss how to determine copyright ownership and to seek permission to use copyright-protected works:
▶ Initial ownership
▶ Works for hire
▶ Collective works
▶ Derivative works
▶ Government works
▶ Other claimants
▶ Copyright transfers
▶ Recovering damages and profits

At the outset, it is important to realize that content authors are not necessarily content owners. As mentioned in Chapter 1, authors are able to transfer all or some of their rights in copyright, and the transferees are themselves able to transfer their rights ad infinitum. Also, in some cases, an author may be determined by law, regardless of actual authorship, as in the case of works for hire. For digital librarians, it is very important to determine who the content owners are (see sidebar at the end of this chapter for resources for finding owners). There are several reasons for this, among them: (1) the content manager (or digital librarian) may want to seek copyright permission from the rights owner or (2) the content manager may want to know whether the content is still copyright-protected, by determining, for example, when the author died. In either case, the inquiry cannot proceed efficiently without conducting a copyright search to determine who the content owners are[1] or having the U.S. Copyright Office conduct the search at a fee, which is currently $165 an hour or fraction of an hour, with a two-hour minimum.

INITIAL OWNERSHIP

Single Author

Initially, copyright is vested in the work's author.[2] Authorship is defined by case law rather than by statute. One does not become an author and thus deserving of a copyright merely by operating digital or other equipment that fixes a work in a tangible medium of expression. For example, in *Lindsay v. RMS Titanic*, a documentary filmmaker who directed the filming but did not himself perform the filming was declared the copyright owner in the film, because he actually created the work by directing and translating the idea in a fixed tangible expression.[3]

Joint Authors

If there is more than one author, then the work becomes a joint work, with all authors as co-owners, having an equal and undivided interest in the whole work, except in the rare case where the authors mutually agree to delineate specific authors as sole authors for specific sections. The legislative history of the 1976 Copyright Act makes clear that authors become joint when there is collaboration with one another and the intention of merging their individual contributions to create "inseparable or interdependent parts of a unitary whole."[4] The intent must be at or before the time of the creation, but there is no requirement that the joint authors be in the same physical space or even work simultaneously. They may never meet at all. In cases of works for hire, discussed in the next section, the relevant intent is that of the owner, not the author.

> ✓ **Checklist 3: Test for Joint Authorship**
> - ❏ Did each author make an independently copyrightable contribution to the work?
> - ❏ Did the authors mutually intend to be coauthors?
> - ❏ Do the facts bear out this intention?

The requirement for independently copyrightable contribution is designed to encourage actual creativity by preventing those who did not contribute creatively from gaining equal rights in a work. The inquiry into the mutuality of the intent is designed to enable consultation without fear of losing rights unintentionally, thus encouraging creativity.

There are other ways a work can become joint, even when there is no joint authorship. For works subject to renewal terms (pre-1976), the renewal rights might have vested in more than one person. Also, the termination rights discussed in Chapters 5 and 6 may vest in more than one person. Furthermore, a copyright may pass by will to two or more persons. The copyright owner may also make a nonexclusive transfer of the copyright to more than one person, thus creating joint ownership. Finally, a work may be subject to community property laws in some states, such that the proceeds of the work, if it was created during the marriage, belong equally to both spouses.

The reader should note that a joint work is different from a collective work, which is a collection of works into a collective whole, with no intention from the authors to create a merged whole work.[5] Where one of the authors is working within the scope of his or her employment, as in works for hire, the employer becomes the joint owner, even though other owners may be independent co-owners. An important point here for digital librarians is that one co-owner of a copyright could grant a nonexclusive license in the copyrighted work without the consent of other co-owners[6] subject only to accounting to the other co-owners, and co-owners cannot be liable for infringement of that copyright to one another.[7] Co-owners are always free to enter into an agreement among themselves on how to exploit the copyrighted material, including granting exclusive rights. The digital librarian should be on the lookout for such agreements. While a licensee is insulated from an infringement action by nonconsenting owners, it is conceivable that a nonconsenting owner could sue the licensee where the licensee's use of the copyrighted work resulted in the work's destruction.

Notable Points 11: Copyright Ownership

- Copyright initially vests in the author.
- Where there are joint authors, copyright is jointly owned by all the authors.
- A co-owner of a copyright is free to independently grant a license for the use of that work.
- Authors become joint where there is collaboration and the intent to create a joint work.
- Other ways a work may become joint:
  - For works subject to renewal terms (pre-1976), the renewal rights for works subject to renewal terms might have vested in more than one person.
  - Termination rights may vest in more than one person.
  - A copyright may pass by will to two or more persons.
  - A copyright owner may make a nonexclusive transfer of the copyright to more than one person, thus creating joint ownership.
  - In some states, a work may be subject to community property laws, creating a right of ownership of copyright proceeds for the nonauthor spouse.

WORK FOR HIRE

Where a work is created by an employee or for some other entity that pays for the creation for certain specified uses, the employer or the entity that commissions the work is considered the author. However, the employee or a commissioned party may enter into a written and signed agreement with the employer regarding the distribution of some or all of the rights.[8] The courts of appeal are split on whether the agreement should be in writing before creation or whether it can be oral and then subsequently in writing. Whether a person is an "employee" is determined by the application of common law of agency, taking into account, for instance, the degree of control the commissioner had on the manner and means of creating the product, among other factors.[9] The Copyright Act defines a work made for hire as a work that is prepared by an employee within the scope of his or her employment or a work especially commissioned or ordered if it falls into one of nine categories.[10] Scope of employment examines several factors, including whether the individual was hired to create works such as the one in question; whether the work was done substantially within the time and space limits of the job; and whether, in creating the work, the purpose was to serve the employer's interest. The work-for-hire doctrine does not generally apply to academic writing, as professors are evaluated for tenure based on what they write.

> ☑ **Checklist 4: Is It a Work for Hire?**
>
> ❑ Is the work for use as:
> ❑ a contribution to a collective work?
> ❑ part of a motion picture or other audiovisual work?
> ❑ a translation?
> ❑ a supplementary work?
> ❑ a compilation?
> ❑ an instructional text?
> ❑ a test?
> ❑ answer material for a test?
> ❑ an atlas?
> ❑ Did the parties expressly agree to have the work considered a work for hire in a written and signed instrument?

The designation "work for hire" can have serious effects regarding the rights of the parties, including initial ownership of the copyright, duration of copyright, termination rights, and renewal rights among others.[11] When it is a work for hire, the employer retains all the rights in the copyright, and the employee has no statutory right, unless there is a written agreement to the contrary. Also, the termination rights, discussed in Chapter 5, do not apply to works for hire, because there is no starving artist here who needs protection. The term of protection is not life-plus 70 years as in works that are not for hire; it is, instead, 95 years from when the work was published or 120 years since it was created. Also, the Visual Artists Rights Act, discussed in Chapter 4, does not apply.

COLLECTIVE WORKS

We began our discussion of collective works and compilations in Chapter 2. When examining content that is part of a collective work, special care should be taken to determine the copyright holder. The separate contributors would normally hold the initial copyright, but the holder of the copyright in the collective work can reproduce and distribute a contribution from the collective work and its revisions, even in a new format. For example, a federal circuit court ruled that publication of a digital archive of articles and photographs from past issues of *National Geographic* magazine was a revision of the previous print formats.[12] Some of the rights of the collective work rights holder include the collection and editing that produced the collective whole, sections that might have been written for the rights holder under work for hire, and transfers of copyright from authors.

OWNERSHIP IN DERIVATIVE WORKS

A basic tenet of copyright law is that the limited monopoly granted to authors is designed to eventually allow a work to enter the public domain, where other creators can use it and build on it. Works that are based on preexisting works, whether they are in or out of the public domain, are independently copyrightable. The copyright extends to the new original material. To merit copyright protection, the new work cannot be a slavish copy of the original and should have more than the modicum of originality required for an original copyrighted work. The deviation of the modified work from the original should be nontrivial.

> **Notable Points 12: Derivative Works**
>
> ▶ A derivative work based on an expired copyright is still copyrightable.
> ▶ The original copyright owner has derivative rights unless specifically transferred.
> ▶ The owner of a derivative copyright does not necessarily own copyright in the underlying work.
> ▶ License agreements for derivatives can be divided up by format of adaptation, such as film.
> ▶ Originality requirement for derivatives cannot be met simply by reproduction in another medium.
> ▶ Derivates made without copyright owner's permission belong to the copyright owner.

The copyright in the original work remains and is part of the derivative work, even though the derivative work may have its own copyright. Thus even where the copyright owner in the derivative is different, the copyright owner in the original protected work retains ownership of that original.

GOVERNMENT WORKS

There is no copyright protection for any work of the U.S. government whether published or unpublished, effectively putting such work in the public domain.[13] A work of the U.S. government is a work that is prepared by an officer or employee of the U.S. government as part of the preparer's official duties.[14] The government essentially produces works for hire with the public as the employer that pays in the form of taxes and other ways, not to mention that this flexibility gives the people the right to have information about their government, in keeping with the aim of the First Amendment and participation in a democracy. The works may include things like maps, meteorological data, and safety manuals. The U.S. government may, however, hold copyrights transferred to it by assignment, bequest, or by other method of transfer.[15] Also, it is worthwhile to note that just because a work of the U.S. government is in the public domain in this country does not mean that it is not protected outside the United States. The legislative history of the Copyright Act clearly shows that the prohibition was not intended to have that effect.[16]

The notes of the committee on the judiciary make it clear that this prohibition does not prevent U.S. government employees or officials from obtaining a copyright on a work created of their own volition and outside the scope of their employment, even when they are writing within their professional fields or the subject matter involves the government work.[17] The legislative history further indicates that the prohibition does not apply to the U.S. Postal Service, which could, for instance, use copyright for the prevention of reproduction of its postage stamps as long as they met the requirements of copyrightability. Where there is joint federal and nonfederal creation, the matter becomes a bit complicated, as the federal author, unlike the nonfederal author, is unable to claim copyright. This results in the unsatisfactory situation of a joint work in which some of the content is copyrightable and some is not.

The continuing controversy is whether government contractors should be able to secure copyright for works created with the use of federal funds. Generally, the federal government retains data rights and federal purpose rights in works that it has commissioned.[18] Federal purpose includes the right of the government to display and use the works. While the contractor can assert copyright in published scientific and technical articles based on the data produced in the performance of the contract, the federal government retains unlimited use rights in the data[19] and a license to reproduce, distribute, prepare derivative work, and display and perform the copyrighted work. The federal digital librarian can digitize and display government-funded and commissioned copyrighted works to audiences within the federal government but would need the copyright holders' permission to digitize and display to the public, unless permitted by data rights.

The Fair Copyright in Research Works Act (H.R. 801) seeks to amend the copyright code to prevent any federal government agency from requiring a transfer of copyright in works created under federal funding or conditioning receipt of federal funds on such a transfer. On the other hand, efforts are intensifying to provide open access to all research that is federally funded. The National Institutes of Health, for example, requires its grantees to post a final prepublication text so that others can have access.

States are not under the same restrictions regarding copyright. However, the intent of copyright protection is to provide an incentive to create by allowing authors to have a limited monopoly. States arguably do not need this incentive, but may copyright their works under certain circumstances. However, even here there are categories of works that cannot be protected. The law, for example, whether it is in the form of legislation or judicial opinion or regulation, is not subject to federal copyright protection.[20] The law is viewed as ideas or facts and thus not subject matter of copyright. In any case, the incentive argument for creativity would seem very odd applied to legislative productivity. However, just because a copyrighted work is referred to by a law or judicial opinions does not make that work "law" and therefore uncopyrightable.[21]

Notable Points 13: Government Works
- No copyright can be applied to works of the federal government.
- Some works of state governments may be copyrighted.
- The law, whether state or federal, does not have copyright protection.

OTHER CLAIMANTS

Despite the law bestowing the initial copyright in the author and requiring in most cases written agreements of changes in ownership, the digital librarian should be on the lookout for other claimants. In California, for example, in a decision that has been widely criticized[22] but not overruled, a court of appeal ruled that copyright constituted divisible community assets and a nonauthor spouse could share equally in the proceeds related to a lawsuit on a copyright.[23] The court found no inconsistency between the federal copyright law and the state's community property laws. The court did not find that the spouse shared ownership in the copyright—only in the proceeds of the copyright. We observe again that not all transfers require that they should be in writing. A grant of a nonexclusive license, for example, may be oral or may be implied from conduct.[24]

COPYRIGHT TRANSFERS

Section 201(e) permits an author to transfer an interest in copyright by conveyance to some other entity. Such a transfer may occur by operation of law, such as within bankruptcy proceedings, or, as discussed in this section, within the context of community property law. It is important to remember that copyright is personal property that can be bequeathed or become subject to laws of succession on its owner's death. The copyright law is silent on the operation of law upon joint owners and inheritance. Again, not all interests in the copyright need be transferred; rights can be separated and transferred, with the new owner having all the copyright law protection to that particular right. Involuntary transfer by government agencies of a copyright owner's rights is specifically prohibited by Title 17 of the U.S. Code, section 201(e).

Transfer of a copyright in a work does not transfer rights in the material object of that work.[25] Likewise, transfer of the material object does not transfer copyright in the work. Thus, there is an important distinction between copyright and the material object within which the copyright is embedded. A digital collection acquiring new, nondigitized works, therefore, does not by virtue of that acquisition acquire copyright in the work; the copyright holder owns the rights, not the work. We explore copyright transfers in more detail in Chapter 6.

RECOVERING DAMAGES AND PROFITS

In bringing suit for infringement, the copyright owner has the right to recover damages and profits, as does a transferee of the copyright, as well as assignees. However, only the owner of the copyright at the time of the infringement can bring suit. Later transferees and assignees can only do so if there is an express assignment of the right to bring suit. Holders of an exclusive right can bring an infringement suit even against the copyright owner's wishes. Similarly, a joint author may bring suit without bringing the coauthors into the suit.[26]

In litigation, one of the defenses available may be lack of ownership. Only an owner has standing to sue. The previous discussion therefore emphasizes the importance of determining the copyright owner, as the determination of this may have the effect of ending the suit. Thus, it is important to determine whether the work had ever been assigned to someone else and whether such an assignment was ever recorded.[27] Recall that one co-owner has the right to allow use of a work without the other co-owners' consent. We discuss infringement litigation in more detail in Chapter 8.

Notable Points 14: Copyright Ownership and Transfer

- Content authors are not necessarily content owners.
- Only owners have standing to sue.
- A copyright co-owner can grant a license in the copyrighted work without co-owners' consent.
- Generally, a licensee is insulated from an infringement action by non-consenting owners.
- Operating digital or other equipment that fixes a work in a tangible medium of expression does not automatically confer copyright on the operator.
- Contributors to a collective work hold separate copyright from the holder of the copyright in the collective work.
- Transfer of copyright may be by written agreement or by operation of law.
- Copyright is personal property that can be bequeathed.
- Exclusive rights can be transferred separately.
- There may be other unforeseen claimants in a copyright.

RESOURCES FOR FINDING COPYRIGHT OWNERS AND CLEARANCES

American Federation of Musicians, http://afm.org
American Society of Composers, Authors, and Publishers (ASCAP), http://ascap.com
American Society of Media Photographers (for photos), http://asmp.org
American Society of Picture Professionals (for photos), http://aspp.com
Art Museum Image Consortium, http://amico.org
Artists Rights Society, http://arsny.com
Association of American Publishers, http://publishers.org
Association of Authors' Representatives, http://aaronline.org
The Authors Guild, http://authorsguild.org
Authors Registry, http://www.authorsregistry.org
Broadcast Music, Inc. (BMI), http://www.bmi.com
Copyright Clearance Center, http://www.copyright.com
The Copyright Licensing Agency (United Kingdom), http://www.cla.co.uk
Copyright Renewal Database (1923–1963), http://collections.stanford.edu/copyrightrenewals/bin/page?forward=home
iCopyright (for web content), http://icopyright.com

(Continued)

> **RESOURCES FOR FINDING COPYRIGHT OWNERS AND CLEARANCES** *(Continued)*
>
> Internet Movie Database, http://www.imdb.com
> Motion Picture Licensing Corporation, http://mplc.org
> National Music Publishers Association (Harry Fox Agency), http://nmpa.org
> Notices of Restored Copyrights, http://copyright.gov/gatt.html
> Search Copyright Information, http://copyright.gov/records/
> SESAC, http://sesac.com
> United States Patent and Trademark Office, http://www.uspto.gov
> The WATCH File: Writers, Artists, and Their Copyright Holders (United Kingdom), http://tyler.hrc.utexas.edu/

> **HYPOTHETICAL #3**
>
> Mr. Rich, a prominent writer, scholar, and thinker, died in an accident when his little plane came down during a heavy thunderstorm. At the reading of his will it was discovered that he left a huge collection of digitized material from his personal library to the New Age Library. The library has given Ms. New Graduate the responsibility "to manage" this new collection. What issues should Ms. Graduate consider?
>
> *A suggested response to this hypothetical question can be found in Appendix 6.*

ENDNOTES

1. See U.S. Copyright Office Circular 22, *How to Investigate the Copyright Status of a Work*, http://www.copyright.gov/circs/circ22.pdf, for detailed information on how to investigate a work's copyright status.
2. 17 U.S.C. § 201 (a) (2006).
3. Lindsay v. Wrecked and Abandoned Vessel R.M.S. Titanic, 52 U.S.P.Q. 2d 1609 (Not published in F.Supp.2d); Community for Creative Non-Violence v. Reid, 490 U.S. 730 (1989).
4. Judiciary Committee Notes, House Report 94-1476.
5. *Id.*
6. McKay v. CBS, 324 F.2d 762 (N.Y. 2d Cir. 1963).
7. Dead Kennedys v. Biafra, 37 F. Supp. 2d 1151 (N.D. Cal. 1999).
8. 17 U.S.C. § 201 (b) (2006).
9. Community for Creative Non-Violence v. Reid, 490 U.S. 730 (1989).
10. 17 U.S.C. § 101 (2006).
11. Alan Wernick, *The Work Made for Hire and Joint Work Copyright Doctrines after CCNV v. Reid: "What! You Mean I Don't Own It Even Though I Paid in Full for It?"* 13 HAMLINE LAW REVIEW (1990), 287–295.

12. Faulkner v. National Geographic Enterprises Inc., 409 F.3d 26 (2d Cir. 2005), cert. denied, 126 S. Ct.. 833, 163 L. Ed. 2d 707 (U.S. 2005).
13. 17 U.S.C. § 105 (2006).
14. 17 U.S.C. § 101 (2006).
15. 17 U.S.C. § 105 (2006).
16. Judiciary Committee Notes, House Report 94-1476.
17. *Id.*
18. 48 C.F.R. 52.227-14.
19. 48 C.F.R. 52.227-14 (b), 48 C.F.R. 52.227-14 (c).
20. John G. Danielson v. Winchester-Conant Properties, Inc., 322 F.3d 26 (1st Cir. 2003).
21. Veeck v. Southern Bldg. Code Congress Internl., Inc., 293 F.3d 791 (5th Cir. 2002).
22. Debora Polacheck, *"Un-Worth-y" Decision: Characterization of a Copyright as Community Property*, 17 HASTINGS COMMUNICATIONS AND ENTERTAINMENT LAW JOURNAL (1995), 601–632.
23. In re Marriage of Worth, 195 Cal. App.3d 768 (Cal App.1.Dist. 1987); Alice Haemmerli, *Take It, It's Mine: Illicit Transfers of Copyright by Operation of Law*, 63 WASHINGTON AND LEE LAW REVIEW (2006), 1011–1054.
24. Carson v. Dynegy, Inc., 344 F.3d 446 (5th Cir. 2003); Jacob Maxwell, Inc. v. Veeck, 110 F.3d 749 (11th Cir. 1997); I.A.E., Inc. v. Shaver, 74 F.3d 768 (7th Cir. 1996).
25. 17 U.S.C. § 202 (2006).
26. 77 AMERICAN JURISPRUDENCE TRIALS (2010), 449.
27. *Id.*

▶4

WHAT RIGHTS DO CONTENT OWNERS HAVE AND WHAT ARE THE LIMITATIONS TO THOSE RIGHTS?

IN THIS CHAPTER

We cover the specific rights granted by copyright as well as the legal limitations to copyright:
- Right of reproduction
- Right to make derivative works
- Right of distribution
- Right of performance
- Right to display
- Visual arts
- Limitations on rights

Copyright law bestows on the author several exclusive rights under Title 17 of the U.S. Code, section 106: the right of reproduction of the copyrighted work; the right of preparing derivative works that are based on the work (adaptation); the right to distribute or transfer the work; the right to perform the work publicly; and the right to publicly display the work. In the case of sound recordings, an additional exclusive right is availed: the right of performance by means of digital audio transmission. We now turn to a discussion of each of these rights, as well as examine some of the limitations of the rights. The limitations are discussed under infringement in Chapter 8.

RIGHT OF REPRODUCTION

The owner of a copyright in a work has the exclusive right to make copies, or to authorize the making of copies, of that work. Generally, authors assign these rights to a publisher who can more efficiently make large numbers of copies. This right of reproduction is subject to certain limitations, including fair use and computer programs discussed later in this section. In the same manner that a copyright owner assigns reproduction rights to a publisher, so can a digital library be assigned (usually by license) those rights.

As discussed, digital libraries have multiple formats, which complicates the analysis of the various exclusive rights. For instance, while showing an image on a screen might be a display, it is not necessarily a reproduction.[1] Reproduction includes the duplication of the material object in which the expression is contained, as well as copying the expression on any other tangible medium that can be perceived by humans or machines. Thus, courts have found infringement of copyright on loading a computer program into an electronic memory device used to control the machine.[2] Analog-to-digital conversion by scanning is also a good example of a digital library action that involves the right of reproduction.

In our previous discussion of ownership of copyright in collective works in Chapter 3, we established that as part of revising the collective work, the owner has the right to reproduce a separately contributed work. However, in converting the content from print to digital, a court found that inclusion of photos that could be viewed alone without reference to the context of their appearance in the magazine was unauthorized reproduction.[3]

Copyright challenges, even litigation, have not stopped digitization efforts and projects. Google has been involved in litigation both in the United States and internationally. As of March 2011, a federal judge had rejected a settlement Google had proposed with publishers on the grounds that the settlement still gave too much control over book digitization to Google.[4] This rejection has implications in terms of reduced access from libraries and book users' points of view. Other digitization efforts include the Internet Archive (http://www.archive.org), the Berkeley Digital Library SunSITE (http://uslibrary3.berkeley.edu/Imaging/), the

> **Notable Points 15: Right of Reproduction**
>
> ▶ Owner of copyright has the exclusive right to make or authorize the reproductions of the work.
> ▶ Authors usually assign the right of reproduction to publishers.
> ▶ Right of reproduction is subject to certain limitations, such as fair use.
> ▶ Showing an image on a computer screen is not necessarily reproduction.
> ▶ Loading a computer program into electronic memory may be reproduction.
> ▶ Analog-to-digital conversion by scanning may be reproduction.
> ▶ Despite the constraints of reproduction, digitization efforts continue.

ever-evolving Alexandria Digital Library at the University of California Santa Barbara (http://www.alexandria.ucsb.edu), which is "a globally distributed georeferenced digital library,"[5] the Digital Public Library of America proposed by the Berkman Center for Internet and Society at Harvard University, and various regional, state, individual, and academic library digitization projects.

RIGHT TO MAKE DERIVATIVE WORKS

The copyright owner has the exclusive right to prepare derivative works. This overlaps but is distinguished from reproduction in that, while reproduction requires fixation in a tangible format, derivatives need not be fixed as, for example, when a novel is performed as an opera. This performance, while not a reproduction, would be an infringement of the copyright owner's exclusive right to prepare derivatives. In Title 17 of the U.S. Code, section 101, the definition of a derivative work is quite exhaustive:

> A "derivative work" is a work based upon one or more preexisting works, such as a translation, musical arrangement, dramatization, fictionalization, motion picture version, sound recording, art reproduction, abridgment, condensation, or any other form in which a work may be recast, transformed, or adapted. A work consisting of editorial revisions, annotations, elaborations, or other modifications which, as a whole, represent an original work of authorship, is a "derivative work."[6]

An important point to note here is the requirement that the work be based on a preexisting copyrighted work. This right is valuable for the copyright owner because sometimes a derivative may bring in more return than the original, for example, the popular *Twilight* novels that became blockbuster movies. An example of a digital library creating a derivative could be if the library takes the television game show *Wheel of Fortune* and develops an online self-guide or orientation based on the show. The copyright in the derivative and the copyright in the underlying works are distinct, such that the digital librarian may need to determine the owner of the underlying copyright before exercising any of the exclusive rights in the derivative.

A note about annotations and metadata: these are pieces of information that are added to a digital document either as a temporary attachment for use by individuals or groups, or as a permanent attachment to the underlying work. The annotations can be single or mixed media. Digital annotations can be derivatives, as contemplated in the Copyright Act, or they can be freestanding copyrightable works that are not connected to the underlying work. This is because the annotator has control and can remove or insert annotations with the right software. Some webmasters may, however, object to unauthorized third-party annotations for lack of control. These characteristics of annotations make it difficult to determine whether a derivative has been made or whether there exists a freestanding copyrightable work in the annotations. This is not something that has preoccupied the courts; but as annotations become more sophisticated and complex, it could be only a matter of time before litigation emerges in this area.

Metadata are usually technical markers providing metainformation about a digital document and rarely involve copyright issues. This metainformation about a digital document—essentially data about data—has been described as the document's DNA. Metadata are growing in significance in the litigation world, as parties increasingly demand their production to determine creation, authenticity, and alteration.[7] A legal digital librarian should make sure that documents stored or sent to opposing counsel do not contain hidden data. Also, trademarks have been abused in metadata in attempts to influence a document's visibility to an Internet search engine. This would constitute a trademark infringement. As well, the possibility exists that changes made to metadata may invoke derivative work problems, as a change in metadata can change the look of the document.

> **Notable Points 16: Right to Make Derivative Works**
>
> ▶ The owner of copyright has the exclusive right to make derivative works.
> ▶ Examples of derivatives include translations, dramatizations, motion picture versions, and art reproductions.
> ▶ A derivative need not be fixed in a tangible medium (e.g., a novel performed as an opera).
> ▶ Work must be based on a preexisting copyrighted work.
> ▶ Copyright in the derivative is distinct from copyright in the underlying work.
> ▶ The digital librarian may need to determine the owner of underlying copyright before exercising rights in the derivative.
> ▶ Digital annotations may be derivatives or freestanding copyrightable works.
> ▶ An issue in the annotations of an electronic record is to what extent the annotation amounts to creating a derivative work.

RIGHT OF DISTRIBUTION

The copyright owner has the exclusive right to distribute the copyrighted work to the public by way of selling it, transferring ownership of the rights, renting, leasing, or lending the work.[8] The copyright owner has control of distribution of the first copy to the public, that is, the right of publication.[9] However, the new copy owner, who may not necessarily be a copyright owner, may rent, lease, or lend that particular copy.[10] This is referred to as the *first-sale doctrine*. The new copy owner, however, has no copyright in the work, unless there is a written agreement to that effect. The copyright owner may continue making other copies and distributing those copies. The first-sale doctrine is of limited application in the digital world. But phonorecords cannot be rented out without permission from the underlying copyright owner, and this would not be considered distribution. An example of a digital library distribution could be where proprietary materials were posted on its website without the copyright owner's permission, assuming there were no issues of fair use (discussion follows) or service provider exceptions discussed in Chapter 10.

Notable Points 17: Right of Distribution and First-Sale Doctrine

- Owner of copyright has exclusive right to distribute work to the public.
- This right of distribution extends to the first copy.
- Under the doctrine of first sale, the new copy owner may distribute that particular copy.
- The new copy owner has no copyright in the copy.
- The doctrine of first sale is unclear in the digital environment.

RIGHT OF PERFORMANCE

The exclusive right to public performance includes a list of areas that are covered: literary, musical, dramatic, and choreographic works, pantomimes, and motion pictures and other audiovisual works.[11] Acts that would be considered performance include reciting, acting, playing, or dancing a work either directly or by means of a device.[12] It does not matter whether the performance was for profit or not. A digital library that made a video clip of a musical available for viewing on a website might be

Notable Points 18: Right of Public Performance

- The copyright owner has the exclusive right to public performance.
- Performance includes reciting, acting, playing, or dancing a work.
- Performance need not be for profit.
- A digital library making a video clip of a musical available on a website may be performing.

in violation of the right of performance, assuming none of the limitations discussed in the next section apply.

RIGHT TO DISPLAY

Like the public performance exclusive right just discussed, the public display right has its own list of covered areas: literary, musical, dramatic, and choreographic works, pantomimes, and pictorial, graphic, or sculptural works, including the individual images of a motion picture or other audiovisual work—a slight expansion of the previous list.[13] Acts that would be considered display include directly showing a copy of the copyrighted work; showing by using a film, slide, television image, or other device or process; and showing individual images in the case of audiovisual work.[14]

Performing and displaying publicly means the performance or display happens in a public place and does not include incidental showings to a "normal circle of a family and its social acquaintances."[15] It also includes transmitting or communicating the work to members of the public, whether the recipients are at the same place, different places, same time, or different times.[16] Note, however, that the act of public performance or display does not in and of itself constitute "publication" of the copyrighted work.[17] Instances of problems with violations of the right of display might involve the digital collections of museums that include protected works displayed without the copyright owner's permission.

> **Notable Points 19: Right of Public Display**
>
> ▶ The copyright owner has the exclusive right to display the work in public.
> ▶ Display includes showing the work either directly or by using audiovisual devices.
> ▶ Public performance and display does not constitute publication of the work.
> ▶ Museums that have digital collections should be particularly aware of this right.

VISUAL ART

Independently of the rights discussed above, authors of visual art have additional rights under the Visual Artists Rights Acts (VARA).[18] These include claiming authorship of a work and preventing others from attributing the author's name to a work that the author did not create. The visual art author also has the right to prevent attribution of his or her name to a work that has been distorted, mutilated, or modified, where such modifications would be likely to harm the author's reputation and honor.[19] This is known as the right of attribution.

Furthermore, the author of a visual art has the right to prevent the intentional distortion, mutilation, or other distortion of a work that would injure his honor or reputation, and if the work is of a recognized stature, to prevent its destruction.[20] This is referred to as the right of integrity. This right can apply to work that is attached to property that the artist does not own, such as the wall of a building.[21] However, modification of work caused by passage of time or inherent nature of the material would not be considered mutilation, distortion, or other proscribed modification.[22]

For digital librarians and other content managers, it is important to note that the author of the visual art does not need to own the copyright to exercise these rights. Likewise, joint authors of a visual art are also co-owners of these rights[23] and can exercise those rights independently. However, only the author of a work can exercise VARA rights. Works for hire are not protected under VARA. The duration of VARA rights is generally the life of the author, or where there are joint authors, the life of the last surviving author.[24] Also, VARA rights may not be transferred, but they can be waived in a written instrument specifically identifying the work and the uses to which the waiver applies. A joint author waives the rights for all authors.[25] The digital librarian should also remember that, absent a written agreement to the contrary, a waiver of VARA rights does not constitute a transfer of the work, and neither does a transfer of ownership of a work constitute a waiver of VARA rights. In other words, ownership of VARA rights is distinct from ownership of copyright.[26]

VARA rights are akin to moral rights derived from French theory. That theory posits an author has some sort of parental rights to his or her creation and that these rights cannot be alienated from the author even after the work and the author are separated, because the work is an extension of the author. Thus, artists are able to continue controlling the work even after he has disposed of his economic interest.

Unlike some countries, moral rights in the United States are limited. Many of the countries that subscribe to moral rights include in their laws the right of integrity, the right of attribution, and the right of disclosure. The right of disclosure refers to the ability of the author to decide when and in what form the work is distributed to the public. A few countries also include the right of withdrawal—or the right to recall a work from circulation, the right to prevent malicious and excessive criticism (remember the work is an extension of the author) that injures the author's reputation. Unlike France, moral rights in other countries may not be perpetual, can be waived, and may be alienated. In passing VARA, the United States attempted, albeit halfheartedly, to comply with the Berne Convention, to be discussed in Chapter 13.

> **Notable Points 20: Visual Artists Rights**
>
> ▶ Authors of visual art have additional rights under the Visual Artists Rights Act (VARA), including:
> - right to claim authorship of a work;
> - right to disclaim attribution of authorship of a work;
> - right to disclaim attribution of authorship of a work that has been distorted or mutilated; and
> - if the work is a recognized stature, right to prevent its destruction.
>
> ▶ Authors of visual art do not need to own copyright in the work to exercise VARA rights.
>
> ▶ Only the author of a work can exercise VARA rights.
>
> ▶ VARA does not protect works for hire.
>
> ▶ VARA rights generally last for the life of the author or, for joint works, the longest surviving coauthor.
>
> ▶ A waiver of rights by a joint author waives rights for all coauthors.
>
> ▶ Many countries have similar or expanded rights, which they term *moral rights*.

LIMITATIONS ON RIGHTS

First-Sale Doctrine

U.S. Congress, in keeping with the constitutional charge to promote the advancement of science and the useful arts by granting authors and copyright owners the exclusive rights previously discussed, also provided some limitations on those rights.

Among the limitations is the first-sale doctrine that we discussed under the right of distribution, which distinguishes between the physical copy and the expression embodied in that copy.[27] Under the first-sale doctrine, a rights holder who sells a particular copy can no longer exercise authority of the further distribution of that particular copy. The sale thus terminates the copyright owner's authority to interfere with subsequent sales or distribution of that copy.[28] This doctrine seems to have very limited application in the digital world, as there is usually no physical copy. However, the term *copy* is still defined as a material object in which the work is fixed by any method from which the work can be perceived or reproduced either directly or with the aid of a device.[29] Thus a "copy" would include digital files, including fixation in a computer random access memory.

Digital First Sale

In the previous discussion, we mentioned the first-sale doctrine[30] that distinguishes between the right to a physical copy and the right to the contents. We saw that having disposed of the physical copy, the rights holder cannot control the further disposal of that physical copy. This is what makes it possible for libraries to rent out books and for individuals to dispose of their physical copy of the copyrighted item. We mentioned that while the first-sale doctrine seems to work well in the physical world, it does not seem to apply as well to the digital world. In this section, we look more closely at the application of the doctrine to digital copies not stored in a physical format such as compact discs.

The Librarian of Congress, pursuant to a requirement to report to Congress on the effects of the Digital Millennium Copyright Act (DMCA), examined the effect of e-commerce and associated technology on the first-sale doctrine. The report distinguished between the transfer of digital physical copies, such as CDs, and the transfer of digital copies that are transferred electronically, and recommended that the first-sale doctrine does not extend to the electronic transmission.[31]

Brian Mencher notes that there is a difference in the traditional notions of ownership and current digital ownership because of the ways copies may be disposed of.[32] After selling the physical copy, the owner no longer has possession. If the copy is obtained through a digital transfer, on the other hand, and in the absence of voluntary deletion—or "forward and delete" technology ensuring automatic deletion from the transmitting computer—the original owner still has a copy of the work, which means the original owner or the transferee made a reproduction, which may be an infringement of the copyright owner's exclusive

Notable Points 21: Digital First Sale

- First-sale doctrine distinguishes between the physical copy and the expression contained in the copy.
- After the sale of the first copy, the rights holder cannot control the further distribution of that copy.
- First-sale doctrine seems to have limited application in the digital environment.
- In a report to Congress, the Librarian of Congress recommended that the first-sale doctrine does not extend to digital transmissions.
- Digital transfers still leave a copy of the transferred copy at the original source.
- Law in this area is unsettled.

right of reproduction. In trying to examine this problem, and despite the report of the U.S. Copyright Office, Mencher explored the question whether the purchaser of a digitally formatted musical work can, under the first-sale doctrine, sell or dispose of the work through a digital transfer. He noted that the law is unsettled in this area.

Mencher begins by criticizing the U.S. Copyright Office's reliance on the then-current state of the art in technology, where "forward and delete" technology did not exist, arguing that the existence of such a technology would negate the "reproduction" concerns. He also criticizes the report's reliance on the argument that copies of digitally transmitted content are not susceptible to degradation as the physical copies of digital content are. He argues that the first-sale doctrine was never about the quality of the digitally transmitted work over the quality of a physically transferred work. He argues that where deletion upon transfer is effected and the digital copy has been obtained lawfully, the digital first-sale doctrine should apply.[33]

Fair Use

Another well-known limitation is that of fair use, provided under Title 17 of the U.S. Code, section 107, which curtails the copyright owner's exclusive right of reproduction and other uses. Fair use is essentially a public policy balancing the need for the public to be well informed against the need to provide incentives to creators to create the information. It is also a necessary element for the implementation of the First Amendment's aim of encouraging dialogue and criticism. Under fair use, the reproduction of copyrighted work for purposes such as criticism, comment, news reporting, teaching, and research would not be considered a copyright infringement. This is not an exhaustive list of permitted purposes. Fair use is considered an affirmative defense to claims of infringement.

A determination of whether a use is fair depends on a consideration of several factors, including the four that the courts have taken into account: (1) purpose and character of use, (2) nature of the copyrighted work, (3) the amount and substantiality of the portion used, and (4) the effect of the use upon the potential market or value of the copyrighted work.

The first and fourth factors are closely related, in as much as they relate commerce and profit. The first factor looks at whether the purpose of use is commercial or nonprofit, and whether the use was transformative, as for example in a parody, and there was good faith or intent to deal fairly. It also looks to see if the use was for news reporting, which is by definition fair use. The fourth factor examines whether the use of the copyrighted work has the effect of substituting the market for the original, so that if such use were to be widespread, there would be an adverse impact on the potential markets for the copyrighted work, including the market for derivatives. Here, the digital librarian dealing with unpublished content should be especially aware of the owner's right to first publication.[34]

The second and third factors are also closely related in that they are looking into the nature and amount of the copyrighted work used. The second factor looks into, among other things, whether the work is factual or fiction or fantasy. A claim of fair use in a work of fiction or fantasy will probably have a steeper hill to climb than in a factual work. The third factor looks into quality and quantity, and examines extent to which the amount used is central to the copyrighted work, in other words, whether it is the "heart of the work." This factor examines whether the quantity and quality of the amount used exceeds what can be considered legitimate for fair use.[35] For computer programs, for example, reproduction of a computer program should not exceed what is necessary to understand the unprotected elements of the protected work.[36] That a work is not published does not by itself extinguish a fair use defense.[37] We examine fair use again in Chapter 8, in the context of infringement.

> **Notable Points 22: Fair Use (Part 1)**
>
> ▸ Fair use is a public policy that balances the needs of the public to access information and the need for incentives to create the information.
> ▸ Fair use is an affirmative defense against infringement claims.
> ▸ Factors in the determination of fair use:
>   - Purpose and character of use
>   - Nature of the copyrighted work
>   - Amount and substantiality of the portion used
>   - Effect of use on the potential market or value of the work

Section 108

Digital libraries and other digital content collections should take special note of another limitation on the copyright owner's exclusive right of reproduction that is provided to libraries and archives under Title 17 of U.S. Code, section 108—a section which has its origin in a mainly print world, but which has implications for digital content. Under this section, libraries or archives, or their employees acting within the scope of their employment, may legally reproduce or distribute one copy of a copyrighted work. This right is subject to certain conditions: there has to be no direct or indirect commercial advantage in the reproduction or distribution of such copy; the library or archival collections must be open to members of the public or available to other persons doing research in a specialized field, and not just those affiliated with the library or archives; and either a notice of copyright or statement that the work may be copyright-protected must be included on the reproduced or distributed copy.[38] This right does not apply to musical, pictorial, graphic or sculptural works, motion pictures, or other audiovisual work not dealing with news.[39]

> ☑ **Checklist 5: Section 108 Eligibility**
>
> ❏ Is there no direct or indirect commercial advantage in the reproduction or distribution of such copy?
> ❏ Is the library or archival collections open to members of the public or available to other persons doing research in a specialized field?
> ❏ Is a notice of copyright or statement that the work may be copyright-protected included on the reproduced or distributed copy?
> ❏ Does the work to be copied belong to a class to which the right does not apply?

If the copies are being reproduced solely for replacement of lost, stolen, damaged, or deteriorated work, or an obsolete format, then the allowable number of reproduced copies increases to three.[40] A format is obsolete if a machine necessary to use the work stored in that format is no longer available in the marketplace or is no longer being manufactured.[41] To utilize this limitation on the author's exclusive right of reproduction, the library or archive has to demonstrate that it has made an unsuccessful reasonable effort to find an unused replacement at a fair market price, and that a copy so reproduced in a digital format is not made available to the public in the digital format outside the library's premises.[42]

> ☑ **Checklist 6: Replacement of Works Under Section 108**
>
> ❏ Is the work lost, stolen, damaged, or deteriorated?
> ❏ Is the work in an obsolete format?
> ❏ Is the machine necessary to use the work no longer available in the marketplace or no longer being manufactured?
> ❏ Has the library or archive made an unsuccessful reasonable effort to find an unused replacement at a fair market value?
> ❏ Will the reproduction in digital format be made unavailable to the public in digital format outside the library's premises?

For unpublished works, the number of copies that can be reproduced or distributed increases to three, where the duplication is solely for preservation and security, or for deposit in another library or archive of the kind previously described.[43] There are limiting conditions here as well: (1) the work to be reproduced or distributed must be currently in the reproducing or distributing library's collection and (2) copies reproduced in a digital format are not distributed in that format or made available to the public outside the library or archive premises.

> ☑ **Checklist 7: Reproduction and Distribution of Unpublished Works**
>
> ☐ Is it solely for preservation and security, or for deposit in another eligible library or archive?
> ☐ Is the work currently in the reproducing or distributing library's collection?
> ☐ Are copies reproduced in a digital format withheld from distribution in that format or not made available to the public outside the library or archive premises?

If a library or archives user is going to own the copy made on the authority of section 108, certain other conditions apply. The library or archives must not have had notice that the copy would be used for purposes other than private study or research, and the library must prominently display a copyright notice at the place where reproduction orders are accepted, following the regulations of the register of copyright. Such reproduction can not exceed more than an article or other contribution to a collection or periodical issue, or a small part of other copyrighted work.[44]

However, the library or archives may copy the entire work or a substantial part of it for a requesting user if the library has determined through reasonable investigation that a copy of the requested work cannot be acquired at a fair price. The conditions on private use and copyright notice still apply in this case.[45] Likewise, owners of computer program copies, including digital collections that own such copies, are not considered infringers when they make or authorize the making of another copy or adaptation of the program if this is done as an essential part of utilizing the program in a machine, or the copy is made for archival purposes where such copy is destroyed when possession of the copy is no longer rightful.[46]

> ☑ **Checklist 8: Copying or Modifying Computer Program Copies by Owners**
>
> ☐ Is the copying or modification done as an essential part of utilizing the program in a machine?
> ☐ Is the copy made for archival purposes?
> ☐ Is the copy destroyed when possession of the copy is no longer rightful?

Section 108 allows a library or archives to escape liability for copyright infringement that is the result of the unsupervised use of its copying equipment, as long as the library displays a notice advising users that copying may be subject to copyright law. It also puts on notice for possible liability those who use such equipment or make copy requests in ways that exceed the fair use exemption. Further, the section makes it clear that it does not limit a library or archive's ability to reproduce or distribute a limited number of copies of audiovisual news programs or excerpts, does not affect the rights of fair use, and does not interfere with contractual obligations the library or archives may have entered into at the time it acquired a copy for its collection.[47]

The benefits of Section 108 were intended to cover sporadic, not systematic, reproduction and distribution of copyrighted work; and do not apply especially where the library or archives is aware it is engaging in related or concerted reproduction of single or multiple copies of the same material over one or more occasions, and the material is intended for aggregate or separate use by individuals or members of a group.[48]

> ☑ **Checklist 9: Ineligibility to Use Section 108**
>
> ❏ Is the reproduction and distribution of copyrighted work systematic, as opposed to sporadic?
> ❏ Is the library or archives aware it is engaging in related or concerted reproduction of single or multiple copies of the same material?
> ❏ Is the material intended for aggregate or separate use by individuals or members of a group?

Notwithstanding the exclusive rights of the copyright owner, a library or archives may reproduce, distribute, display, or perform in digital form a copy of a work that is within the last 20 years of its copyright term. This allowance does not apply if, after a reasonable investigation, the library or archives finds that the work is subject to commercial exploitation; the work can be obtained at a reasonable price; or the copyright owner provides notice that the work is subject to commercial exploitation and can be obtained at a reasonable price.[49]

> ☑ **Checklist 10: Copying a Work within the Last 20 Years of Its Copyright Term**
>
> ❏ The library or archive has, after a reasonable investigation, found that work is not subject to commercial exploitation,
> ❏ the work cannot be obtained at a reasonable price, or
> ❏ the copyright owner has not provided notice that the work is subject to commercial exploitation.

In 2005, a study group was convened to reexamine and update section 108 library and archives exceptions and limitations to the digital world. It issued its report in 2008 and made several recommendations, including legislative changes that would make museums eligible to take advantages of section 108 and requiring some additional eligibility criteria for libraries and archives, among others.[50] Work on library rights and limitations continues at the international level by the Standing Committee on Copyright and Related Rights (SCRR) of the World Intellectual Property Organization (WIPO), which has added three working days in its November 2011 meeting dedicated to limitations and exceptions for libraries and archives.[51]

The exclusive rights of the copyright owner are further curtailed by Title 17 of the U.S. Code, section 110, in the context of teaching, religious service, and personal use, which we shall discuss later. The effect of transfers as a limitation on the exclusive rights is discussed in Chapter 6. Likewise, the TEACH (Technology, Education, and Copyright Harmonization) Act as a limitation on the exclusive rights is discussed in Chapter 8. The subject of infringement is also discussed in more detail in Chapter 8.

Notable Points 23: Summary of Copyright Owner's Rights and Limitations

- A copyright owner can authorize a digital library to reproduce protected work.
- Because of mixed media, there may be multiple copyright owners.
- Conversion from print to digital without the copyright owner's permission may infringe on right of reproduction.
- Derivatives need not be fixed to violate the copyright owner's right of performance.
- The rights under copyright have several limitations, including the fair use exemption to infringement.
- Authors of visual art may have moral rights that continue even after they have parted with the copyright.
- Certain libraries have an exemption from copyright infringement in reproduction under section 108 of the copyright code.

HYPOTHETICAL #4

Ms. New Graduate from Hypothetical #3 has determined who owns the copyrights in Mr. Rich's collection and is now planning to have the collection available to the public. She wants to further redigitize the collection in the new Everlasting Format that has just been introduced, and she wants to create an archive of the collection. What additional issues should she now address?

A suggested response to this hypothetical question can be found in Appendix 6.

ENDNOTES

1. Notes of Committee on the Judiciary, House Report No. 94-1476.
2. See Williams Electronics, Inc. v. Artic Intern., Inc., 685 F.2d 870 (3d Cir. 1982); Atari Games Corp. v. Nintendo of America Inc., 975 F.2d 832 (Fed. Circ. 1992).
3. Auscape Intern. v. National Geographic Soc., 409 F.Supp.2d 235 (S.D.N.Y. 2004).
4. Laurie Segall, *Judge Rejects Google's Attempt to Create a Universal Library* (March 22, 2011), http://money.cnn.com/2011/03/22/technology/google_books_lawsuit/index.htm.
5. Alexandria Digital Library Project (2011), http://www.alexandria.ucsb.edu.
6. 17 U.S.C. § 101 (2006).
7. E-Discovery: Metadata Grows in Legal Significance (June 27, 2009), http://www.theposselist.com/2009/01/23/e-discovery-metadata-grows-in-legal-significance/.
8. 17 U.S.C. § 106 (3) (2006).
9. 17 U.S.C. § 101 (2006).
10. 17 U.S.C. § 109 (2006).
11. 17 U.S.C. § 106 (4) (2006).
12. 17 U.S.C. § 101 (2006).
13. 17 U.S.C. § 106 (5) (2006).
14. 17 U.S.C. § 101 (2006).
15. *Id.*
16. *Id.*
17. *Id.*
18. 17 U.S.C. § 106A (2006).
19. 17 U.S.C. § 106A (a) (2) (2006).
20. 17 U.S.C. § 106A (a) (3) (B) (2006).
21. 17 U.S.C. § 113 (d) (2006).
22. 17 U.S.C. § 106A (c) (2006).
23. 17 U.S.C. § 106A (b) (2006).
24. 17 U.S.C. § 106A (d) (2006).
25. 17 U.S.C. § 106A (e) (1) (2006).
26. 17 U.S.C. § 106A (e) (2) (2006).
27. 17 U.S.C. § 202 (2006).
28. Parfums Givenchy, Inc. v. Drug Emporium, Inc., 38 F.3d 477 (9th Cir. 1994).
29. 17 U.S.C. § 101 (2006).
30. 17 U.S.C. § 109 (a) (2006).
31. U.S. Copyright Office, Digital Millennium Copyright Act, § 104 Report (August 29, 2001); Brian Mencher, *Digital Transmission: To Boldly Go Where No First Sale Doctrine Has Gone Before*, 10 UCLA ENTERTAINMENT LAW REVIEW (2002), 47–68.
32. Mencher, *supra*, note 30.
33. *Id.*
34. Harper & Row Publisher v. Nation Enterprises, 471 U.S. 539 (1985).

35. Castle Rock Entertainment, Inc. v. Carol Publishing Group, Inc., 150 F.3d 132 (2nd Cir. 1998).
36. *Atari Games*, 975 F.2d 832.
37. 17 U.S.C. § 107 (2006).
38. 17 U.S.C. § 108 (a) (2006).
39. 17 U.S.C. § 108 (i) (2006).
40. 17 U.S.C. § 108 (c) (2006).
41. *Id.*
42. *Id.*
43. 17 U.S.C. § 108 (b) (2006).
44. 17 U.S.C. § 108 (d) (2006).
45. 17 U.S.C. § 108 (e) (2006).
46. 17 U.S.C. § 117 (2006).
47. 17 U.S.C. § 108 (f) (2006).
48. 17 U.S.C. § 108 (g) (2006).
49. 17 U.S.C. § 108 (h) (2006).
50. The Section 108 Study Group Report (March 2008), http://section108.gov/docs/Sec108StudyGroupReport.pdf.
51. World Intellectual Property Organization (WIPO), Standing Committee on Copyright and Related Rights (SCCR), *Conclusions* (November 8–10, 2010), http://www.wipo.int/edocs/mdocs/copyright/en/sccr_21/sccr_21_conclusions.pdf.

5
HOW LONG DO THE RIGHTS LAST?

IN THIS CHAPTER

We analyze the duration of the rights provided by copyright, including a discussion of the restoration of rights lost:
- Post-1978 rights
- Preexisting works
- Termination of transfers and licenses for pre-1978 works
- Effect of formalities on the duration of copyright
- Expiration of copyrights

One of the most controversial issues of copyright in the twentieth century has revolved around the duration of copyright protection. The constitutional clause that grants U.S. Congress the power to give authors some exclusive rights also mandates a "limited term" for the exercise of those rights. At the end of this limited term, works are supposed to enter the public domain and there provide resources for new creativity. Whether a work is still under copyright protection or has entered the public domain is an important concern of digital libraries. Under the Copyright Act of 1976, works of individual authorship were protected for the life of the author plus 50 years, and corporate works were protected for 75 years from the date of first publication. Under the Copyright Extension Act of 1998 (also known as the Sonny Bono Copyright Term Extension Act), these terms were extended by 20 years.

POST-1978 WORKS

Currently, a copyrightable work created on or after January 1, 1978, acquires protection upon its creation for a term consisting of the life of the author plus 70 years after that author's death.[1] Where the work has joint authors, the copyright lasts during the life of the last surviving author plus 70 years after that surviving author's death.[2] A literal reading of the statute suggests that a work published after the death of the author would be protected from the date of creation plus 70 years after the author's death—or for 70 years after the author's death, if it was created on the eve of the author's death. Also, unpublished or uncopyrighted works that were created before January 1, 1978, enjoyed the new term extension, with the earliest expiration set at December 31, 2002. If the works were published on or before December 21, 2002, the copyright protection term would not expire until December 31, 2047.[3] This was obviously a big incentive to take those pre-1978 unpublished manuscripts out of the attic and publish them.

Notable Points 24: Copyright Duration for Single and Multiple Authors

- Single-authored works have copyright protection for the life of the author plus 70 years.
- Multiple-author works are protected for the life of the last surviving author plus 70 years.
- The copyright assignee takes the remainder of the term.
- The copyright in some unpublished or uncopyrighted works created before January 1, 1978, expired on December 31, 2002.
- The copyright in some uncopyrighted works created before January 1, 1978, but published on or before December 21, 2002, will expire December 31, 2047.

Currently, works for hire, anonymous works, and pseudonymous work have copyright protection for 95 years from the date of first publication, or 120 years since they were created, whichever expires first. A special caveat applies in the case of anonymous or pseudonymous works: where the identity of the author or authors is later revealed, the term will revert back to protection based on the life of the author or last surviving author plus 70 years.[4] Where a collection contains anonymous or pseudonymous works, it is important that the digital librarian examine the copyright registration records of the U.S. Copyright Office, as the record may have been corrected to reflect the identity of the author(s) in accordance with Title 17 of the U.S. Code.[5] This is also a good place to try to determine if an author is still living or has died. If the work in the collection is 95 years old from when it was first published, or 120 years have passed since it was first created, and the register's records do not indicate whether the author is still living or has been dead for less than 70 years, any person obtaining a certified report to this effect is entitled to the assumption that the author has been dead for more than 70 years. Such a reliance on this assumption that is in good faith offers a complete defense to infringement.[6]

Before Title 17 of the U.S. Code, section 301 went into effect on January 1, 1978, unpublished works essentially had perpetual protection under common law. Section 301, whose main impact was to federalize copyright law by preempting state statutes, also erased the distinction between published and unpublished works as far as copyright protection was concerned.

Notable Points 25: Copyright Duration for Anonymous Works, Pseudonymous Works, and Works for Hire

- Anonymous works, pseudonymous works, and works for hire are protected for 95 years from publication or 120 years from creation.
- If the author of an anonymous or pseudonymous work is later revealed, the term of protection reverts back to life of the author plus 70 years, or the life of the last surviving author plus 70 years.
- The digital librarian should examine the registration records in the Copyright Office to determine if an author's identity has been ascertained.
- The digital librarian should examine the registration records in the Copyright Office to determine if an author is still living.
- Where a work is:
  - 95 years old from when it was first published or
  - 120 years have passed since it was created and
  - there is no indication in the register's record that the author is alive or has been dead for less than 70 years, a certified report creating the assumption that the author has been dead for more than 70 years may be obtained from the Copyright Office.
- Good faith reliance on the certified report is a complete defense to infringement.

PREEXISTING WORKS

If the work was already in the public domain, it remained there. However, to comply with the Berne Convention (discussed in Chapter 13), the rights of foreign authors that had been lost due to noncompliance with copyright registration formalities and whose works had fallen into the public domain were restored. We discuss restoration of rights later in this chapter. Preexisting copyrighted works whose first term of protection was still in effect as of January 1, 1978, got an extension of 28 years from when the copyright was first secured.[7] This means that for most works in this class, the duration of the copyright had expired by 2006. In terms of renewable works falling under the 1909 act, the act allowed an initial 28 years' protection, plus a renewal term of another 28 years. The 1976 act added another 19 years, and the 1998 Copyright Term Extension Act added yet another 20 years, resulting in a potential 95 years' protection from the date of publication. Generally speaking, works published on or before 1922 are in the public domain, while copyright for works that were published between 1923 and 1963 and were renewed will expire on January 1, 2019. Copyrights in works published after 1964 were automatically renewed. Stanford University has an excellent resource in the form of a searchable and downloadable copyright renewal database for books published between 1923 and 1963.[8]

> **Notable Points 26: Example of Duration for Work Published in 1925**
>
> As an example of duration, we use a work that was first published in 1925:
> Is the work in the public domain due to formalities failure?
> > Yes. It stays in the public domain.
> > No. It has an additional 28 years' protection (until 1953).
> > > Was the work properly renewed?
> > > > No. Copyright expires December 31, 1953.
> > > > Yes. It has an additional 28 years' protection (to 1981).
> > > > > If still protected, in 1976 it has an additional 19 years' protection (to 2000).
> > > > > If still protected, in 1998 it has an additional 20 years' protection (to December 31, 2020).

In the case of posthumous (that is, first published after author's death) composites such as periodicals, encyclopedia, and works for hire, the owners of such subsisting copyrights were allowed to extend the duration of copyright protection by another 67 years, meaning a work in this class could be protected until 2045.[9] Also, where the author was no longer living, the author's heirs or next of kin were entitled to seek a similar extension of the duration of copyright protection.[10]

Absent an application for a renewal, the 67-year term extension is automatically vested in the person or entity that was the copyright's proprietor on the last day of the copyright's original term—or to any other entitled person.[11] Certificates of registration of renewal and extensions of copyright term made within one year of the copyright's expiration are prima facie evidence of the validity of the copyright and the facts stated in the certificate, during the extended term.[12] In any case, all copyrights that were still in their renewal term on the implementation of the Sonny Bono Copyright Term Extension Act were declared to have a 95-year term from the date of the original copyright.[13]

TERMINATION OF TRANSFERS AND LICENSES FOR PRE-1978 WORKS

This extension for preexisting works has been much criticized. Even the *New York Times* criticized the extension in an editorial, despite the fact that it is a big content owner.[14] Moreover, presumably to help heirs capture some of the posthumous benefits of an author's work, Congress provided for the termination of transfers and licenses of the renewal copyright, other than those bequeathed by will or works for hire that were executed before January 1, 1978, by certain persons under specific conditions. An author who had executed a grant could terminate it. Where more than one author had executed the grant, an author could terminate his or her share of the grant or, if no longer living, certain persons could also terminate the grant. A surviving spouse would own the entire termination interest in the first instance but would own only one-half of the author's interest where there are surviving children of the author or surviving children of any deceased child of the author.[15] The other half is divided among the children or grandchildren, as the case may be.[16] However, in the case of the children of a deceased author's child, only a majority can exercise the termination interest.[17] Where neither a surviving spouse nor children or grandchildren exist, the executor, administrator, or personal representative of the author retains the termination interest.[18]

> **Notable Points 27: Example of Distribution of Termination Rights**
>
> The author is married and has no children.
> The spouse has full termination rights.
> The author is married and has three children: X, Y, and Z.
> The author dies:
> > The spouse has one-half of the author's interest.
> > Children X, Y, and Z have the other half, divided equally among them.
> > The spouse dies:
> > > Children X, Y, and Z own the entire termination interest, divided equally among them.
> > If child X dies:
> > > His interest passes on to his children, divided equally among them (their share in a termination interest can only be exercised by the majority).
> The author dies, spouse dies, and there are no surviving children or grandchildren:
> > The author's executor, administrator, personal representative, or trustee owns the entire termination interest.

The right of termination runs for a period of five years following the later of 56 years since the copyright was originally secured or beginning January 1, 1978.[19] The termination is achieved by notifying the grantee or successor, in writing, not less than two years or more than ten years before the effective date of termination, which must fall within the five-year window. This notice of termination (see Appendix 1) must be recorded in the U.S Copyright Office.[20] If the grant was not originally executed by the author, then all those entitled to terminate the grant are required to sign the notification.[21] Multiple authors or successors of multiple authors shall sign proportionately to their termination interest. Even where there had been a previous agreement not to terminate, the termination may still be effected.[22] The expected future rights upon termination vest on the date of the notification.[23]

Section 304(c) was designed to provide authors with added benefits and to stimulate creativity by mitigating the consequences of unwise grants they may have made before they had realized the value of their works. The courts are split on the inalienability of the termination right. The second circuit has held that the right to terminate is inalienable and cannot be surrendered or transferred. The ninth circuit, on the other hand, has allowed a voluntary agreement that benefits the author's family as an alternative to the use of the termination right.[24]

> **Notable Points 28: Termination of Rights for Pre-1978 Works**
>
> ▶ For pre-1978 works, the window for exercising the termination runs during the five years following 56 years since the original copyright, or beginning January 1, 1978, whichever is later. Thus, if a copyright was secured on January 1, 1977, the right could potentially be available during a five-year window beginning 2033.
>
> ▶ Termination right is exercised by notifying the grantee or successor in writing two to ten years before the effective date of termination.
>
> ▶ Notice must be recorded in the U.S. Copyright Office.
>
> ▶ The termination is effected regardless of prior agreement not to terminate.
>
> ▶ Termination right is designed to ameliorate the consequences of unwise grants before the value of a work is known.

Effect of Termination

Upon termination of grants and licenses, the rights revert back to the author, author's heirs, or to others who are entitled to terminate the grant.[25] However, these reversionary rights do not bring with them a transfer of any contractual rights that the grantee had with third parties.[26] Derivative rights pursuant to a transfer or license continue to operate during the term of the renewed and extended term, even where no application to register or extend the term of the work's original copyright had been made, as well as following termination of grant, provided no further derivatives were made based on such a transferred, licensed, or terminated grant.[27] Further grants on a terminated grant are valid only if made after the termination's effective date, except that an agreement to make a future grant between an author or an author's successors and an original grantee following the serving of the notice of termination is valid.[28] Even for termination rights that had expired on the effective date of the Sonny Bono Copyright Term Extension Act, the above conditions (17 USC 304(c)(1-6)) apply for terminations during the last 20 years of the current copyright term. Also, for such expired rights, termination may still be effected during a five-year window beginning at the end of 75 years from the date the copyright was originally obtained.[29]

Termination rights are essentially there to protect authors from adverse consequences of contracts they may have entered into, where, for example, a work became more valuable later than when they entered into the contract. This was supposed to protect the starving author and his family, by allowing them to recoup the later success of a work; essentially a clawback giving the author an opportunity for a new deal.

Transfers made on or after January 1, 1978, are governed by section 203 and generally follow the same formula as in works made before 1978. These will be discussed in the next chapter.

> **Notable Points 29: Reversion of Termination Rights**
>
> ▶ The rights of terminated grants revert back to the author or successors.
> ▶ Contractual rights grantee had with third parties are not included in the reversionary rights.
> ▶ Derivative rights transferred or licensed are allowed to continue following termination, as long as no new derivates are made from the terminated rights.
> ▶ Further grants on a terminated grant are not valid unless made after the termination's effective date.

FORMALITIES AND THEIR EFFECT ON DURATION OF COPYRIGHT

We noted that post 1976, there is no requirement for formalities in order to obtain copyright protection. Before 1976, there were several formalities: publication, notice, registration, and deposit of copies with the Library of Congress. It was thought that by complying with formalities, it was easier for owners to register a work than for others to find out if the work was copyrighted. Also the copyright notice alerted all to the fact that a work was protected.

Some of the consequences of not following formalities were dire; for example, "general publication" without compliance with formalities effectively put a pre-1976 work in the public domain. Limited publication, for example, in giving lectures or dramatic compositions, sometimes led to less drastic results. For works that were generally published between January 1, 1978, and March 1, 1989 (the effective date of the Berne Convention Implementation Act of 1988), a copyright notice was required and copyright owners were allowed to "cure" the lack of notice by adding it.[30] Failure to cure entitled infringers to claim "innocent infringement" if they had relied on the lack of notice.[31]

The removal of formalities was mainly driven by the desire of the United States to conform to the Berne Convention. However, there are several advantages for observing some of the formalities, including registration (an online application form for copyright registration is available at http://www.copyright.gov/forms/notice.html). For example, not only does one get federal jurisdiction for infringement actions when one registers, but it is also a requirement in bringing suit for copyright infringement, as well as for obtaining statutory damages and attorney fees, provided the registration is timely—before commencement of the infringement or within three months of publication.[32] Registration is also prima facie evidence of copyrightability, dispensing with an "innocent infringer" defense.[33]

Restoration of Lost Rights Due to Formalities

As mentioned, foreign authors who lost their copyright for not following U.S. copyright formalities had their copyrights restored. This represents a big trap for the unwary digital librarian, who might have and use content that is mistakenly believed to be in the public domain. Congress took this action in 1994 when it passed section 104A in the Copyright Act, essentially to comply with the Rule of Retroactivity of the Berne Convention.[34] With that move, a large body of work that was previously thought to be in the public domain was suddenly protected again.

The restoration applies to works by authors from countries that are members of the Berne Convention treaty or the World Trade Organization, whose protection under U.S. copyright law had been lost due to failure to comply with formalities such as renewal or proper notice. Restoration of copyright protection was automatic, as long as the works were still protected under the laws of the country of origin and the copyright was never owned by a government.[35] For most countries, the restoration of lost rights went into effect on January 1, 1996. The period of protection is the remainder of the time that a copyright would have been in effect in the United States if the work had not entered into the public domain.[36]

Notable Points 30: Restoration of Rights Lost Due to Formalities Noncompliance

- Beware: Not all pre-1976 works not complying with formalities are in the public domain.
- Copyrights were restored to foreign authors who had lost them because of not complying with U.S. formalities.
- Only authors from the Berne Convention or World Trade Organization member countries are eligible for the restoration.
- If work was still protected in the country of origin, restoration of rights was automatic.
- Rights for most countries were restored with effect from January 1, 1996.
- Protection is for the remainder of the time copyright protection would have been available in the United States if the work had not entered the public domain.

For the restored copyright, ownership reverts initially to the author or initial right holder, based on the law of the country where the work originated.[37] Upon the restoration of the copyright, the owner may give notice of intent to enforce the copyright or an exclusive right to a party that had relied on the fact the work was in the public domain, either by filing the notice with the U.S. Copyright Office or by serving the relying party directly. This notice is equally effective as to other reliance parties with actual knowledge of the service to any party. The *Federal Register* publishes these notices for public access. An example of a list of restored copyrights for which Notices of Intent to Enforce were processed can be accessed at http://www.copyright.gov/fedreg/1998/63fr5141.html.

A party that created derivative works based on the restored copyrighted work before December 8, 1994 (the enactment of the Uruguay Round Agreements Act, discussed in Chapter 13) is free to continue exploiting the work but must pay a

> **☑ Checklist 11: Lost Copyrights Due to Noncompliance with Formalities**
>
> ☐ Was the copyright lost in the United States due to noncompliance with formalities?
>
> ☐ Was the copyright owner from a country that is a Berne Convention or World Trade Organization member?
>
> ☐ Is the work still protected in its country of origin?
>
> ☐ Have you been served with a notice of intent to enforce copyright or an exclusive right, or has the owner filed such a notice with the U.S. Copyright Office, or are you aware of any such service of notice on another party?

reasonable compensation for such use. The compensation is determined by a U.S. district court and reflects the effect on the actual or potential market for the work, as well as the relative contributions of the author of the original work and the party exploiting the derivative work.[38]

EXPIRATION OF COPYRIGHTS

When the term of copyright protection expires, the work enters the public domain, free for anyone to use and reuse. This is in keeping with the intent of the intellectual property clause in the U.S. Constitution. We should note that copyright terms run to the end of the year in which they would expire[39] and that when a copyright expires, contractual rights and obligations based on that copyright also expire.[40] Furthermore, works not "created" in the sense of being fixed in a tangible medium are still protected by common law; this is because they are not a proper subject matter for copyright protection and thus such laws would not be preempted by the federal copyright law as provided by section 301.[41]

Note also that for works protected by multiple copyrights—an original work and a derivative, for example—a copyright may expire for the derivative but may still be in effect for the original (this is probably going to occur with material that was subject to renewal requirements). For example, the copyright in the play *Pygmalion* was still in effect, while copyright in the movie based on the play had expired. Defendants took the movie, which was now in the public domain, and distributed it. The owners of the copyright in the play sued, and the court ruled that the derivative copyright protected only the new material, not the material derived from the underlying work.[42]

> **Notable Points 31: Expiration of Copyrights**
>
> ▶ Even though most individual works have copyright protection that covers the life of the author plus 20 years, and corporate works have protection between 95 and 120 years, the actual period of protection may vary depending on the particular circumstances of the works.
>
> ▶ Copyrights for works created after 1978 cannot be lost to the public domain because of failure to follow formalities.
>
> ▶ Copyright transfers and licenses subject to renewal can be terminated by the granting author or legally authorized persons during a specific window, which for most works runs until 2034.
>
> ▶ Contractual rights and obligations based on a copyright expire when that copyright expires.

> **HYPOTHETICAL #5**
>
> Refer back to Hypothetical #3 for situation background. However, in this instance, a significant portion of the collection is by anonymous and pseudonymous authors, and some of it is previously unpublished. Also, a small portion of the collection might be in the public domain, because the authors were foreigners who had not complied with the former copyright registration formalities. Some pieces were published in 1921, others in 1925. In addition, some authors transferred their copyrights to Mr. Rich in 1977, and some licensed to him the right to create derivative works. What additional issues should Ms. Graduate be concerned with?
>
> *A suggested response to this hypothetical question can be found in Appendix 6.*

ENDNOTES

1. 17 U.S.C. § 302 (a) (2006).
2. 17 U.S.C. § 302 (b) (2006).
3. 17 U.S.C. § 303 (a) (2006).
4. 17 U.S.C. § 302 (c) (2006).
5. 17 U.S.C. § 408 (d) (2006).
6. 17 U.S.C. § 302 (e) (2006).
7. 17 U.S.C. § 304 (a) (2006).
8. Stanford University, Libraries and Academic Information Resources, *Copyright Renewal Database* (2011), http://collections.stanford.edu/copyrightrenewals/bin/page?forward=home.
9. 17 U.S.C. § 304 (B) (2006).
10. 17 U.S.C. § 304 (C) (2006).
11. 17 U.S.C. § 304 (2) (2006); 17 U.S.C. § 304 (3) (2006).
12. 17 U.S.C. § 304 (4) (B) (2006).
13. 17 U.S.C. § 304 (b) (2006).
14. *Keeping Copyright in Balance* [Editorial], NEW YORK TIMES (February 21, 1998), http://www.nytimes.com/1998/02/21/opinion/keeping-copyright-in-balance.html.
15. 17 U.S.C. § 304 (c) (2006).
16. 17 U.S.C. § 304 (c) (2) (A–B) (2006).
17. 17 U.S.C. § 304 (c) (2) (C) (2006).
18. 17 U.S.C. § 304 (c) (2) (D) (2006).
19. 17 U.S.C. § 304 (c) (3) (2006).
20. 17 U.S.C. § 304 (c) (4) (A) (2006).
21. 17 U.S.C. § 304 (c) (4) (2006).
22. 17 U.S.C. § 304 (c) (5) (2006).
23. 17 U.S.C. § 304 (c) (6) (B) (2006).

24. Allison M. Scott, *O Bother: Milne, Steinbeck, and Emerging Circuit Split over the Alienability of Copyright Termination Rights*, 14 JOURNAL OF INTELLECTUAL PROPERTY LAW (2007), 357–388.
25. 17 U.S.C. § 304 (c) (6) (2006).
26. Mills Music, Inc. v. Snyder, 469 U.S. 153 (1985).
27. 17 U.S.C. § 304 (4) (A) (2006); 17 U.S.C. § 304 (6) (A) (2006).
28. 17 U.S.C. § 304 (c) (6) (D) (2006).
29. 17 U.S.C. § 304 (d) (2006).
30. 17 U.S.C. § 405 (2006).
31. 17 U.S.C. § 405 (b) (2006).
32. 17 U.S.C. § 412 (2006).
33. 17 U.S.C. § 410 (c) (2006).
34. Dam Things from Denmark v. Russ Berrie & Company, 290 F.3d 548 (3rd Cir. 2002).
35. 17 U.S.C. § 104A (a) (2) (2006).
36. 17 U.S.C. § 104A (a) (1) (B) (2006).
37. 17 U.S.C. § 104A (b) (2006).
38. 17 U.S.C. § 104A (d) (3) (B) (2006).
39. 17 U.S.C. § 305 (2006).
40. Shoptalk, Ltd. v. Concorde-New Horizons Corp., 168 F.3d 586 (2nd Cir. 1999).
41. 17 U.S.C. § 301 (2006).
42. Russell v. Price, 612 F.2d 1123 (9th Cir. 1979).

6
HOW ARE RIGHTS ACQUIRED FROM OWNERS?

IN THIS CHAPTER

We discuss the acquisition of rights as well as the termination of copyright transfers and licenses and the reversion of those rights:
- Transfer of copyright
- Termination of rights granted after January 1, 1978
- Reacquistion of rights and licenses through reversion

TRANSFER OF COPYRIGHT

The Copyright Act of 1976 defines a transfer of copyright ownership as an assignment, mortgage, exclusive license, or any other conveyance, alienation, or hypothecation of a copyright or of any of the exclusive rights comprised in a copyright, whether or not it is limited in time or place of effect, but not including a nonexclusive license.[1] As discussed in previous chapters, an owner of a copyright is free to transfer the complete bundle of rights contained in the copyright, or any specific rights from the bundle, to other parties by way of conveyance or by operation of law or licensing. The new owner of any specific, separately transferred right from the bundle is entitled to all the protection and remedies that the original copyright owner had.[2] This is a departure from the Copyright Act of 1909, where a copyright was indivisible; only the owner of the entire copyright had standing to sue for infringement.

The transfer may also be bequeathed by will and may pass as personal property through intestate succession laws. A government body or official cannot force the transfer rights of copyright ownership that the copyright owner has not previously voluntarily transferred.[3] In proceedings for bankruptcy and mortgage foreclosures, however, this prohibition does not apply because the copyright owners have voluntarily subjected themselves to the legal proceedings.[4]

A transfer of copyright ownership or exclusive license has to be accomplished in writing by an instrument of conveyance or other note or memorandum of transfer;

this document must also be signed by the rights' owner or an authorized agent, at the time of the agreement, unless the transfer has been accomplished by operation of law, such as the court's interpretation of express or implied consent in an agreement. Because the Copyright Act does differentiate between a transfer of ownership of a copyright and transfer of ownership of a copy, this can present special problems relating to computer software. Whether a transfer was of a copy or the copyright in software was the subject of the case in *Shugrue v. Continental Airlines*.[5] The court in that case ruled that a contract granting "all right, title and interest" in a software was a transfer of copyright, where it was clear from the language of the contract that the parties intended to transfer all rights, including copyrights, and not merely to license those rights. However, if the language had been ambiguous, then a contract would not be read to have transferred copyright ownership. Instead, the court would have looked to see if it merely amounted to a transfer of the material object. Even though we previously indicated that there is no need to use the magic word *copyright* when executing a transfer agreement, the absence of that word may lead to ambiguity about what exactly is being transferred.[6]

Notarization is not a requirement but may be useful as prima facie evidence of the transfer's execution. If a purported transfer is not in writing and signed, then it is not valid, unless the transfer is by operation of law.[7] However, when it comes to infringement litigation where the original copyright owner and a copyright transferee both agree as to the ownership of copyright, a defendant cannot invoke the writing requirement to avoid suit.[8] An oral agreement that is followed by the execution of a writing is valid[9] as long as the oral agreement has not expired.[10] Also, a nonexclusive license agreement can be oral[11] or even implied[12] because it does not involve a transfer of copyright ownership. In fact, the court in *Conwell v. Gray Loon Outdoor Marketing Group* was of the opinion that nonexclusive licenses are not within the purview of copyright law.[13] It is important for the digital librarian to remember the concept of copyright divisibility: when we are talking about a copyright owner, we may be talking about an owner of just one of the exclusive rights that has been transferred, while the remaining rights may have been transferred to other parties. The owner of the exclusive right can sue a party for infringement, independently of other owners of the remaining rights.

To record a transfer of copyright ownership in the U.S. Copyright Office it is necessary that the conveying document pertains to a copyright (it does not have to bear the magic word *copyright*; see the Recordation information at http://www.copyright.gov/forms/ for recording optional cover sheet) and bears the actual signature of the executing person or is accompanied by a sworn or official certification that it is a true copy.[14] The legislative history indicates that the recording can be of any signed document that relates to copyright, including grants of nonexclusive licenses or other assignments[15] and any means of conveyance can transfer copyright.[16] Such a recordation provides constructive notice to others of the facts stated in the document, if the recorded document specifically identifies a work such that a reasonable title or registration number search would reveal the work after indexing by the register of copyrights. To be recorded, the work has to be registered, a topic that will be discussed more in Chapter 14.[17]

Failure to record does not affect the validity of the transfer, but it does affect conflicting transfers. Where there are conflicting transfers, the one executed and recorded first prevails, unless, without notice of the earlier transfer, the later transfer was recorded first in good faith and for valuable consideration.[18] However, a nonexclusive license will prevail over a conflicting transfer of copyright ownership where the license was granted before the execution of the transfer or, without notice of the transfer, was granted before the transfer was recorded. The nonexclusive license has to be evidenced by a written instrument signed by the rights' owner or authorized agent.[19] Also, priority does not arise in cases of bad faith where, for example, the second transferee knew of an earlier transfer. Because of the scope for fraud, transfers in the form of gifts do not take priority.

The purpose of the recordation requirements is to protect licensees, assignees, and other bona fide purchasers by revealing the copyright owner's true identity so that they are able to contact such owner for permission to use a copyrighted work.[20] Creditors may also obtain a security interest in copyright from a copyright owner and may record a copyright mortgage or an agreement to such effect in the Copyright Office.[21] This would perfect the security interest, provided the underlying work is also registered in the Copyright Office.[22] Perfection of security interests is the process of providing constructive public notice of an interest in a secured property by possessing or controlling the property or by complying with applicable laws. For copyright, one may perfect the security interest by recording under section 9-302 of the Uniform Commercial Code (UCC) or under section 205 of the Copyright Act, or both.[23] It is important to note that federal copyright law does not preempt state law with respect to perfection and priority of security interests in unregistered copyrights, as the Copyright Act does not provide for the rights of parties that are secured by unregistered copyrights.[24] Indeed, Ward noted this conflict between state law, as reflected in the UCC, and federal law, as reflected in copyright law.[25]

The digital librarian licensee must be careful not to go beyond the rights transferred. Grantors will probably try not to have a new technology provide a windfall to the licensee, while the licensee will seek as broad a coverage of future technologies as possible. Most cases in this area are determined on the basis of contract law, where the issue turns not so much on copyright law but on the interpretation of nonexclusive or implied grants. Thus, courts use contract interpretation principles from state laws in the construing of licenses and copyright transfers.[26] It is important to note, however, that when copyright owners transfer a copyright, they lose all the exclusive rights provided by the Copyright Act, unless they have reserved some of those rights. This means they cannot reproduce, distribute, publicly perform or display the work, or create any derivatives of the work. This is true even where the transferor is the original author.[27]

> **Notable Points 32: Copyright Transfers**
>
> ▶ Copyright ownership is property that can be transferred.
> ▶ The rights in copyright are divisible and can be separately transferred, thus different rights may belong to different parties.
> ▶ Copyright ownership rights cannot involuntarily be transferred from an owner by government.
> ▶ Transfer of copyright or an exclusive license must be by a written and signed instrument of conveyance by the copyright owner.
> ▶ A court may interpret an agreement to find express or implied transfer.
> ▶ A nonexclusive license agreement can be oral or even implied, because it does not involve a transfer of copyright.
> ▶ Recording of the copyright transfer conveyance instrument gives constructive notice of the identity of the copyright owner and resolves the priority of conflicting transfers: the first executed and recorded transfer prevails. It also serves to perfect security interests in copyrights.
> ▶ A nonexclusive license granted before the execution and recording of a transfer prevails over a conflicting transfer of copyright ownership.
> ▶ The courts use principles of contract law to interpret copyright transfers.

TERMINATION OF RIGHTS IN TRANSFERS AND LICENSES GRANTED AFTER JANUARY 1, 1978

Termination of transfers and licenses operate as acquisition or reacquisition of rights that had previously been alienated. Again, this is to rectify the situation where a creator alienated rights in a creation well before the full value of such creation became evident and is designed to benefit the surviving spouse, children, and grandchildren. In the previous chapter we discussed termination of transfers and licenses pertaining to works whose term of copyright renewal was still on as of January 1, 1978. In this section we look at termination of transfers and licenses granted by the author on or after January 1, 1978, many of which will begin to be exercised by 2013.

Following the 1976 Copyright Act, there was no longer any need to renew copyrights, but termination rights were retained. Other than for works made for hire, the exclusive or nonexclusive grants of transfers and licenses of copyright that an author executes on or after January 1, 1978, other than by a will, may be terminated by the author, if living, or by persons entitled to exercise more than one-half of the author's termination interest, as described in this section. Where there are joint authors, the majority of the authors who executed the grant may also terminate it; if any such author is dead, his or her successors in interest may terminate.[28] Furthermore, termination may occur whether or not there was any agreement to the contrary, including agreements to make a will or future grants.[29] Thus, Congress intended to make termination rights inalienable.[30]

The termination period runs during the five-year period beginning at the end of 35 years following the execution of the grant or, if the grant is for publication rights, during the period beginning at the end of 35 years from the date of the work's publication, or 40 years from the date of the grant's execution, whichever is earlier.[31] This rule acknowledges the fact that some time could elapse between the signing of the contract for publication and the actual publication.[32] To effect the termination, a written advance notice to the grantee or successor in title is required (see Appendix 1). The notice should be signed by the required number and proportion of owners of the termination interest, or their agents, and must state the effective date of termination falling within the five-year termination period. The notice must be served not less than two years or more than ten years before the effective date of termination, and a copy of the notice must be recorded in the Copyright Office before the effective date of termination.[33] The notice must specifically state that the termination is being made under section 203 and must identify each grantee whose interest is being terminated, the addresses to which the notice is being sent, the date the grant had been executed, the title and name of the author or authors, the copyright registration number where available, the effective termination date, and a statement that all persons necessary to sign the termination of the grant have done so.[34]

If the author is dead, the statute prescribes ownership of the termination interest as follows: the entire interest is owned by the surviving spouse, but the spouse owns only one-half interest if there are surviving children or grandchildren of the author.[35] If there is no surviving spouse, the author's surviving children and the surviving children of any deceased child own the entire termination interest.[36] The interests of the author's surviving children and grandchildren are divided and exercised among them per stirpes, according to the numbers represented, and only a majority of the children of a deceased child can exercise the share of one of them who is deceased.[37] In the previous chapter, we saw an example of how this distribution works. The author's executor, administrator, personal representative, or trustee owns the entire termination interest where no surviving spouse, children, or grandchildren are known.[38]

> **Notable Points 33: Termination of Copyright Transfers**
> - Previously made copyright transfers may be terminated during a specific window of time.
> - This right allows copyright owners to enjoy the later success of their works whose rights they transferred before their full value was known.
> - For post-1978 works, many termination rights will begin to be exercised in 2013.
> - Termination rights can be exercised despite agreements to the contrary.
> - Only a living author, or persons entitled to exercise more than one-half of the author's termination interest, may terminate.
> - Notice of termination must be served on the transferee not less than two years or more than ten years before the effective date of termination and must be recorded in the Copyright Office before the date the termination is to become effective.

REACQUISITION OF RIGHTS AND LICENSES BY REVERSION

Upon termination, the rights to the terminated grants revert to the author(s) or other lawful holders of the termination interests, including those who did not sign the required advance notice of termination to the grantee or successors to the grantee.[39] However, rights to derivative works that were granted before the termination can continue to be exercised under the grant's terms but cannot expand to the preparation of other derivative works based upon the copyrighted work that is covered by the terminated grant.[40] Thus, there is no right to create new derivative works after the rights to the original work have been terminated.

On the date that the notice of termination of grant is served, the future reversionary rights become vested in the author(s) or other lawful successors in interest in the same proportion as ownership in the termination rights.[41] Any further grant or agreement to make a grant covered by the terminated grant, by owners in whom the rights have vested, must be signed by the same number and proportion of owners as were required to terminate the grant but covers those eligible persons who did not sign. Persons who die after rights have vested are represented by their heirs at law or legal representatives.[42] Such further grants or agreements to make a grant are valid only if made after the effective termination date of the original grant, except for agreements made between the vested beneficiaries and the original grantee or the original grantee's successor in title, which are valid after the service of the notice of termination.[43] It should be noted that the right of termination is not automatic: it is an option that has to be exercised.

Grants that are not terminated continue to the end of the copyright protection term.[44]

The policy interests that termination and reversion of rights are designed to ameliorate are the unequal bargaining positions of authors stemming from the difficulties in determining a work's value prior to its being exploited. This maneuver in effect terminates any prior deals of copyright transfers or licenses, and provides the authors or their heirs an opportunity to make a new deal. However, this also presents a threat to publishers and film producers because a valid notice of termination could erase any rights to future profits.[45] It also brings uncertainty to digital content managers who have acquired copyright by transfer, because those transfers can be terminated.

In the next chapter, we take a closer look into the issue of licensing—especially licensing in the special case of the digital media environment.

Notable Points 34: Effect of Termination of Copyright Transfers

▶ Rights to terminated grants revert to the author or successors in interest.
▶ Previously granted rights to make derivative works survive the termination under the terms of the original grant.
▶ New derivative works may not be made based upon the terminated work.
▶ A copyright transfer termination right is not automatic; it has to be exercised.
▶ Transfers that are not terminated continue to the end of the copyright protection term.

HYPOTHETICAL #6

Imagine the same situation as Hypothetical #4. In this instance, Ms. Graduate is interested in the New Digital Library acquiring rights from some of the copyright owners. What *additional* issues should Ms. Graduate be concerned with?

A suggested response to this hypothetical question can be found in Appendix 6.

ENDNOTES

1. 17 U.S.C. § 101 (2006).
2. 17 U.S.C. § 201 (d) (2006).
3. 17 U.S.C. § 201 (e) (2006).
4. Notes of Committee on the Judiciary, House Report 94-1476.

5. Shugrue v. Continental Airlines, Inc., 977 F.Supp. 280 (S.D.N.Y. 1997).
6. Raymond Nimmer, *Intellectual Property Issues*, 4 LAW OF COMPUTER TECHNOLOGY (2010), 29.
7. 17 U.S.C. § 204 (2006).
8. Monroig v. RMM Records and Video Corp., 194 F.R.D. 388 (D. Puerto Rico 2000).
9. Valente-Kritzer Video v. Pinckney, 881 F.2d 772 (9th Cir. 1989).
10. A & A Plush Inc. v. SKM (USA) Enterprises Inc., 47 U.S.P.Q.2d (BNA) 1438 (C.D. Cal. 1998).
11. Conwell v. Gray Loon Outdoor Marketing Group, Inc., 906 N.E.2d 805 (Ind. 2009).
12. Effects Associates, Inc. v. Cohen, 908 F.2d 555 (9th Cir. 1990).
13. *Conwell*, 906 N.E.2d 805.
14. 17 U.S.C. § 205 (a) (2006).
15. Notes of the Committee on the Judiciary, House Report 94-1476.
16. Jules Jordan Video, Inc. v. 144942 Canada Inc., 617 F.3d 1146 (9th Cir. 2010).
17. 17 U.S.C. § 205 (c) (2006).
18. 17 U.S.C. § 205 (d) (2006).
19. 17 U.S.C. § 205 (e) (2006).
20. Northern Songs, Ltd. v. Distinguished Productions, Inc., 581 F.Supp. 638 (S.D.N.Y. 1984); Gaiman v. McFarlane, 360 F.3d 644 (7th Cir. 2004).
21. In re Peregrine Entertainment, Ltd., 116 B.R. 194 (C.D. Cal. 1990).
22. In re AEG Acquisition Corp., 127 B.R. 34 (C.D. Cal. 1993), affirmed in 161 B.R. 50 (9th Cir. 1993).
23. Elise B. May, *Where Your Priorities Should Be: Analysis of the Perfection and Priority of Security Interests in Copyrights As It Affects Bankruptcy*, 11 BANKRUPTCY DEVELOPMENTS JOURNAL (1995), 509–540.
24. In re World Auxiliary Power Co., 303 F.3d 1120 (9th Cir. 2002).
25. Thomas M. Ward, *Creating and Perfecting Security Interests in Intellectual Property*, MAINE BAR JOURNAL (1994), 154–164.
26. Yount v. Acuff Rose-Opryland, 103 F.3d 830 (9th Cir. 1996).
27. Nimmer, *supra*, note 6.
28. 17 U.S.C. § 203 (a) (1) (2006).
29. 17 U.S.C. § 203 (a) (5) (2006).
30. Allison M. Scott, *O Bother: Milne, Steinbeck, and Emerging Circuit Split over the Alienability of Copyright Termination Rights*, 14 JOURNAL OF INTELLECTUAL PROPERTY LAW (2007), 357–388.
31. 17 U.S.C. § 203 (a) (3) (2006).
32. Notes of Committee on Judiciary, House Report No. 94-1476.
33. 17 U.S.C. § 203 (a) (4) (2006).
34. 37 C.F.R. 201.10.
35. 17 U.S.C. § 203 (a) (2) (A) (2006).
36. 17 U.S.C. § 203 (a) (2) (B) (2006).
37. 17 U.S.C. § 203 (a) (2) (C) (2006).

38. 17 U.S.C. § 203 (a) (2) (D) (2006).
39. 17 U.S.C. § 203 (b) (2006).
40. 17 U.S.C. § 203 (b) (1) (2006).
41. 17 U.S.C. § 203 (b) (2) (2006).
42. 17 U.S.C. § 203 (b) (3) (2006).
43. 17 U.S.C. § 203 (b) (4) (2006).
44. 17 U.S.C. § 203 (b) (6) (2006).
45. Scott, *supra*, note 30.

7

WHAT SHOULD YOU KNOW ABOUT DIGITAL MEDIA LICENSES?

IN THIS CHAPTER

We take a closer look at digital media licenses, particularly how the content of licenses and interaction with multiple parties can impact how digital media are used and exploited:
- Need to interact with multiple parties
- Examining the license
- Compulsory licenses for copyrighted music

INTRODUCTION

A license is essentially a contract between the content owner and a party wishing to use that content. The intellectual property license is of course based on the underlying rights conferred by the property. In the case of copyright, these would be the exclusive rights provided by copyright law. The license specifies the uses allowed by the copyright owner that will not trigger an infringement suit. In return, the copyright owner is compensated in the form of a license fee or royalty. Thus, the owner continues to maintain ownership but makes use possible, thereby enabling the progress of science and the useful arts that the Constitution intended.

The license may be nonexclusive or exclusive. In a nonexclusive license, the copyright owners can grant the same license to multiple parties for the same rights and may continue to use the rights themselves. This license can be oral or in writing; it can even be implied. But it would need to be in writing to be recorded in the Copyright Office.

If exclusive, it must be in writing and the owner of the right being licensed must sign. When a copyright owner grants an "exclusive" license, this does not mean that the entire copyright has been transferred. Only one or more rights have been transferred, and the owner retains some rights, which he may subsequently transfer as an exclusive grant to some other licensee. As we shall discuss, the license may be limited in its terms to a specific duration, use or uses, territory of use, media, and even language of use. An exclusive licensee may sublicense the right. However, some courts recognize the right to sublicense only if it is expressly provided for in writing by the copyright owner.[1] Because a licensee cannot grant greater rights than he or she has in the sublicense, the rights in the sublicense expire upon termination of the original license. The owner of the exclusive license may bring suit on infringement regardless of the consent of the copyright owner.

> **Notable Points 35: Licenses**
>
> ▶ Intellectual property license is based on the underlying rights conferred by the copyrighted work.
> ▶ Unlike a copyright transfer, a license allows the copyright holder to retain copyright while allowing others to use some of the owner's rights.
> ▶ A license can be exclusive or nonexclusive; if exclusive, it must be in writing.
> ▶ An owner of an exclusive license has standing to bring suit on infringement of the licensed right.

NEED TO INTERACT WITH MULTIPLE PARTIES

One of the principal considerations in licensing is to establish whether the parties to the contract have the authority to enter into an agreement. As we discussed in Chapter 2, one of the challenges of digital media licensing is the need to interact with multiple parties and obtain multiple licenses for the same work. Because the work is often multimedia, the digital collection manager will find that a separate license may be needed for the sound, video, and nonmedia data portions of the work. This gives rise to the need to identify all the rights holders because there may be layers upon layers of rights, and these may overlap in ways that are sometimes unpredictable.

The periods of copyright protection may also vary for some of the rights, depending on when the particular aspect of the work was first created and whether the entity that created the particular work was an individual, joint, or corporate author. Also, as discussed in the previous chapter, because copyrights can be assigned, authors are not necessarily the rights holders, and because of copyright divisibility, copyright holders may not necessarily hold all the exclusive rights. Where the work has several authors and is therefore joint, it is important for the digital content manager acquiring a license to remember that each author has the right to separately grant nonexclusive licenses for the same right to multiple parties without the need for consent from the other authors. Thus it is important to perform some due diligence to verify that there are no conflicting licenses to third parties and to obtain a written warranty as to the ownership and the right to license a particular right. This is in addition to conducting a copyright and licenses records search at the Copyright Office.

> **Notable Points 36: Licenses and Multiple Copyright Owners**
>
> ▶ In digital media licensing, there is often need to interact with multiple rights owners.
> ▶ The duration of copyright protection varies.
> ▶ Authors may not necessarily hold all the exclusive rights.
> ▶ It is important to conduct due diligence to ensure no conflict with licenses granted to third parties.

EXAMINING THE LICENSE

Because a license is a contract, it is important to examine its terms carefully.[2] This is especially important where the license is unilateral, rather than bi- or multilateral. Unilateral licenses tend to be of the shrink-wrap kind, a contract contained in software packaging that is activated by the user's opening of the packaging. It may also come in the form of a web-wrap (or click-wrap), where a user is asked to click Yes or No to an electronic license for digital content. Unlike shrink-wrap, the litigation in this area centers on whether a particular unilateral license is enforceable. The results of such litigation vary from jurisdiction to jurisdiction. *ProCD v. Zeidenberg*, for example, found shrink-wrap licenses enforceable.[3] *Vault v. Quaid* had earlier held that a license agreement prohibiting decompilation or disassembly of a program was unenforceable, as it was preempted by copyright law.[4] Bilateral or multilateral (between a vendor and more than one institution) licenses are usually subject to negotiations between the parties, whereas unilateral licenses are not. Also, a license may contain a choice of law statement, which essentially spells out the jurisdictional law that is to govern the agreement. The jurisdiction and the law may not always be convenient and favorable to licensees.

The Liblicense website of the Yale University Library has some very useful resources for typical license agreement clauses.[5] A typical license, for example, will contain statements regarding who the parties to the contract are; a definition of major terms used in the agreement; the subject matter or rights being granted by the license; the obligations of the parties; the duration of the license and the terms for renewal; fees and methods of payment; conditions of use and scope of the license (including whether it is exclusive or nonexclusive; single site or multisite; single user or multiple users; authorized users, etc.); when the contract may be terminated; choice of law; alternative dispute resolution mechanism; a statement on whether the license can be assigned; nonwaiver of failure to enforce a breach of a clause; the level of support or documentation provided; a severability clause that protects the agreement if some clauses are found to be unenforceable; and a confidentiality clause.

The agreement might also contain clauses requiring the licensee to protect copyright and other intellectual property; a requirement to provide usage and other statistics to the licensor, some of which may raise privacy issues; a declaration to hold the licensor harmless or indemnification for liability for third-party damages; a statement on amendments to the agreement; and a statement that the parties signing the agreement are authorized to do so. In this context, it is important to remember that licenses fall under contract law, which is covered under state laws, which can vary from state to state.[6]

In some cases, however, a digital content manager may simply want to use content under copyright. In that case, there may already be collective licensing entities set up to collect license fees or royalties. The Copyright Clearance Center (http://www.copyright.com) is the best known resource for mostly nondigital content. For multimedia formats, resources include the American Society of Composers, Authors, and Publishers (ASCAP) (http://ascap.com) for music royalties and the Motion Picture Licensing Corporation (MPLC) (http://www.mplc.org) for film.

It is important to note that the license cannot exceed the purpose for which it was granted. In *Gilliam v. ABC*, for example, the plaintiffs, who created the television show *Monty Python*, sued ABC because the television network broadcast episodes that had been heavily edited to allow commercial interruption. The plaintiffs claimed that the edited episodes impaired the integrity of the original work. The court concluded that ABC's editing went beyond what the plaintiffs had authorized and not only impaired the plaintiffs' right of attribution but also created an infringing derivative.[7]

For software, it may sometimes be necessary to have an escrow service for source code. In this scenario, a licensor deposits the software source code with a third party. In the event the licensor becomes insolvent, the licensee can obtain the source code from the escrow service. Also, it may be necessary to include in the terms of the license an indemnification clause covering third-party claims of copyright infringement.

New Uses and Geographical Considerations

Also, questions often arise over whether the licenses negotiated cover novel uses that are made possible by advances in technology. In addition to the need for acquiring multiple licenses for a work, the license may also cover different areas of consideration. One such area may involve a limitation of geographic territory. Where a geographic restriction is present, repercussions can occur where the content is opened up for access through the Internet.

Likewise, a limitation on language may be set, where, for example, the license might require use in specific language territories or markets. For example, the product may be used in Spanish-speaking countries but not in Chinese-speaking countries. Also, a license can be exclusive or nonexclusive, with an exclusive license generally demanding a premium fee. Though increasingly rare, a license may also include restriction on platform use, such that there would be a different fee for using the license on a Mac operating platform as opposed to a Windows platform, especially where the digital material is designed to work on one and not the other platform. Allowing sublicensees to use software without the licensor's permission may open up the licensee to vicarious or contributory infringement.

Alteration or Modification of Content

For video or audio clips, there may also be limitations on the portion that can be used or the ability to alter or modify content. As discussed, certain media may necessitate licensing from multiple rights owners. A music recording, for example, may require a license from the copyright holder of the music and lyrics, as well as the copyright holder of the sound recording. But performers may also have some rights that would need to be licensed. Sometimes the owner of both of these rights may be a single individual, usually a producer or a recording company that has been assigned all of the underlying copyrights. The license should make explicit who owns modifications and/or derivatives, if the right to modify is included in the license. Generally, the licensee will own the modification and will grant back a license to the licensor. Else, there may be an express assignment of rights to the licensor. However, the licensor may not want the responsibility for the modified code.

Some of the licensing issues include permissions to synchronize music with images, which means obtaining rights from both the music rights owner and the image rights owner, as well as releases from actors, if it is a film.[8] Todd Brabec and Jeffrey Brabec give examples of nine options for synchronization licenses for a song in a television production: a period-determinate free television license; Internet streaming; life-of-copyright free television license; downloads; all television rights for life of copyright; all media rights excluding theatrical; home video buyout including mobile phones; theatrical use outside the United States; and use of song in promos.[9] The duration of the license is always a negotiable issue but can in no case be longer than the copyright protection of the underlying work. Licenses may also limit reproduction of copies, conditions or prohibitions of multiple and simultaneous uses on single or multiple computers, as well as limitations of content vendor liability. More seriously, licenses may infringe on fair use rights.

> **Notable Points 37: Scope of Licenses**
> - Shrink-wrap licenses are enforceable.
> - Instead of obtaining a license, some content may be used by paying a royalty to a royalty collection agency.
> - The use of a license cannot exceed the purpose for which it was granted.
> - An escrow service can be utilized for software source code.
> - Read the small print in licenses:
>   - Use of a license may be limited by such restrictions as geography, language, or even platform use.
>   - There may also be restrictions on the ability to alter or modify content.
> - A license cannot exceed the period of the copyright protection of the underlying work.

COMPULSORY LICENSES FOR COPYRIGHTED MUSIC

The exclusive rights in nondramatic musical works to reproduce and distribute copies or phonorecords of the copyrighted work to the public are subject to compulsory licensing.[10] A compulsory license requires the owner of an intellectual property to license the use of that property at a fixed rate determined by statute or by judicial decision.[11] Compulsory licensing to make and distribute phonorecords of a work is available where, under the copyright owner's authority, the work has been distributed to the public in the United States. Again, the compulsory license does not apply to works like movie soundtracks, ballet scores, and such; reproduction of this type of work requires permission from the copyright owner. Persons seeking the compulsory license must have as their primary purpose distribution to the public for private use, including distribution by means of digital delivery. Such licenses are available only for sound recordings that were originally fixed lawfully.[12] This compulsory license includes the privilege of rearranging the music to conform to the style of a particular performance, as long as no derivative protection is sought for the new arrangement.[13]

A person wishing to obtain the compulsory license has 30 days after making the phonorecords to notify the copyright holder of the intention to do so. Such notice must be served before the work is distributed. Where the owner cannot be located or identified, the notice can be filed with the Copyright Office (see the form Notice of Use of Sound Recordings Under Statutory License at http://www.copyright.gov/forms/). When distribution commences before the filing of such a notice of intent, the opportunity for a compulsory license is lost and the making and distribution become infringing acts, unless a negotiated license is in existence.[14]

Distribution in this sense means the person exercising the compulsory license has permanently and voluntarily given up possession.[15] Persons entitled to obtain compulsory licenses may negotiate royalty rates with copyright owners of nondramatic musical works, provisions of the antitrust laws notwithstanding.[16] The Copyright Office sets periodic mechanical royalty rates (current rates can be obtained at http://www.copyright.gov/carp/m200a.html). Failure to pay royalty terminates a compulsory license.[17] There are agencies, such as Harry Fox Agency, that collect royalties and issue mechanical and synchronization licenses. We examine royalties in Chapter 11.

Digital phonorecord delivery under a compulsory license has to carry any information encoded in the sound recording identifying performing artist, title, and related information, including the underlying musical work and writer.[18] Sound recording copyright owners may be liable for infringement of copyrights in a nondramatic musical work that is embodied in the sound recording.[19] Section 118 also provides a compulsory license for using certain works in connection with noncommercial broadcasting.[20]

The compulsory license has not been without its critics. Howard Abrams, for example, considers the compulsory license as sanctioning the creation and exploitation of a derivative work (the sound recording) without the authorization of the copyright owner of the underlying work (the musical composition), in violation of the copyright owner's exclusive right to make derivatives.[21]

Notable Points 38: Compulsory Licenses

▶ Despite their controversy, compulsory licenses are available to make or distribute phonorecords of nondramatic musical works, if the work has been distributed to the public under the copyright owner's authority.

▶ Compulsory licenses apply only to those sound recordings that were originally lawfully made.

▶ The copyright owner must be provided with a Notice of Intent to Use a compulsory license.

▶ Failure to pay royalty terminates a compulsory license.

With the developing technology in mobile devices come old issues wrapped in new contexts. One of the issues involves whether downloading a digital file that embodies a song constitutes a public performance.[22] Courts have not found a performance right for a copyright owner in a download but recognize a mechanical right in a ringtone (see http://www.copyright.gov/carp/m200a.html for the mechanical rate on a ringtone). This puts the United States at odds with many other countries that recognize performance rights in a download.[23]

> **HYPOTHETICAL #7**
>
> In working on Hypothetical #6, Ms. Graduate discovers that she has to obtain a license for the use of some of the content in Mr. Rich's collection. What *additional* issues should Ms. Graduate be concerned with?
>
> *A suggested response to this hypothetical question can be found in Appendix 6.*

ENDNOTES

1. Gardner v. Nike, Inc., 279 F.3d 774 (9th Cir. 2002).
2. ARLENE BIELEFIELD and LAWRENCE CHEESEMAN, TECHNOLOGY AND COPYRIGHT LAW (New York: Neal-Schuman, 2007).
3. ProCD, Inc. v. Zeidenberg, 908 F.Supp. 640 rev'd 86 F.3d 1447 (1996).
4. Vault Corp. v. Quaid Software, 847 F.2d 255 (5th Cir. 1988).
5. Yale University Library, *Liblicense* (2011), http://www.liblicense.com.
6. Bielefield and Cheeseman, *supra*, note 2, at 146.
7. Gilliam v. American Broadcasting Companies, 538 F.2d 14 (2nd Cir. 1976).
8. Todd Brabec and Jeffrey J. Brabec, *The New and Complex World of Television Music Licensing*, 27 ENTERTAINMENT AND SPORTS LAWYER (2010), 1–7.
9. Todd Brabec and Jeffrey J. Brabec, *Mobile Music Licensing: A New Model, a Variation of the Old, or Just Something New and Different*, PRACTISING LAW INSTITUTE (April–May 2010), PLI/Pat 425.
10. 17 U.S.C. § 115 (2006).
11. ROGER D. BLAIR and THOMAS F. COTTER, INTELLECTUAL PROPERTY: ECONOMIC AND LEGAL DIMENSIONS OF RIGHTS AND REMEDIES (Cambridge, England: Cambridge University Press, 2005).
12. 17 U.S.C. § 115 (a) (1) (2006).
13. 17 U.S.C. § 115 (a) (2) (2006).
14. 17 U.S.C. § 115 (b) (2006).
15. 17 U.S.C. § 115 (c) (2) (2006).
16. 17 U.S.C. § 115 (3) (B) (2006).
17. 17 U.S.C. § 115 (6) (2006).
18. 17 U.S.C. § 115 (3) (F) (2006).
19. 17 U.S.C. § 115 (3) (H) (2006).
20. 17 U.S.C. § 118 (2006).
21. Howard B. Abrams, *Copyright's First Compulsory License*, 26 SANTA CLARA COMPUTER AND HIGH TECHNOLOGY LAW JOURNAL (2010), 215–253.
22. Brabec and Brabec, *supra*, note 8.
23. *Id.*

8

WHAT IS INFRINGEMENT AND WHAT ARE THE RESULTS OF INFRINGEMENT?

IN THIS CHAPTER

We examine the infringement arena, an area that is a background concern throughout this book:
▶ Infringement
▶ Noninfringement
▶ Action for infringement
▶ Remedies for infringement
▶ Damages for infringement

INFRINGEMENT

Copyright infringement is not confined, as we often think, to simply copying a protected work. Technically, an infringer is anyone who violates any of the rights provided to the copyright owner by the Copyright Act. The violation of any of the exclusive rights of a copyright owner may be considered an infringement.[1] Anyone, including a state, an instrumentality of a state, an official or employee acting in an official capacity, can be an infringer and is subject to sanctions just like any nongovernmental entity.[2]

Thus infringement may be found where, without the copyright owner's permission, one reproduces copies; prepares derivative works that are based on the protected work; distributes copies to the public by sale, rental, lease, or lending; performs or displays the work publicly, including, in the case of sound recordings, performing the work by means of digital audio transmission.[3] Infringement also includes violation of the rights of authors of visual art to attribution and integrity, which include the right of the author to claim authorship of a work, and to prevent the use of the author's name as the author of a work that has been mutilated or otherwise distorted.[4] The intentional mutilation, distortion, or other modification of a visual work that is prejudicial to the author's honor or reputation, as well as the destruction of a work of recognized stature, would also be an infringement of the author's rights.

It is also an infringement to import into the United States copies of a work that have been acquired outside the United States, without permission of the copyright owner.[5] Such importation is an infringement on the copyright owner's exclusive right to distribute under section 106 of Title 17 of the U.S. Code. Likewise, it is an infringement to export infringing copies from the United States.[6]

Digital scanning is essentially copying, which, if unauthorized, is infringing. In *Phillips v. Kidsoft* a court found infringement by the defendant who had scanned some 30 mazes from the plaintiff's books into a computer, altered them, and published them on a website.[7] The court took pains to distinguish between the mazes in which the plaintiff had no copyright and the "book of mazes," in which he had copyright. Similarly, the court in *Tiffany Design v. Reno–Tahoe Specialty* found the defendants' act of scanning the plaintiff's photograph into a computer violated the plaintiff's exclusive right of reproduction.[8]

Courts investigate copying by looking into whether there is direct or circumstantial evidence of direct copying. Circumstantial evidence would include access to the copyrighted work and or substantial similarity, such that the latter work could not have been independently created. There is a split in the courts about whether to look for substantial similarity in the work as a whole or to first remove uncopyrightable elements of the copied material—the so-called abstraction-filtration–comparison analysis.[9] The courts may also examine whether it is a case of improper appropriation where an ordinary observer or intended audience would see substantial similarities between two works. However, independently created works, though substantially similar, would have independent copyrights. This is because copyright law encourages creativity while punishing copiers. Uploading of digital content to media devices may also infringe on patents issued to cover such uploading. A case was filed on February 23, 2011, in a U.S. district court in Texas against, among others, Samsung and Facebook for using proprietary technology to enable file uploads to smartphones, tablets, and webpages.[10]

When courts examine infringement claims, they first establish whether the plaintiff has ownership of a valid copyright. If the plaintiff has a certificate of copyright registration, this would be prima facie evidence that the subject matter is indeed copyrightable and a valid copyright exists. The burden would then shift to the defendant to prove the invalidity of the copyright.

Copyright infringement is a strict liability offense, which means there is neither an intent requirement, nor a need to prove causation and damages. Intent, however, may be relevant when the issue concerns fair use.

Certain media may present interesting problems, because more than one type of intellectual property may be at issue. In hosting a computer game on an Internet bulletin board, for example, one may be violating the copyright in the game as well as the trademark of the game's producer.[11]

> **Notable Points 39: Prima Facie Infringement**
> - Elements of prima facie infringement:
>   - Existence of a valid copyright
>   - Infringement of an exclusive right
> - Elements of prima facie copying:
>   - Access to the copyrighted work
>   - Substantial similarity to the copyrighted work

Contributory Infringement

One need not have committed the infringing act to be held liable for infringement. One can be held accountable as a contributory infringer. Contributory infringement is to induce, cause, or materially contribute to infringing conduct by third parties while knowing of the infringing activity.[12] This may include supplying the instruments for committing the infringement. However, the mere design and distribution of a product which can be used for substantial lawful means but which is in fact used for unlawful purposes does not necessarily impute secondary liability to the designer or distributor.[13] Contributory infringement may be imposed even when there was no intention to infringe.[14] Knowledge of infringement is a substantial element of contributory infringement, as is an act or participation in the infringement. If, for example, the content provider has previously received cease-and-desist letters, knowledge may be imputed.

Vicarious Infringement

Vicarious infringement occurs when one profits from direct infringement while not taking any steps to exercise a right to stop or limit the infringement.[15] The theory of respondeat superior holds an employer liable for infringing acts his or her employee makes while the employee is acting within the scope of employment, even when the employer has no knowledge of the activity—and even when the employer has prohibited such activity.[16] However, it is not necessary to have an employer-employee relationship; any special relationship can generate vicarious liability.[17] As noted in the following section, a library or archives is not liable for vicarious infringement when others have used its unsupervised equipment to infringe copyright, provided there is a copyright notice displayed on such equipment.

Notable Points 40: Contributory and Vicarious Infringement

- Inducing, causing, or materially contributing to infringing conduct by third parties can lead to liability for contributory infringement.
- Supplying the instruments for committing the infringement may also lead to contributory infringement.
- No intent is required for a finding of contributory infringement.
- Acts of infringement by a person or entity that you control may lead to liability for vicarious infringement.
- A library is not liable for vicarious infringement liability in cases where unsupervised reproduction equipment is used by third parties, as long as where such equipment displays a copyright notice.

NOT INFRINGEMENT

In spite of the prohibition against importing or exporting copies without the copyright owner's permission, it is not an infringement when the importation or export is done under authority of the federal or state government, except for copies for use in schools or copies of any audiovisual work not imported for archival use. Also, the prohibition does not include the importation or export of a copy for personal use, including the importation by scholarly or religious organization of copies for lending or archival purposes that are not part of a systematic reproduction or distribution.[18]

Fair Use

There are situations where action that would be considered infringement is nevertheless excused, for example, whether an action is considered fair use. Fair use is a long-established judicial doctrine that has now been set into statutory code, and as discussed in Chapter 4, is one of the limitations to a copyright owner's exclusive rights. Purposes generally considered fair use, and thus not infringing, include criticism, comment, news reporting, teaching, and scholarship.[19]

The courts consider several factors in determining whether a use of protected work is fair and therefore noninfringing: the purpose and character of the use, whether or not it is commercial; the nature of the work; the amount and substantiality of the portion used in relation to the work as a whole; and the market and economic impact of the use.[20]

Unfortunately, the determination of fair use and thus noninfringement is a fact-specific exercise, and thus it is difficult to predict the outcome of an infringement claim. One of the telltale signs of misuse of the fair use doctrine is bad faith. Where, for example, a magazine obtained an unauthorized copy of a president's memoirs and then preempted a book publisher in the publication of the memoirs, the court found infringement because—even though news reporting is generally fair use—in this case the manuscripts were unpublished and the magazine published what was the "heart of the book," and what was published essentially supplemented the market for the original work.[21] Digital librarians often deal with unpublished content, and though the Harper & Row case was predigital, it has not been overruled.

The legislative history shows that at the time of passing the section 107 amendment, various stakeholders gave their views to the Judiciary Committee. The Ad Hoc Committee of Educational Institutions and Organizations on Copyright Law Revision, the Authors League of America, Inc., and the Association of American Publishers, Inc., for example, came up with an agreement worked out between authors and publishers that laid out guidelines for classroom copying in educational institutions[22] that would later be largely superseded by the TEACH Act in 2002,[23] discussed in the next section. Likewise, representatives of the music industry came out with their guidelines for the educational use of music.[24]

At this point, it is worth mentioning that although not strictly a part of the fair use doctrine, it is not an infringement for authorized entities to reproduce and distribute copies of nondramatic literary work in specialized formats, including Braille, audio, or digital text, for the exclusive use of persons with disabilities.[25] Such copies must bear (1) a notice that reproduction in any other format is an infringement and (2) a copyright notice identifying the copyright owner and the date of original publication.[26] Authorized entities are government bodies or nonprofit organizations that have as a primary mission to provide specialized training services to people who qualify as blind or disabled.[27]

Notable Points 41: Fair Use (Part 2)

▶ Fair use is a judiciary-derived limitation of the copyright owners' exclusive rights, which has now been codified in the Copyright Act.

▶ Among the factors considered by a court to determine fair use are:
- purpose and character of the use,
- nature of the work,
- amount and substantiality of the portion used in relation to the work as a whole, and
- market and economic impact of the use.

▶ A finding of fair use depends on the specific facts of the case.

Library and Archives Reproduction

Section 108 of Title 17 specifically exempts libraries and archives (hereinafter libraries) that meet certain criteria from infringement liability if they make or distribute one copy of a work, provided the reproduction or distribution is not for the purpose of direct or indirect commercial exploitation; the library collections are open to the public and other researchers; and reproduced or distributed work includes a copyright notice, or a statement that the work may be protected by copyright. The library may also reproduce up to three copies of an unpublished work for preservation and security purposes or for deposit in a library whose collections are open to the public. The copy to be reproduced has to be currently in the reproducing library's collection. If the reproduction is in a digital format, the digital reproduction shall be used only inside the library premises and shall not otherwise be distributed in that format outside those premises.

It is also not an infringement to reproduce up to three copies of a published work to replace a copy that is damaged, that is lost or stolen, or that is deteriorating. This exemption also applies to a work stored in a format that has become obsolete. If a machine or device that can read the format is no longer manufactured or reasonably commercially available, then the format is considered obsolete.[28] To take advantage of this exemption, the library has to demonstrate that after a reasonable effort it has determined that an unused copy of the work could not be obtained at a fair price. It also has to ensure that copies reproduced in a digital format are not made available to the public in that format outside the library premises. This right of reproduction and distribution applies where the copy of no more than one article or other contribution to a collection or periodical issue becomes the property of the user, provided the library has had no notice that the copy would be used for other than scholarly purposes and it prominently displays a warning notice that the material may be protected by copyright laws.[29] This exemption also applies where the copy of an entire work or a substantial part of the work becomes the property of a user, provided the library has after a reasonable effort determined that a copy could not be obtained at a fair market price, provided, again, that the library has no prior notice of uses other than scholarly and prominently displays a copyright warning at the place where reproduction orders are taken.[30]

A library will be relieved from infringement liability for the unsupervised use of reproduction equipment provided the equipment displays a warning indicating that copying may be subject to copyright laws. However, persons using such equipment or requesting copies are liable for infringement if use exceeds fair use.[31] Systematic copying or reproduction is also infringement, but libraries are allowed to participate in interlibrary arrangements that may include systematic reproduction of multiple copies provided they do not have as a purpose providing a subscription substitute.[32]

Furthermore, it is not infringement for a library to copy a work (including in digital form) during the last 20 years of the copyright protection term for preservation and scholarly purposes provided the library has after a reasonable investigation determined, or there is no contrary notice from the copyright owner, that (1) the work is not subject to normal commercial exploitation or (2) a copy of the work cannot be obtained elsewhere at a reasonable price.[33] These reproduction rights do not apply to musical, pictorial, graphic or sculptural works, motion pictures or other nonnews audiovisual work, except in cases of preservation and security or research use, or for the replacement of damaged, lost, or stolen works.[34]

Performance and Display for Teaching and Instruction

It is not an infringement for instructors or students to perform or display a work during face-to-face teaching activities in a classroom or similar space of a nonprofit educational institution that is devoted to instruction. However, it is an infringement where a copy of a motion picture or other audiovisual work displayed or performed was made illegally and the person displaying or performing the copy knew or had reason to know the copy was illegally made.[35] This exemption worked well in the traditional classroom but less well in distance education.

Responding to changes in technology and the growing use of online distance education, Congress in 2002 passed the Technology, Education, and Copyright Harmonization (TEACH) Act. The idea was to limit infringement liability for education activities that involved the uploading, transmission, and storing of digital content by enabling the use of copyrighted material in distance education in the same way such content could have been used in a live classroom setting.

According to the TEACH Act, it is not an infringement to perform a nondramatic literary or musical work or limited portions of other work, or to display a work in an amount comparable to what is typically displayed during a live classroom session. This does not apply to works produced or marketed primarily for display or performance as part of mediated instructional activities that are digitally transmitted.[36]

There are several requirements, however, for taking advantage of the exemptions in section 110 (2). The performance or display has to be (1) made by or at the direction or actual supervision of an instructor and (2) an integral part of a class session offered as a regular part of the systematic mediated instructional activities of (3) a government body or an accredited nonprofit educational institution.[37] The performance and display transmission also has to be directly related and of material assistance to the teaching content. The transmission, to the extent technology will allow, has to be made solely for the students enrolled in the course or government body officials as part of their official duties or employment.[38] In addition, the transmitting body has to have in place copyright policies and copyright information that it relates to its users and must provide notice to the users that the course material may be subject to copyright protection. For digital transmissions, the transmitting body has to apply technological measures that prevent retention of the work that is in an accessible form by recipients beyond the end of the class session and prevents further dissemination of the work to others by the recipients. Furthermore, the transmitting body must not itself engage in conduct that would interfere with technological measures put into place by copyright owners to prevent such retention or further unauthorized dissemination.[39]

During services at a place of worship or other religious assembly, it is not an infringement to perform a nondramatic literary or musical work or a religious dramatico-musical work.[40] Also, if the performance of a nondramatic literary or musical work that is not transmitted to the public is not for commercial purpose and the performers, organizers, and promoters have not been compensated, then this, too, is not an infringement.[41] However, to take advantage of this exemption, (1) there should be no direct or indirect admission charge, or the net proceeds are used not for private gain but for educational, charitable, or religious purposes, and (2) the copyright owner has not served a written and signed notice objecting to the performance to the person responsible for the performance. Such notice shall be served seven days before the date of performance and shall state reasons for the objection.[42] Other exemptions include freedom from vicarious liability for governmental bodies or nonprofit horticultural organizations for performances by others at an agricultural show,[43] or the performance of a nondramatic musical work designed for handicapped persons that is noncommercial and transmitted through the facilities of a governmental body or a noncommercial education broadcasting station.[44] Exemptions from copyright infringement arising out of performing exist also for nonprofit veteran or other nonprofit fraternal organizations. College and university fraternal organizations do not enjoy this exemption unless the performance is a social function held solely to raise money for a specific charitable purpose.[45] Further, a transmitting organization is exempt from infringement liability if it is licensed to transmit to the public or performance or display of the work, or to make a copy of the transmission for its own use, provided it

> **Notable Points 42: Fair Use (Part 3)**
>
> ▶ For teaching purposes, a work comparable to what would be typically displayed in a live classroom session may be digitally transmitted under section 110(2) of Title 17 in the U.S. Code.
>
> ▶ Works that are produced or marketed primarily for display or performance as part of mediated instructional activities are not covered by this exemption.

destroys such a copy within six months of the transmission, unless the copy is made exclusively for archival purposes.[46] Such an organization may also convert print or other analog versions of works into a digital format if no digital version of the work is available to the institution or if the digital version available is so protected by technological protection measures that it cannot be used under the TEACH Act.[47]

☑ **Checklist 12: TEACH Act Exemptions**

- ❏ Is the performance or display:
  - ❏ made by, at the direction of, or under the actual supervision of an instructor?
  - ❏ an integral part of a class session offered as a regular part of the systematic mediated instructional activities of a government body or an accredited nonprofit educational institution?
  - ❏ directly related and of material assistance to the teaching content?
- ❏ Is the transmission, to the extent technology will allow, made solely for the students enrolled in the course or government body officials as part of their official duties or employment?
- ❏ Does the transmitting body have copyright policies and copyright information that it relates to its users?
  - ❏ Does it provide notice to the users that the course material may be subject to copyright protection?
- ❏ Has the transmitting body applied technological measures to prevent retention of the work that is in an accessible form by recipients beyond the end of the class session?
  - ❏ If so, do these measures prevent further dissemination of the work to others by the recipients?
- ❏ Has the transmitting body refrained from engaging in conduct that would interfere with technological measures put into place by copyright owners to prevent such retention or further unauthorized dissemination?

Computer Programs

For an owner of a computer program, it is not an infringement to make a copy or adapt the computer program as long as the new copy or adaptation is created as an essential step in the utilization of the computer program on a machine used for utilizing such programs, or the new copy or adaptation is only for archival purposes and all archival copies are destroyed when rightful possession of the computer program ceases.[48] Exact copies made under this exemption may be transferred along with the original copies as part of a lease, sale, or transfer of all the rights in the program. However, the copyright owner's permission will be required to transfer any adaptations.[49] Likewise, it is not an infringement for the owner or lessee of a machine to make or authorize the making of a copy of a computer program to activate a machine containing an authorized copy of the program for the purpose of repairing or maintaining the machine.[50] A copy so made must not be used in any other manner and must be destroyed immediately after the completion of the repair or maintenance, and no part of the computer program that is not necessary for such repair or maintenance shall be accessed.[51]

OTHER NONINFRINGING ACTIVITIES

In *Ticketmaster v. Tickets.com* (2000), the plaintiff alleged infringement because the defendant had copied entire pages from the plaintiff's website in order to extract factual data, had republished the factual data on the defendant's website and had provided users with deep links to internal pages of the plaintiff's website.[52] Based on the teachings of *Feist Publications v. Rural Telephone Service,* the court in this particular case found no infringement in the copying of factual data and also did not find infringement in providing deep links to the plaintiff's website.[53]

ACTION FOR INFRINGEMENT

Where there is an infringement of an exclusive right under a copyright, the legal or beneficial owner of that right is entitled to bring suit against the infringer.[54] A beneficial owner may include a former copyright holder who has given up the copyright in exchange for royalties. The litigant is required to register a copyright claim before commencing litigation, or show that application to register had been attempted and refused.[55] The court may require the owner of the right to give notice to any person whom copyright office records has shown to have an interest in the exclusive right and may require others having or claiming an interest in the copyright to join in the lawsuit.[56] A copyright infringement plaintiff is required to specify the particular original works subject to the copyright claim, demonstrate that he or she owns the copyright in those works, that the copyrights have been registered as required by statute, and then specify when and how the defendant infringed the copyright.[57]

REMEDIES FOR INFRINGEMENT

Several remedies are available to an owner of a right that has been or is being infringed. These include injunctions, impounding, and destruction of the infringing articles.

Injunctions

A court having proper jurisdiction may issue a temporary or final injunction to restrain or prevent copyright infringement.[58] The granting of an injunction is a discretionary power of the court, may be served to anyone anywhere in the United States, and is enforceable by any U.S. court having jurisdiction on the person served.[59] A temporary injunction preserves the status quo so that no party is further injured until a case is determined.[60] To determine whether a temporary injunction should be issued, a court looks into several factors. The first factor the court examines is whether there is reasonable likelihood that a party will succeed on the merits of the case. The second factor looks into whether the lack of an injunction will result in irreparable harm to the plaintiff. The third factor is a balance test between the likely injury to the plaintiff as opposed to harm to the defendant. The last factor the court looks into is whether it is in the public interest to issue or deny the injunction.[61] The issuance of a temporary injunction may be accompanied by a bond by the plaintiff protecting the defendant against damages caused by the injunction, should it turn out that the injunction was in error. Permanent injunctions are more likely to be given where repeat violations are likely.

Impound and Disposition

During the time that an action for infringement is pending, a court may order produced all copies claimed to be infringing and all articles which may be used for the reproduction of the offending articles, and may take under the custody of the court all records documenting the manufacture, sale, or receipt of articles involved in the infringing activities.[62] There is no need to wait for an injunction: the seizure may happen at any time a suit has been filed, without waiting for an injunction. The court may enter a protective order protecting the confidentiality and proprietary information in the records under its custody.[63] The court may order the destruction or other reasonable disposition of infringing copies and all articles used for reproduction as part of a final judgment or decree.[64]

DAMAGES FOR INFRINGEMENT

Civil

A copyright infringer is generally liable for the copyright owner's actual damages suffered as a result of the infringement. The copyright owner can also recover any profits the infringer has made that can be attributed to the infringement. The copyright owner is required only to allege the infringer's gross revenue, and then it is up to the infringer to prove deductibles and parts of the profit not attributable to the infringement.[65]

However, instead of actual damages and profits, the copyright owner may elect to pursue statutory damages, for infringement of any one work, of not less than $750 and not more than $30,000. Parts of a derivate work or a compilation will count as one work.[66] But where a copyright owner can prove willful infringement, the court may increase the statutory damages to not more than $150,000. Likewise, where the infringers are able to prove that they were not aware they were infringing or had no reason to believe their acts constituted an infringement, the court may reduce the statutory damages to not less than $200.[67] An example of such an infringement might involve the use of a restored copyright under the Berne Convention. The copyright owner must have registered the copyright to be eligible for statutory damages.

If the infringer was an employee or agent of a nonprofit educational institution, library, or archives acting within the scope of his or her employment and believed use of the copyrighted material was fair use, the court shall remit statutory damages,[68] sometimes to nothing. Providing false contact information to a domain name registrar for a domain name used in connection with the infringement creates a rebuttable presumption of willful infringement.[69] The court may allow recovery of the full costs of litigation except against the United States or an officer of the United States; it may also award reasonable attorney fees to the prevailing party.[70] Again, the copyright must have been registered to get the attorney fees.

Criminal

A person who willfully infringes a copyright for commercial exploitation or personal financial gain may be subject to criminal punishment if the reproduction, including by digital means, involves copies with a total retail value of $1,000 or makes available a work that he or she knows is being prepared for commercial distribution on a computer accessible by members of the public.[71] Works falling under this section include computer programs, musical works, motion pictures or other audiovisual work, and sound recordings. Works being prepared for commercial distribution refers to where the copyright owner has a reasonable expectation of commercial distribution, the copies have not been commercially distributed, or, in the case of a motion picture, it has been exhibited in an exhibition facility but not made available for sale to the general public in a format intended for the viewing public.[72]

Persons putting a false copyright notice or words implying such a notice on an article and who, with fraudulent intent, publicly distribute or import for public distribution an article bearing such notice are subject to a criminal fine of up to $2,500.[73] Similarly, a person who, with fraudulent intent, removes a copyright notice from a copyrighted work is subject to a fine of the same amount.[74] Making a false representation of a material fact in the process of an application for copyright registration is also subject to up to a $2,500 criminal fine.[75]

Criminal proceedings have a five-year statute of limitation, while civil actions have a three-year statute of limitation,[76] unless there is fraudulent concealment, which would toll the statute. The main pushers of criminal sanctions in copyright law have been the media and publishing industry, especially the Recording Industry Association of America, when it comes to digital file sharing. In 2008, President George W. Bush signed into law P.L. 110-403, the Prioritizing Resources and Organization for Intellectual Property (PRO-IP) Act, which created the Office of the U.S. Intellectual Property Enforcement Representative, allowed the Department of Justice to bring civil suits on copyright holders' behalf, and essentially enhanced criminal and civil penalties for intellectual property infringement. In March 2011, the White House issued a white paper proposing to make illegal streaming of content a federal felony and arguing that Congress must fix the law to facilitate the enforcement of intellectual property laws. Streaming is different from downloading in that it is nonpermanent and does not store content on the end user's device.[77] Among the recommendations is one giving law enforcement authority to seek a wiretap for criminal trademark and copyright offenses.[78]

In Chapter 10, we discuss the relief available for Internet service providers under Title 17, section 512, of the U.S. Code.

Notable Points 43: Remedies for Infringement

▶ A legal or beneficial owner of a copyright right is entitled to bring suit against an infringer.

▶ Remedies for injunction may include:
- injunctions against the infringer and/or
- impound and disposition of the infringing articles.

▶ Penalties for infringement may be civil or criminal.

▶ Civil actions must be brought within three years after the infringement is discovered.

▶ Criminal infringement action must be brought within five years.

HYPOTHETICAL #8

Ten months into managing Mr. Rich's collection, New Age Library recognizes Ms. Graduate's high quality of work and gives her the additional responsibilities of managing the works in Hypothetical #2. Despite her best efforts to comply with copyright law, Ms. Graduate begins to worry that she may be infringing some copyrights on some of the works in the collection. What are some of the issues she would need to address?

A suggested response to this hypothetical question can be found in Appendix 6.

ENDNOTES

1. 17 U.S.C. § 106–122 (2006).
2. 17 U.S.C. § 501 (2006).
3. 17 U.S.C. § 106 (2006); 17 U.S.C. § 501 (2006).
4. 17 U.S.C. § 106A (2006).
5. 17 U.S.C. § 602 (2006).
6. 17 U.S.C. § 602 (2) (2006).
7. Phillips v. Kidsoft LLC, 52 U.S.P.Q.2d 1102 (D. Md. 1999).
8. Tiffany Design v. Reno–Tahoe Specialty, 55 F.Supp.2d 1113 (D. Nevada 1999).
9. Computer Associates Intern v. Altai, 982 F.2s 693 (2d Cir. 1992).
10. Summit 6 v. Research In Motion, 2011 WL 645157 (N.D. Texas, 2011).
11. Sega Enterprises v. MAPHIA, 857 F.Supp 679 (N.D. Cal. 1994).
12. Intellectual Reserve v. Utah Lighthouse Ministry, 75 F.Supp.2d 1290 (C.D. Utah 1999).
13. Metro–Goldwyn–Mayer Studios v. Grokster, 545 U.S. 913 (2005).
14. F.E.L. Publications v. National Conference of Catholic Bishops, 466 Supp. 1034 (N.D. Ill. 1978).
15. *Metro–Goldwyn–Mayer Studios*, 545 U.S. 913.
16. Gershwin Pub. Corp v. Columbia Artists Management, 443 F.2d 1159 (2nd Cir. 1971).
17. *F.E.L. Publications*, 466 Supp. 1034.
18. 17 U.S.C. § 602 (3) (A–C) (2006); 17 U.S.C. § 108 (g) (2) (2006).
19. 17 U.S.C. § 107 (2006).
20. 17 U.S.C. § 107 (1–4) (2006).
21. Harper & Row Publishers v. Nation Enterprises, 471 U.S. 539 (1985).
22. See Notes on the Committee of the Judiciary, House Report 94-1476.
23. 17 U.S.C. § 110 (2) (2006).
24. U.S. COPYRIGHT OFFICE, *Circular 21: Reproduction of Copyrighted Works by Educators and Librarians* (Washington, DC: U.S. Copyright Office, 2009).
25. 17 U.S.C. § 121 (2006).
26. 17 U.S.C. § 121 (2) (2006).
27. 2 U.S.C. § 135a (2006).
28. 17 U.S.C. § 108 (c) (2006).
29. 17 U.S.C. § 108 (d) (2006).
30. 17 U.S.C. § 108 (e) (2006).
31. 17 U.S.C. § 108 (f) (2006).
32. 17 U.S.C. § 108 (g) (2006).
33. 17 U.S.C. § 108 (h) (2006).
34. 17 U.S.C. § 108 (i) (2006).
35. 17 U.S.C. § 110 (1) (2006).

36. 17 U.S.C. § 110 (2) (2006).
37. 17 U.S.C. § 110 (2) (A) (2006).
38. 17 U.S.C. § 110 (2) (B–C) (2006).
39. 17 U.S.C. § 110 (2) (C–D) (2006).
40. 17 U.S.C. § 110 (3) (2006).
41. 17 U.S.C. § 110 (4) (2006).
42. *Id.*
43. 17 U.S.C. § 110 (6) (2006).
44. 17 U.S.C. § 110 (8) (2006).
45. 17 U.S.C. § 110 (10) (2006).
46. 17 U.S.C. § 112 (2006).
47. 17 U.S.C. § 112 (f) (2006).
48. 17 U.S.C. § 117 (a) (2006).
49. 17 U.S.C. § 117 (b) (2006).
50. 17 U.S.C. § 117 (c) (2006).
51. 17 U.S.C. § 117 (c) (1–2) (2006).
52. Ticketmaster v. Tickets.com, 2000 WL 525390 (Not published in F.Supp.).
53. Feist Publications v. Rural Telephone Service, 499 U.S. 340 (1991).
54. 17 U.S.C. § 501 (b) (2006).
55. 17 U.S.C. § 411 (a) (2006).
56. 17 U.S.C. § 501 (2006).
57. Lindsay v. RMS Titanic, 52 U.S.P.Q.2d 1609 (Not published in F.Supp.) (1999).
58. 17 U.S.C. § 502 (a) (2006).
59. 17 U.S.C. § 502 (b) (2006).
60. Tom Doherty Associates v. Saba Entertainment, 60 F.3d 27 (2d Cir. 1995).
61. Johnson v. Couturier, 572 F.3d 1067 (9th Cir. 2009).
62. 17 U.S.C. § 503 (a) (2006).
63. 17 U.S.C. § 503 (2) (2006).
64. 17 U.S.C. § 503 (3) (b) (2006).
65. 17 U.S.C. § 504 (a) (2006).
66. 17 U.S.C. § 504 (c) (1) (2006).
67. 17 U.S.C. § 504 (c) (2) (2006).
68. *Id.*
69. 17 U.S.C. § 504 (c) (3) (2006).
70. 17 U.S.C. § 505 (2006).
71. 17 U.S.C. § 506 (2006).
72. 17 U.S.C. § 506 (a) (2006).
73. 17 U.S.C. § 506 (c) (2006).
74. 17 U.S.C. § 506 (d) (2006).
75. 17 U.S.C. § 506 (e) (2006).
76. 17 U.S.C. § 507 (2006).

77. Joseph Magri, *New Media—New Rules: The Digital Performance Right and Streaming Music over the Internet*, 6 VANDERBILT JOURNAL OF ENTERTAINMENT LAW AND PRACTICE (2003), 55–81.
78. Executive Office of the President of the United States, Administration's White Paper on Intellectual Property Enforcement Legislative Recommendations (Washington, DC: EOPUS, 2011).

9

WHAT SHOULD YOU BE AWARE OF IN DIGITAL RIGHTS MANAGEMENT SYSTEMS?

IN THIS CHAPTER

We examine digital rights management within the context of the Digital Millennium Copyright Act (1998) and discuss the various exemptions for violation claims provided for under the act:
- Violations of the DMCA
- Analog devices compliance
- DMCA challenges
- Fair use and the DMCA

INTRODUCTION

Digital rights management (DRM) systems are software technological measures that assist copyright owners to prevent unauthorized access to content. However, such measures have sometimes been criticized as going beyond what is protected by copyright and locking up material that should be in the public domain.

Following pressure from rights owners, Congress passed the Digital Millennium Copyright Act (DMCA) in 1998. A section of this act prohibits the circumvention of technological measures that a copyrighted work's owner has embedded in a work to prevent unauthorized access to the content.[1]

In an attempt to monitor the effect of the DMCA, Congress requested the Librarian of Congress to make a ruling at three-year intervals whether users of copyrighted works are likely to be adversely affected by the circumvention prohibition in their ability to make noninfringing uses of copyrighted works in a particular class. In doing so, the Librarian of Congress would examine the availability of copyrighted works for use; the availability for use of works for nonprofit preservation, educational, and archival purposes; impact on news reporting, criticism, and scholarship; the effect of circumvention of technological measures on value or market for copyrighted works; and other factors the Librarian may consider appropriate.[2]

If the Librarian publishes a class of copyrighted works the use of which would be adversely affected by the circumvention prohibition (as per Appendix 2), then the prohibition would not apply to that class for the three years following such publication.[3]

VIOLATIONS OF THE DMCA

The DMCA also prohibits the manufacturing, importing, trafficking, offering, or providing to the public any technology or service that is (1) primarily produced or designed for circumvention of technological measures effectively controlling access to protected works, (2) has only limited commercially significant purpose other than circumvention, or (3) is marketed with knowledge that it is for use in circumventing a technological measure.[4] For technological measures, circumvention is defined as, without the permission of the copyright owner, undertaking any of the following actions: descrambling a scrambled work; decrypting an encrypted work; or otherwise avoiding, bypassing, removing, deactivating, or impairing a technological measure[5] that effectively protects a copyright owner's right. A technological measure effectively protects a copyright owner's right in a work if in its ordinary operation it prevents, restricts, or otherwise limits the exercise of a copyright owner's right.[6] Effective protection is found regardless of whether the encryption is based on a weak or strong encryption, so long as the technological measure's function was to control access.[7]

> **Notable Points 44: Digital Rights Management**
>
> ▶ Digital rights management systems are software technological measures that assist copyright owners to prevent unauthorized access to content.
>
> ▶ The Digital Millennium Copyright Act prohibits the circumvention of technological measures that a copyrighted work's owner has embedded in a work to prevent unauthorized access to the content.
>
> ▶ Circumvention is defined as descrambling a scrambled work, decrypting an encrypted work, or otherwise avoiding, bypassing, removing, deactivating, or impairing a technological measure that effectively protects a copyright owner's right, without the copyright owner's permission.
>
> ▶ The DMCA prohibits the manufacturing, importation, offering to the public, providing, or otherwise trafficking in certain analog devices that do not conform to automatic gain control copy control technology.

Likewise, DMCA prohibits the manufacturing, importing, trafficking, offering, or providing to the public any technology or service that is (1) primarily produced or designed for the purpose of circumventing protection afforded by a technological measure that effectively protects a copyright owner's right, (2) has only limited commercially significant purpose other than to circumvent protection, or (3) is marketed by a person or others with that person's knowledge for use in circumventing protective technology.[8] Circumventing protection afforded by a technological measure is defined as avoiding, bypassing, removing, deactivating, or otherwise impairing a technological measure.[9]

Exemptions for Libraries and Similar Institutions

The DMCA makes a significant exemption for nonprofit libraries, archives, and educational institutions when they circumvent to gain access for the purposes of determining if they wish to acquire the work. There are provisos, however: (1) the accessed work may not be retained longer than is necessary to make a good faith determination and (2) the accessed work may not be used for any other purpose.[10] Moreover, the exemption applies only when an identical copy of a work is not reasonably available in another form.[11] Willful violation of this exemption for commercial purposes or financial gain exposes the library, archives, or educational institution to actual damages or statutory damages of between $200 and $2,500 per circumvention act.[12] Proof that such institutions were not aware or had no reason to believe their acts constituted a violation will result in a court remitting the damages.[13] However, for repeated offenses, the institution shall also forfeit the anticircumvention exemption.[14]

Regardless of the exemption, however, libraries or educational institutions may not manufacture, import, offer to the public, provide, or otherwise traffic in technology or service that circumvents a technological measure.[15] The collections must also be open to the public and available to other researchers in a specialized field.[16] Law enforcement and government intelligence activities are exempted from the anticircumvention law.[17]

Reverse Engineering Exemptions

Also exempted is an individual who has lawfully obtained a computer program and wants to circumvent a technological measure effectively controlling a particular portion of the program for the sole purpose of identifying and analyzing interoperability of an independently created computer program with other programs that have not been previously available to that person.[18] Interoperability here is defined as the ability of computer programs to exchange information and for the programs to mutually use the exchanged information.[19]

In addition to the identification and analysis permitted, the DMCA also allows a person to develop and employ technological means to circumvent a technological measure, and to circumvent a protection, in order to enable interoperability if the means are necessary to achieve such interoperability.[20] Information acquired through the identification and analysis of interoperability, as well as the development and employment of the circumvention technological measures, may be shared with others if the person provides the information solely for the purpose of enabling interoperability of an independently created program with other programs, as long as doing this does not otherwise constitute infringement.[21]

Encryption Research Exemption

The DMCA also grants an exemption to persons who circumvent a technological measure in a copy, phonorecord, performance, or display of a published work in an act of good faith encryption research.[22]

Encryption research refers to the activities conducted to advance the state of knowledge in encryption technology or to assist in the development of encryption products that are necessary to identify and analyze vulnerabilities and flaws of encryption technologies in copyrighted works. Encryption technologies in this sense refer to the scrambling or descrambling of information, mathematical algorithms, and formulas.[23]

To avail oneself of the exemption, (1) the person has to have lawfully obtained the encrypted copy, phonorecord, performance, or display of the published work; (2) the act would have to be necessary to conduct the encryption research; (3) a good faith effort to obtain authorization was made before the circumvention; and (4) the act does not otherwise constitute infringement under another section of the law.[24]

Several factors are considered to determine whether a person qualifies for the encryption research exemption. They include (1) dissemination of the research, (2) legitimacy of the research endeavor, and (3) sharing of the research results with the work's copyright holder. The first factor looks at whether the findings of the research were disseminated and whether the dissemination was in a manner reasonably calculated to advance the state of knowledge in encryption technology or in a manner that facilitates infringement or is a breach of security or a violation of privacy. The second factor looks to whether the person claiming the exemption is engaged in a legitimate course of study, is employed, or is appropriately trained and experienced in the field of encryption technology. The third factor examines whether the researcher provides the protected work's copyright owner with notice of the research findings and documentation, and when such notice was given.[25]

The exemption for good faith encryption research extends to the researcher providing the technological means used to circumvent to a research collaborator. The technological means may also be shared with another person for the purpose of verification of the research.[26]

Privacy Exemption

Any person may circumvent a technological measure that effectively controls access to a protected work that (1) collects or disseminates personally indentifying information reflecting the online activities of a natural person seeking to gain access to the protected work and (2) collects this information in the course of its operation without providing to the user a conspicuous notice of such collection or dissemination and without providing that user with the capability to prevent or restrict such collection or dissemination. To enjoy the exemption, the circumventing act has to have the sole effect of identifying and disabling the collection and dissemination of the personally identifying information and be carried out solely for the purpose of preventing such collection and dissemination and not otherwise be in violation of any other law.[27]

Security Testing Exemption

Security testing is defined under the DMCA as accessing a computer, computer system, or network solely for the purpose of good faith testing, investigating, or correcting a security flaw or vulnerability with the computer system or network owner's authorization.[28] Thus, in spite of the DMCA's prohibition of circumvention, a person may engage in an act of security testing that does not otherwise constitute infringement or violate any other applicable law,[29] such as the Computer Fraud and Abuse Act of 1986.[30] To determine whether a person qualifies for the security testing exemption, the DMCA provides several factors to consider, including whether (1) the information derived from the testing was used solely to promote the security of the owner of the computer of the computer system or network or shared with the developer of such computer system or network and (2) the information was used or maintained in a manner that does not facilitate copyright infringement or is not a violation of privacy or breach of security.[31] Under this same exemption, a person may develop, produce, distribute, or employ circumventing technological means for the purpose of performing the acts of security testing.[32]

ANALOG DEVICES COMPLIANCE

Prior to the widespread availability and use of digital recording devices, analog recording devices were perceived as a threat to audiovisual content owners,

> **Notable Points 45: Exemptions to the Anticircumvention Prohibition**
>
> ▶ Exemptions for libraries and similar institutions allow circumventing to gain access for the purposes of determining if they wish to acquire the work.
> ▶ Reverse engineering allows for identifying and analyzing interoperability of computer programs.
> ▶ The encryption research exemption allows persons to circumvent a technological measure in a published work in an act of good faith encryption research.
> ▶ A privacy exemption allows the circumvention of a technological measure that effectively controls access to a protected work that collects or disseminates personally identifying information reflecting online activities without providing the user with a conspicuous notice of such collection or a means of preventing or restricting such collection or dissemination.
> ▶ A security testing exemption can be made for the purpose of good faith testing, investigating, or correcting a security flaw or vulnerability with the computer system or network owner's authorization.
> ▶ The Librarian of Congress makes rulings at three-year intervals whether users of copyrighted works are likely to be adversely affected in their ability to make noninfringing uses of copyrighted works in a particular class and publishes this list as being exempt from the prohibition. Factors to consider:
>   - Availability of copyrighted works for use
>   - Availability for use of works for nonprofit preservation, educational, and archival purposes
>   - Impact on news reporting, criticism, and scholarship
>   - Effect of circumvention of technological measures on value or market for copyrighted works
>   - Other factors the Librarian may consider appropriate

specifically the motion picture industry. Following the passage of the DMCA, therefore, manufacturing, importing, offering to the public, providing, or otherwise trafficking in certain analog devices that do not conform to the automatic gain control copy control technology was prohibited. Gain control is a technology that essentially changes a receiver's amplification to maintain constancy in spite of input signal strength variations. Copy control is an anti–copy protection device. The following devices must conform to the automatic gain control copy control technology: VHS format analog video cassette recorder, 8 mm format analog video cassette recorder or camcorder, Beta format analog video cassette recorder, and any video cassette recorder that uses the NTSC video input format.[33] The reader will notice that most (if not all) of these technologies have died and been superseded by their digital equivalents, although many libraries continue to have them and are systematically digitizing them. Also, the manufacture, import, and offer to the public of such devices where the design has been modified from a state of previously conforming to the automatic gain control copy control technology to a nonconforming state is prohibited, and new manufacturers of VHS and 8 mm format recorders are required to conform to the four-line colorstripe copy control technology for any new devices.[34] An analog video cassette recorder is said to be conforming to the four-line colorstripe copy control technology if it detects one or more of the elements of such a technology and does not record the motion picture or transmission that is recorded by such technology or records a signal that exhibits a meaningfully distorted or degraded display when played back.[35]

Consumers are somewhat protected from the implementation of automatic gain control copy control technology to prevent or limit consumer copying, except for a single transmission or specified group of transmissions of a per-fee live event which the consumer has selected, or copying from a physical medium containing prerecorded audiovisual works.[36] The nonconformity prohibition also does not require analog VCRs to conform to the automatic gain copy control technology for video received through the lens of a camera, nor does it apply to the manufacture, import, offer for sale, or other trafficking of any professional analog videocassette recorder.[37] A professional analog videocassette recorder is one that is designed and intended for a commercial use by a person who regularly uses such a device for lawful business or industrial use.[38]

DMCA CHALLENGES

The DMCA has been challenged in courts as being fundamentally inconsistent with the Intellectual Property Clause of the U.S. Constitution. However, courts have held that protecting the exclusive rights of authors is consistent with giving Congress power to "promote the useful arts and sciences," because it protects against unlawful piracy and trafficking in tools that would promote widespread piracy and infringement.[39] In response to challenges on First Amendment grounds, the courts have held that the DMCA provisions as applied to computer programs that decrypt digitally encrypted movies on DVD constitute content-neutral restriction on speech. Even challenges claiming DMCA is overly broad—in that it prevents users from accessing material they would be entitled to under fair use—have not been too successful.[40]

> **Notable Points 46: Challenges to DMCA**
>
> ▶ Most court challenges to the DMCA have been unsuccessful.
> ▶ Challenges have included:
>   - that the DMCA is inconsistent with the intellectual property clause of the Constitution;
>   - First Amendment challenges; and
>   - that the DMCA is overly broad and prevents access to unprotected material.

To maintain an allegation of violation of the DMCA anticircumvention provision, the plaintiffs would have to prove (1) they own a valid copyright on the protected work, (2) the work is effectively controlled by a technological measure that the defendant has circumvented, and (3) third parties can now access the work without authorization, in a manner that infringes or facilitates infringing a protected right because of a product that the defendant either (a) produced or designed primarily for circumvention, (b) made available despite only limited commercial significance other than circumvention, or (c) marketed for use in circumvention of the controlling technological measure.[41]

FAIR USE AND THE DMCA

The DMCA purports to preserve fair use, free speech, and other rights—and remedies copyright use—in the use of consumer electronics, telecommunications, or computing products.[42] For example, a "user exemption" is implicitly authorized that allows a consumer to make a backup copy of a DVD for the user's personal use, but this exemption is only for an individual who has gained lawful access and is circumventing the protection measures pursuant to make fair use of the work, which is lawful conduct.[43]

While fair use may be an affirmative defense to copyright infringement, it does not exempt from liability circumvention tools that are otherwise deemed unlawful under the DMCA.[44] The court in *Realnetworks v. DVD Copy Control Association* (2009) was of the view that fair use is not a defense to trafficking products used to circumvent effective technological measures which prevent unauthorized access and/or copying of a copyrighted work. But while fair use is inapplicable in the act of circumvention itself to gain access, copying of a work may be fair under appropriate circumstances, and thus the act of circumventing a technological measure that prevents copying may not be prohibited under the DMCA, while the act of circumventing a technological measure that prevents access is definitely prohibited under the DMCA.[45] This would suggest that an individual who has gained lawful access may circumvent the copy control technologies pursuant to a fair use. The question then still remains: if the access was unlawful, could copying for fair use be lawful? One court put it very well: while it is not unlawful to circumvent for the purpose of engaging in fair use, it is unlawful to traffic in tools that allow fair use circumvention.[46] Thus, it would be difficult to engage in fair use if the tools of access were not readily available. This puzzle may occupy the courts for some time.

> **Notable Points 47: DMCA and Fair Use**
> ▶ There is tension between the DMCA and the fair use doctrine.
> ▶ To utilize fair use, one must have gained lawful access to the content.
> ▶ Circumvention of access control is not lawful access.
> ▶ It is unclear whether copying for fair use would be lawful after an unlawful access.

HYPOTHETICAL #9

While worrying about Hypothetical #8, Ms. Graduate discovers that some of the items are protected by DRM systems. What *additional* issues should Ms. Graduate now address?

A suggested response to this hypothetical question can be found in Appendix 6.

ENDNOTES

1. 17 U.S.C. § 1201 (a) (1) (A) (2006).
2. 17 U.S.C. § 1201 (a) (1) (C) (2006).
3. 17 U.S.C. § 1201 (a) (1) (D) (2006).
4. 17 U.S.C. § 1201 (a) (2) (2006).
5. 17 U.S.C. § 1201 (a) (3) (A) (2006).
6. 17 U.S.C. § 1201 (a) (3) (B) (2006).
7. Universal City Studios v. Reimerdes, 111 F.Supp.2d 294, affirmed 273 F.3d 429 (2000).
8. 17 U.S.C. § 1201 (b) (1) (2006).
9. 17 U.S.C. § 1201 (b) (2) (2006).
10. 17 U.S.C. § 1201 (d) (1) (2006).
11. 17 U.S.C. § 1201 (d) (2) (2006).
12. 17 U.S.C. § 1203 (c) (2006).
13. 17 U.S.C. § 1203 (c) (5) (B) (ii) (2006).
14. 17 U.S.C. § 1201 (d) (3) (2006).
15. 17 U.S.C. § 1201 (d) (4) (2006).

16. 17 U.S.C. § 1201 (d) (5) (2006).
17. 17 U.S.C. § 1201 (e) (2006).
18. 17 U.S.C. § 1201 (f) (1) (2006).
19. 17 U.S.C. § 1201 (g) (2006).
20. 17 U.S.C. § 1201 (f) (2) (2006).
21. 17 U.S.C. § 1201 (f) (3) (2006).
22. 17 U.S.C. § 1201 (2) (2006).
23. 17 U.S.C. § 1201 (g) (1) (2006).
24. 17 U.S.C. § 1201 (g) (2) (2006).
25. 17 U.S.C. § 1201 (g) (3) (2006).
26. 17 U.S.C. § 1201 (g) (4) (2006).
27. 17 U.S.C. § 1201 (i) (2006).
28. 17 U.S.C. § 1201 (j) (1) (2006).
29. 17 U.S.C. § 1201 (j) (2) (2006).
30. 18 U.S.C. § 1030 (2006).
31. 17 U.S.C. § 1201 (j) (3) (2006).
32. 17 U.S.C. § 1201 (j) (4) (2006).
33. 17 U.S.C. § 1201 (k) (1) (A) (2006).
34. 17 U.S.C. § 1201 (k) (1) (B) (2006).
35. 17 U.S.C. § 1201 (k) (4) (C) (2006).
36. 17 U.S.C. § 1201 (k) (2) (2006).
37. 17 U.S.C. § 1201 (k) (3) (2006).
38. 17 U.S.C. § 1201 (k) (4) (D) (2006).
39. U.S. v. Elcom Ltd., 203 F.Supp.2d 1111 (2002).
40. *Universal City Studios*, 111 F.Supp.2d 294.
41. Chamberlain Group v. Skylink Technologies, 381 F.3d 1178, 1203 (2004).
42. 17 U.S.C. § 1201 (c) (1–4) (2006).
43. Realnetworks v. DVD Copy Control Association, 641 F.Supp.2d 913 (2009).
44. *Id.*
45. *Id.*, at 942.
46. *U.S. v. Elcom*, 203 F.Supp.2d, at 1125.

10

WHAT ARE SERVICE PROVIDERS AND WHAT IS THE SERVICE PROVIDER SAFE HARBOR?

IN THIS CHAPTER

We discuss the safe harbor granted service providers whose systems are used by third parties in infringing activities, including the various requirements for eligibility of such protection, as well as notifications and takedown requirements for infringing material:
- Service providers
- Designated agent requirement
- Transitory transmissions
- Intermediate storage
- Preaccess conditions and removal of infringing material
- Innocent service provider
- Linking exemption
- Nonprofit educational institutions
- Takedown or disable liability and counternotifications
- Identifying infringers
- Injunctions to service providers

INTRODUCTION

In Chapter 9, we discussed digital rights management (DRM) systems, especially as they relate to the anticircumvention provision of the Digital Millennium Copyright Act (DMCA). The DMCA was also broadly designed to preserve copyright enforcement on the Internet. Section 512 of the Copyright Act is a safe harbor for Internet service providers (ISPs) who find themselves providing service to customers who are infringers of copyrights online, including violators of the DMCA prohibitions. Essentially, it protects ISPs from liability by infringing action of third parties. Whether or not a service provider qualifies for limitation on liability will be determined on the criteria established for such a limitation described in this chapter.[1] In October 2011, the United States signed the Anti-Counterfeiting Trade Agreement (ACTA), an international treaty that may have an impact on safe harbor for service providers.

SERVICE PROVIDERS

Section 512 of Title 17 defines service providers as entities that offer the transmission, routing, or connections for digital communications between and among points specified by a user, where the user has chosen the transmitted material and the service provider has not modified the content.[2] Service providers include online services, network service providers, or operators of facilities that provide such services.[3] Thus, generally, these are companies that offer backbone connectivity or provide end users with Internet access and would span the range from major national providers to local Internet access providers.

Depending on circumstances, digital libraries and educational institutions can be viewed as ISPs. Libraries do provide online services or network access within the meaning of the statutory definition, which includes "a provider of online services or network access, or the operator of facilities therefore."[4] There is no requirement that an Internet service provider, including a library, take advantage of the safe harbor. Not doing so, however, exposes the library to the sort of liability the safe harbor provisions were meant to prevent. If it is a large library system with its own servers, with webpage portals to other resources, or, as many libraries are currently doing, utilizes Web 2.0 technologies that allow users to post material on its website, then it should consider the benefits of safe harbor.

DESIGNATED AGENT REQUIREMENT

To take advantage of the section 512 limitations on liability, especially for material residing on systems or networks at the direction of users, the service provider must designate an agent who will receive notifications of claimed infringement (see http://www.copyright.gov/onlinesp/agent.pdf for optional interim designation form and http://www.copyright.gov/onlinesp/agenta.pdf for the amended form). The service designates an agent by providing the following information to the Copyright Office, including a location accessible to the public on its website: (1) the agent's name, address, phone number, and e-mail address and (2) other contact information the registrar of copyrights may deem appropriate. A current directory of such agents is kept by the registrar of copyrights and is made available for inspection by the public.[5]

An effective notification of infringement to the designated agent must be in writing and must substantially include the following elements:

1. the physical or electronic signature of a person authorized to act on behalf of the copyright's owner;
2. identification of the work or works claimed to be infringed;
3. identification of material that are claimed to be infringing, and that should be removed or access disabled, with reasonably sufficient information to enable the service provider to locate the material;
4. contact information of the complaining party;
5. a statement that the complaining party has a good faith belief that use of the material complained of is not lawfully authorized by the copyright owner, agent, or other law; and
6. a statement under penalty of perjury from the complaining party that the notification information is accurate and that the party is authorized to act on behalf of the owner of the exclusive right alleged to be infringed.[6]

Notifications that fail to substantially comply with these requirements shall not be considered in determining whether the service provider had actual knowledge or was aware of facts or circumstances that would indicate infringing activity.[7] When the notification lacks the required signature, the service provider must show that it promptly attempted to contact the person making the notification or took other reasonable steps to assist the complainer to substantially comply with the notification elements.[8]

> **Notable Points 48: Infringement and Internet Service Providers**
>
> ▶ ISPs are generally companies that offer backbone connectivity or provide end users with Internet access.
> ▶ Depending on circumstances, digital libraries and educational institutions can be viewed as ISPs.
> ▶ Section 512 of the Copyright Act protects ISPs from liability by infringing action of third parties.
> ▶ To qualify for this protection, ISPs must designate an agent to receive notices of claimed infringing actions.
> ▶ Notices of infringement must be in writing and meet requirements of the act.

TRANSITORY TRANSMISSIONS

Under certain conditions, service providers are protected from monetary liability, and sometimes from injunctive or other equitable relief, for claims of infringement based on the provider's transmission, routing, or provision of connections for material through a system or network controlled or operated by or for the service provider, or because of the intermediate or transient storage of that material in the course of such transmission, routing, or providing connections. The protection applies if:

1. the transmission was initiated by or at the direction of a person other than the service provider;
2. the material transmitted is not selected by the provider; rather, the transmission, routing, provision of connections, or storage is carried out through an automatic technical process;
3. the service provider does not select the recipients of the material but automatically responds to another person's request;
4. in the course of such intermediate or transient storage, no copy of the material made by the service provider is maintained in a manner ordinarily accessible to other than the anticipated recipients or is maintained for a period longer than is necessary for such transmission; and
5. the material is transmitted without modification to its content.[9]

INTERMEDIATE STORAGE

Service providers are also under certain conditions protected from monetary liability, and sometimes from injunctive or other equitable relief, for claims of infringement based on the intermediate and temporary storage of material on a system or network controlled or operated by or for the service provider. This protection applies where:

1. the material is made available online by a person other than the service provider;
2. the material is transmitted from such person through the system or network to another person at the direction of such other person; and
3. storage occurs through an automatic technical process for the purpose of making the material available to system users who request access to the transmitted material from a person other than the service provider.[10]

However, there are several conditions for taking advantage of this exemption. The service provider must transmit the material to the users without modification of its content. Also, the service provider has to comply with rules regarding refreshing, reloading, or other updating of the material that are specified by the person making the material available online, in accordance with a generally accepted industry standard data communications protocol for the system or network that the person making the material available uses. These rules, however, cannot be used by the person providing the material to prevent or unreasonably impair the intermediate storage by the service provider.[11]

The service provider must also not interfere with technology in the material that would provide the feedback information that would have been available to the person providing the material had the subsequent users obtained the information directly from the person making the material available. Several caveats apply here, too. The information feedback technology must not significantly interfere with the service provider's system or network performance or with the intermediate storage. The technology must also be consistent with generally accepted industry standard communications protocols and must not extract other information from the service provider's network or system.[12]

PREACCESS CONDITIONS AND REMOVAL OF INFRINGING MATERIAL

The person providing the material may have set conditions for access to the material. These conditions may include a fee payment or providing a password and/or other information. The service provider must permit access to the stored material in significant part only to system or network users who meet those conditions and only in accordance with those conditions.[13]

Where the person providing the material does so without the copyright owner's permission, the service provider has to expeditiously respond to a notification of claimed infringement by removing or disabling access to the material claimed to be infringing. This responsibility applies where (1) the material has been previously

> **Notable Points 49: Internet Service Providers Conditions for Infringement Liability Protection (Part 1)**
>
> ▶ An ISP may be protected from liability for infringing claims based on the ISP's mere transmission or intermediate or transient storage, without modification, of infringing material on its network.
>
> ▶ An ISP cannot interfere with information feedback technology provided by the person supplying the content.
>
> ▶ The information feedback technology cannot interfere with the ISP's system or network.
>
> ▶ The ISP must provide access only to those users who meet the content owner's preaccess conditions.
>
> ▶ The ISP must respond to notification of a claimed infringement.

removed from the originating site or access to the material has been disabled; or a court has ordered for the removal of the material from the originating site; or has ordered the disabling of access to the material; and (2) the notifying party includes a statement confirming the removal of the material or disablement of access to the offending material from the originating site; or that a court has ordered such removal or disability of access.[14]

INNOCENT SERVICE PROVIDER

Users may sometimes store infringing material on a service provider's system or network. A service provider is exempted from liability from monetary relief and may be exempted from injunctive relief for copyright infringement from storing such material on a system or network controlled or operated by or for the service provider. To benefit from this exemption, the service provider has to show that there was no actual or implied knowledge of infringing material or activity. The service provider shows this by demonstrating that (1) there was no actual knowledge that the material or an activity using the material on the system or network was infringing, (2) even though there was no actual knowledge, there was no awareness of facts or circumstances from which infringing activity would be apparent, or (3) the service provider acted expeditiously to remove or disable access to the material upon obtaining such knowledge or awareness. The service provider also has to show that where it had the right and ability to control infringing activity, there was no financial benefit to the provider that was directly attributable to the infringing activity.[15] This of course means that a provider would not be able to take advantage of the DMCA or the Communications Decency Act's safe harbors for material its own employees have posted.[16]

> ☑ **Checklist 13: Innocent Service Provider**
> ❏ The ISP had no actual knowledge material or activity of network was infringing.
> ❏ The ISP had no awareness of facts or circumstances indicating infringing activity.
> ❏ The ISP acted expeditiously to remove or disable access to material upon knowledge or awareness of infringing activity.
> ❏ No financial benefit to the ISP was directly attributable to the infringing activity.

LINKING EXEMPTION

Service providers are protected from monetary liability, and sometimes from injunctive or other equitable relief, for claims of infringement based on the provider referring or linking users to an online location that has infringing material or activity by use of information location tools. Such tools include directories, indexes, references, pointers, or hypertext links. The service provider (1) must have had no actual knowledge that the activity or material is infringing or was not aware of facts or circumstances from which infringing activity is apparent, and (2) upon obtaining awareness or knowledge of infringement, the service provider acted expeditiously to remove or disable access to infringing material.[17] Also, the service provider must not have received a financial benefit that is directly attributable to the infringing activity, where the service provider has the right and ability to control such activity, and responded expeditiously to remove or disable access to the material or activity upon notification that it was infringing.[18] The required notification information in this case is identification of the reference or link to the material or activity claimed to be infringing and sufficient information for the provider to locate the link or reference.[19]

To take advantage of the limitations on liability, a service provider is not required to monitor its service and affirmatively seek facts indicating infringing activity, except where this is consistent with a complying standard technical measure used to protect copyrighted works. Nor is it required to gain access to, disable access to, or remove material where the law prohibits such conduct.[20]

Notable Points 50: Internet Service Providers Conditions for Infringement Liability Protection (Part 2)

- Service providers may be protected from infringing claims based on providing users links to sites with infringing material or activity.
- Service providers are not required to monitor their service or affirmatively seek facts indicating infringing activity.

NONPROFIT EDUCATIONAL INSTITUTIONS

Under certain circumstances, graduate student or faculty member knowledge of their infringing activities while performing a teaching or research function, while employees of a nonprofit higher education institution that is a service provider, shall not be attributed to the institution. These circumstances are that (1) the infringing activity does not involve provision of online access to instructional material that were required or recommended within the preceding three-year period for a course taught by the faculty member or graduate student, (2) the institution has not received more than two notifications of claimed infringement by that graduate student or faculty member within the preceding three-year period as such notifications were not actionable because of material misrepresentation, and (3) the institution provides informational material accurately describing and promoting compliance with copyright laws to all users of its system or network.[21]

TAKEDOWN OR DISABLE LIABILITY AND COUNTERNOTIFICATIONS

Whether or not material is ultimately determined to be infringing, a service provider is generally not liable for any claim based on the provider's good faith removal or disabling of access to material claimed to be infringing or based on facts or circumstances from which infringing activity is apparent.[22] However, with respect to material residing at the direction of a subscriber on a system or network controlled or operated by or for the service provider, and which the service provider removes or disables access pursuant to notification, the service provider is required to fulfill certain conditions to enjoy this limitation on liability. The service provider has to take reasonable steps to promptly notify the subscriber of the removal or disabling of access. Upon receiving a counternotification objecting to the removal or disabling of access, the service provider has to promptly provide the person who provided the notification with a copy of the counternotification, notifying such person that the service provider will replace the removed material or cease disabling access to the material in 10 business days. The provider then replaces the removed material and ceases disabling access between 10 and 14 business days after receiving the counternotice, unless the provider's designated agent first receives notice that the complainant who notified the provider of the infringing activity has filed a court action seeking an order to restrain the subscriber from engaging in infringing activity related to the material on the service provider's network or system.[23]

A valid counternotification needs to be in writing, must be provided to the service provider's designated agent, and must substantially include the following:

1. the subscriber's physical or digital signature;
2. identification of the removed material or to which access has been disabled and the location where the material appeared before it was removed or before access was disabled;
3. a statement under penalty of perjury that the subscriber has a good faith belief the material was mistakenly removed or had been misidentified; and
4. the subscriber's contact information and a statement consenting to jurisdiction of the federal district court for the jurisdiction in which the subscriber's address is located, or any judicial district in which the service provider may be found if the subscriber's address is located outside the United States, and that the subscriber will accept service of process from the person or agent of the person that provided notification of infringing material or activity.[24]

Persons who materially misrepresent that material is infringing or that material was removed or disabled by mistake or misidentification are liable for any damages, including costs and attorney fees that are incurred by the alleged infringer, by any copyright holder, or a service provider who is injured by such misrepresentation as a result of the service provider relying on such misrepresentation to remove the material or disable access to the material or activity claimed to be infringing or in restoring or enabling access to the material.[25]

A service provider can take advantage of the limitations on liability described in this chapter only if it meets two conditions: One, the service provider has to have adopted a policy providing for termination of service to subscribers who are repeat infringers, must have informed subscribers of this policy, and must reasonably have implemented the policy. Two, in implementing the policy, the service provider accommodates and does not interfere with standard technical measures designed to protect copyrighted works.[26] As defined by this section of the law, a standard technical measure is one which is used by copyright owners to identify or protect copyrighted works, which was developed following a broad consensus of copyright owners and service providers and is available to anyone on terms that are reasonable and nondiscriminatory, and which does not impose substantial costs or burdens on service providers and their networks.[27]

IDENTIFYING INFRINGERS

In order to identify an alleged infringer, the copyright owner or one authorized to act on the owner's behalf may request the clerk of any United States district court to issue a subpoena to a service provider. The request should be accompanied by a copy of the notification of infringement provided to the service provider, the proposed subpoena, and a sworn declaration that the subpoena's purpose is to obtain the identity of an alleged infringer and that the information obtained will be used only for the purposes of protecting the owner's rights.[28] If the notification, the proposed subpoena, and the declaration are in proper form and properly executed, the clerk expeditiously issues and signs the proposed subpoena, returning it to the requestor for delivery to the service provider.[29]

By this subpoena, the service provider receiving the notification will be ordered and authorized, to the extent that such information is available to the service provider, to expeditiously disclose to the requester information sufficient to identify the alleged infringer.[30] Upon receiving an issued subpoena, the service provider shall then have an obligation to provide the copyright owner or designate with the information required by the subpoena, regardless of any other provisions of the law.[31] The provisions of the Federal Rules of Civil Procedure applicable to issuance, service, and enforcement of subpoenas shall generally govern the rules for issuing and delivering such subpoenas.[32]

INJUNCTIONS TO SERVICE PROVIDERS

As discussed in Chapter 8, injunctions are available under section 502 of Title 17 in the U.S. Code as one form of remedy to stop infringing activity. Likewise, injunctions are available against service providers. A court may grant an injunctive order against a service provider, where the service provider is not subject to monetary remedies, as discussed, and where the conduct falls outside of that qualifying for the limitation on remedies. The order may be one restraining the service provider from providing access to material or activity that is infringing and is on a particular online site on the provider's system or one restraining the provider from providing service access to a particular subscriber engaged in infringing activity by terminating the account of such a subscriber. The court may also issue any other order it may consider necessary to restrain or prevent infringement specified in the order, if such an order is the least burdensome to the service provider.[33] For service providers qualifying for the limitation on remedies discussed, the order may include termination of services, restraining the service provider from providing access by blocking access to specific online locations outside the United States, or both.[34]

The court considers several criteria when deciding to issue an injunction. The court considers whether the injunction or a combination of such injunctions would significantly burden the provider or the operation of the provider's system or network. It also considers the magnitude of the copyright owner's likely harm in the digital network environment of the infringement if steps are not taken to restrain the infringement. Furthermore, the court considers the technical feasibility and effectiveness of implementing the injunction, and whether access to non-infringing material at other online locations would be affected. Finally, the court considers the availability of other comparably effective, less burdensome means of preventing or restraining access to infringing material.[35]

CONCLUSION

The DMCA is most often identified with the probation against circumventing technological measures that content owners have put into place to prevent access or infringing activity. However, it is also the part of the copyright law that provides relief for Internet service providers for infringing activity that may occur on their systems. As discussed, libraries—and particularly digital collections—can be considered service providers if they provide online services or network access that allows them to post or link to content or allow users to post or manage content. Whether it is worth the trouble of complying with the requirements for taking advantage of the safe harbor will depend on the individual digital content manager.

> **HYPOTHETICAL #10**
>
> Consider the same scenario as in Hypothetical #1, but in addition, Mr. Digital Librarian has developed a webpage within the library website that allows his colleagues and other users to post comments about the search engine, as well as share their own experiences with other proprietary search engines. Mr. Librarian does not edit or modify the material posted in any way. What *additional* issues should Mr. Librarian be concerned with?
>
> *A suggested response to this hypothetical question can be found in Appendix 6.*

ENDNOTES

1. 17 U.S.C. § 512 (n) (2006).
2. 17 U.S.C. § 512 (k) (1) (A) (2006).
3. 17 U.S.C. § 512 (k) (1) (B) (2006).
4. 17 U.S.C. § 512 (k) (1) (B) (2006).
5. 17 U.S.C. § 512 (c) (2) (2006).
6. 17 U.S.C. § 512 (c) (3) (A) (2006).
7. 17 U.S.C. § 512 (c) (3) (B) (i) (2006).
8. 17 U.S.C. § 512 (c) (3) (B) (ii) (2006).
9. 17 U.S.C. § 512 (a) (2006).
10. 17 U.S.C. § 512 (b) (1) (2006).
11. 17 U.S.C. § 512 (b) (2) (A–B) (2006).
12. 17 U.S.C. § 512 (b) (2) (C) (2006).
13. 17 U.S.C. § 512 (b) (2) (D) (2006).
14. 17 U.S.C. § 512 (b) (2) (E) (2006).
15. 17 U.S.C. § 512 (c) (1) (2006).
16. John F. Delaney, *Poking and Tweeting: Social Media Overview*, 1034 PRACTICING LAW INSTITUTE (February–March 2011), PLI/Pat 43; 47 U.S.C. § 230 (2006).
17. 17 U.S.C. § 512 (d) (1) (2006).
18. 17 U.S.C. § 512(d) (2–3) (2006).
19. 17 U.S.C. § 512 (d) (3) (2006).
20. 17 U.S.C. § 512 (m) (2006).
21. 17 U.S.C. § 512 (e) (2006).
22. 17 U.S.C. § 512 (g) (1) (2006).
23. 17 U.S.C. § 512 (g) (2) (2006).
24. 17 U.S.C. § 512 (g) (3) (2006).
25. 17 U.S.C. § 512 (f) (2006).
26. 17 U.S.C. § 512 (i) (1) (2006).
27. 17 U.S.C. § 512 (i) (2) (2006).
28. 17 U.S.C. § 512 (h) (1–2) (2006).

29. 17 U.S.C. § 512 (h) (4) (2006).
30. 17 U.S.C. § 512 (h) (3) (2006).
31. 17 U.S.C. § 512 (h) (5) (2006).
32. 17 U.S.C. § 512(h) (6) (2006).
33. 17 U.S.C. § 512 (j) (1) (A) (2006).
34. 17 U.S.C. § 512 (j) (1) (B) (2006).
35. 17 U.S.C. § 512 (j) (2) (2006).

11
WHAT ARE COPYRIGHT ROYALTIES?

IN THIS CHAPTER

We discuss the royalty system under the Copyright Act and examine the extraordinary powers of the Librarian of Congress in the royalty litigation system:
- Compulsory license royalties and copyright royalty judges
- Former copyright arbitration panels
- Copyright Clearance Center

INTRODUCTION

As media converge as a result of digitization, many digital content managers find themselves dealing with issues of new ways of using content in areas where they did not imagine themselves to be in the past. For example, digital content managers may find themselves in the area of broadcasting on the Internet, through interactive or noninteractive webcasting and streaming content. Or they may find themselves wanting to reproduce, post, and share digital content online on their websites. When this happens, the topic of royalties comes to the fore.

Royalties derive from the incentive provided by the limited-term monopoly envisioned by article I, section 8, clause 8 of the U.S. Constitution:

> The Congress shall have Power... to promote the Progress of science and useful Arts, by securing for limited Times to Authors and Inventors the exclusive Right to their respective Writings and Discoveries.

It would be indeed a hollow "exclusive Right" if it allowed the holder to exercise only the exclusive rights enumerated in copyright law. Royalties, then, are a tool to assist the copyright holder to allow others to exercise some or all of the exclusive rights while still maintaining ownership.

Notable Points 51: Royalties

▶ Royalties are the mainstay of the incentive provided by the limited-term monopoly envisioned in the Constitution.

▶ Royalties allow the copyright holder to permit use of the exclusive rights by others.

▶ Royalties may be based on contract or set by law.

COMPULSORY LICENSE ROYALTIES AND COPYRIGHT ROYALTY JUDGES

In most instances, royalties are free-market transactions between copyright holders and copyright users that result in voluntarily negotiated license agreements. But in some areas, compulsory (or statutory) licenses are allowed. Especially in the area of compulsory licenses in sound recordings, nondramatic musical works, money-operated phonorecord players, and cable services, copyright royalties are designed to meet several objectives:

1. They should seek to ensure that the availability of creative works to the public is maximized.
2. They should also seek to ensure that the copyright owner is afforded a fair return for the creative works and the copyright user is provided an opportunity to make a fair income, that is, the copyright user can still make a profit even after paying a royalty to the copyright owner.
3. The royalty rates should also reflect the relative contributions between the copyright owner and the copyright user in creativity, technology, capital investment, cost, risk and opening up of new markets for creative expression and media.
4. The rates should also minimize any disruptive impact on the structure and generally prevailing practices of the industries involved.[1]

Notable Points 52: Goals of Royalties

Copyright royalties seek to:

▶ ensure that the availability of creative works to the public is maximized,

▶ ensure a fair return for the creative works to the copyright owner, and

▶ provide the copyright user an opportunity to make a fair income even after paying royalty.

The area of copyright royalties in the cable services industry is probably the only place where a librarian is empowered to appoint judges anywhere in these United States. The Librarian of Congress is vested with the power to appoint three full-time copyright royalty judges, upon consultation with the register of copyrights. The Librarian also appoints one of the three judges as the chief copyright royalty judge.[2] These judges and their staff have their offices in the Library of Congress.[3]

To qualify to be a copyright royalty judge, the person must be an attorney with at least seven years of legal experience. At least five years' experience with adjudication, trials, or arbitrations is required for the chief copyright royalty judge. The act specifies that one of the two other judges must have knowledge of copyright law and the other must have knowledge of economics.[4] The judges serve for six-year terms but may be reappointed to subsequent terms and may serve until a successor is selected to serve a new term.[5] The judges are not given performance reviews.[6]

Besides setting and adjusting reasonable rates that reflect the objectives just discussed, copyright royalty judges also authorize the distribution of royalties collected subject to compulsory licenses, as well as accept or reject royalty claims and petitions.[7] When they are not performing their judicial duties, the judges may also perform other duties as assigned by the register of copyrights within the Library of Congress,[8] providing these duties do not conflict with their duties as copyright royalty judges.[9] The Librarian of Congress establishes rules regarding standards of conduct for the judges, including conflicts of interest,[10] and the Librarian may sanction or remove a judge for violations of such standards, other misconduct, or disqualifying disability, after giving the judge notice and opportunity for a hearing. However, pending such a hearing, the Llibrarian may suspend the judge and appoint an interim judge.[11]

Copyright royalty judges preside over proceeding hearings en banc (i.e., as a whole panel). However, the chief copyright royalty judge may designate an individual judge to preside over collateral and administrative proceedings or any other proceedings the chief judge might consider appropriate. However, a majority final is required for the final determinations of the copyright royalty judges, and a dissenting judge may file his or her own dissenting opinion, to be included in the determination.[12]

To enable them to carry out their functions, copyright royalty judges may issue regulations. Such regulations are subject to the approval of the Llibrarian of Congress and are also subject to judicial review.[13] Hearings are set in motion by a notice of commencement of proceedings published in the *Federal Register* by the copyright royalty judges, inviting the filing of petitions.[14] There are varying date requirements, with many petitions not eligible to be filed until after 2015, and every subsequent fifth calendar year thereafter.[15] The copyright royalty judges may make a determination that a petition is facially invalid or that the petitioner lacks significant interest in the proceeding.[16] There then follows a three-month period of voluntary negotiations between the copyright holders and the copyright users, which may make further proceedings unnecessary.[17] There is also an option for an abbreviated small claims procedure, where the contested amount is $10,000 or less. Making a bad faith statement that the amount in controversy exceeds $10,000 to escape the small claims procedure invites a fine from the copyright royalty judges.[18]

The determinations of the judges are to be supported by the written record and should indicate the findings of fact that the judges relied upon for the determination.[19] The judges may also issue protective orders to protect confidential information.[20] The Librarian of Congress is responsible for the publication of the determination in the *Federal Register*, as well as publicizing it in appropriate ways, including Internet publication. The Librarian also makes the determination available to the public for inspection and copying.[21]

Appeals from the determinations of the copyright royalty judges go straight to the U.S. court of appeals for the District of Columbia circuit, and determinations become

---

Notable Points 53: Powers of Librarian of Congress to Appoint Judges

▶ The Librarian of Congress is empowered to appoint copyright royalty judges, including the chief copyright royalty judge.

▶ Copyright royalty judges:
- set and adjust royalty rates,
- authorize distribution of collected royalties, and
- accept royalty claims and petitions.

▶ The Librarian of Congress makes the appointments in consultation with the register of copyrights.

▶ The Librarian of Congress may sanction or remove a judge for violation of standards of conduct for judges, after giving notice and providing the judge an opportunity for a hearing.

▶ A royalty judge must be an attorney with seven years' legal experience.

▶ One of the three judges must have knowledge of copyright law.

▶ Another one of the three judges must have knowledge of economics.

▶ Judges serve for six-year terms with the possibility of renewal.

▶ Determinations of the judges must be supported by a written record indicating findings of fact relied on.

▶ The Librarian of Congress is responsible for the publication of the determinations in the *Federal Register*.

▶ Appeals to determinations go straight to the U.S. court of appeals for the District of Columbia circuit.

final if not appealed within 30 days after publication in the Federal Register.[22] The court of appeals may vacate the determination of the copyright royalty judges and substitute its own determination or may remand the case back to the copyright royalty judges for further proceedings.[23]

FORMER COPYRIGHT ARBITRATION PANELS

Before the establishment of the Copyright Royalty Board and its three copyright royalty judges, royalties were arbitrated by ad hoc panels, put together for each proceeding. These panels were phased out in 2004, with the passage of Public Law 108-419, the Copyright Royalty and Distribution Reform Act. For historical purposes, it is interesting to compare the setup between the present system of judges with the prior system of arbitration panels.

Upon the recommendation of the register of copyright, the Librarian of Congress had the power to appoint and convene a copyright arbitration panel for the purposes of determining royalty rates for cable compulsory licenses, ephemeral recordings, public performance of sound recording by certain digital transmissions, making and distributing phonorecords (including digital delivery), jukeboxes (after the expiration or termination of a negotiated license that is not replaced by another license), use by noncommercial educational broadcasting stations, and satellite carrier compulsory licenses. This panel may also determine the distribution of royalty fees deposited with the register of copyrights from cable and satellite carriers, digital audio recording devices, and other media payments.[24]

The arbitration panels were composed from lists of persons qualified to serve as arbitrators, submitted by any professional arbitration association or organization.[25] The minimum qualifications to serve as an arbitrator were admission to practice law in the Unites States or its territories, legal practice for ten or more years, and experience in conducting or facilitating arbitration proceedings and resolution of disputes.[26] The Librarian of Congress then published a list of 30 to 75 such qualified persons, who could reasonably be expected to serve in the arbitration panel for the calendar year, in the *Federal Register*.[27] Parties in rate adjustment or royalty proceedings could file an objection with the Librarian of Congress to one or more persons in the arbitration list, within a specified period, and state the grounds and reasons for the objection.[28]

In an arbitration proceeding, the Librarian of Congress, upon the recommendation of the register of copyright, selected two arbitrators from the list to constitute a copyright arbitration royalty panel. The two selected then chose a third arbitrator from the same list, and this third member became the chair of the panel during the proceedings. If the two could not agree on a third member, then the Librarian of Congress would select the third member from the same arbitrator list.[29] The Librarian of Congress could order the suspension of arbitration proceedings under way, where the Librarian considered it necessary and fully justifiable. This could include, for example, the necessity for the removal or replacement of an arbitrator due to a serious emergency or other reason specified by statute.[30]

Panel meetings were generally open to the public,[31] but, upon a vote of the majority of the arbitrators,[32] could be closed or partially closed and information withheld from the public under certain circumstances where, for example, the matter under discussion had been specifically authorized by executive order to be kept secret; or the matter was solely regarding internal practices of the panel; or the matter had been specifically exempted from disclosure by statute; or the matter involved privileged or confidential trade secrets or financial information; or the discussion resulted in the accusation of any person for a crime or formal censure; or there would be an unwarranted invasion of personal privacy; or the matter would have disclosed investigatory records compiled for law enforcement, where such disclosure would have interfered with enforcement proceedings or deprived a person of the right to a fair trial or have been an unwarranted invasion of personal privacy or disclosed the identity of a confidential source or revealed confidential information furnished only by a confidential source or disclosed investigative techniques or endangered law enforcement personnel.[33] Except for meetings of internal deliberations of arbitrators carried out pursuant to their duties and obligations, information in closed meetings had to be published in the *Federal Register*, disclosing each arbitrator's vote, what exemption applied for closing the meeting, and a list of all persons expected to attend the meeting, as well as their affiliations.[34] Any person, upon request stating reasons and contact information, could request to close or open a meeting, or to withhold or disclose information.[35] Transcripts and minutes of closed meetings were kept by the U.S Copyright Office for at least two years and could be authorized for public disclosure at a later time.[36]

The copyright arbitration panel could issue rulings or orders necessary to resolve issues in a proceeding, subject to statutory rules.[37] Parties could file with the Librarian of Congress a petition to modify or set aside the panel's determination, stating the reasons for modification or reversal.[38] The Librarian of Congress could within 90 days of the receipt of the panel's report of determination issue an order accepting the panel's determination or substituting the Librarian's own determination, with reasons for not accepting the panel's determination, and the facts that the Librarian found relevant to reject the determination. The Librarian was required to adopt the panel's determination unless the Librarian found the determination arbitrary or contrary to copyright law.[39] Official determinations of the copyright arbitration panel were published in the *Federal Register* and included the relevant facts and reasons for the determinations. With a few exemptions, all records of the panel and all records of the Librarian of Congress created or assembled for arbitration purposes could be inspected and copied at the U.S Copyright Office.[40]

COPYRIGHT CLEARANCE CENTER

The Copyright Clearance Center is technically not a royalty program but a licensing program.[41] However, it operates like a royalty program, because it collects copyright clearance fees on behalf of copyright owners, eliminating the need to obtain permission from individual rights holders, much like the American Society of Composers, Authors, and Publishers (ASCAP) and Broadcast Music, Inc. (BMI), do for the music industry. The Copyright Clearance Center (CCC) was established in 1978 and is a self-described global rights broker for print and digital content, providing convenient licensing for intellectual property content use. It provides both pay-per-use and annual copyright licenses. Upon appropriate payment, the licenses allow both profit and nonprofit entities to reproduce content, post and share digital content on websites and e-mails, among many other uses. A university, for example, can purchase an annual multiuse license that allows users to share content campus-wide. There is even a license available just for images. However, users are still liable for uses of content not in the CCC's database of subscribing content owners; that is, a publisher of content used that is not in the CCC database could still sue for infringement. Nor can the uses go beyond the scope permitted by the license.[42]

For content owners, the CCC provides services such as tracking royalty payments and approving permission requests. In the recent past, however, the CCC came under criticism for helping fund litigation of a publisher against an academic library in the case of e-reserves,[43] even though it was established as a not-for-profit organization. Nevertheless, as Tracey Armstrong notes, automating the copyright process has dividends, in that it promotes compliance with copyright law, while at the same time providing convenient access to information.[44]

> **Notable Points 54: Copyright Clearance Center**
> - The Copyright Clearance Center (CCC) collects copyright clearance fees on behalf of copyright owners.
> - Though established in the United States, the CCC is international in scope.
> - The CCC provides both pay-per-use and annual copyright use licenses.
> - The CCC provides content owners with services that include royalty payment tracking as well as approving permission requests.
> - CCC has recently been criticized for joining with a publisher in litigation against an academic library.

It is important to note that although the CCC was established in the United States, it has a strong international presence. The CCC is a member of the International Federation of Reproduction Rights Organisations (IFRRO) and has bilateral agreements with other member organizations that promote a content-use global licensing system.[45] The alternative would be to negotiate a license with each content rights holder. However, the problem remains that only a fraction of all available works are covered in the CCC database.

CONCLUSION

Less than a decade ago, librarians seldom worried about compulsory licensing and royalty issues. The convergence of digital media and the new ways of delivering information have changed all that. Now issues that seemed far removed from the library world are taking center stage there.

Although the issues in this chapter focus on royalties as they apply to broadcast media, it is worth emphasizing that royalty issues are found in all kinds of other digital content, as well as in the traditional print world. Compared to the print world, however, licensing and royalty issues in the digital world not only are complex but will likely become even more complex in the future. Libraries are now in the business of broadcasting in all kinds of digital media including, for instance, podcasts. Congress is struggling to enact legislation that tries to keep pace with these changes. Much of what we have discussed in this chapter is sure to be affected by future legislation. In the meantime, the Librarian of Congress continues to possess immense but little-known judicial powers.

> ### HYPOTHETICAL #11
>
> It turns out that some of the rights New Age Library acquired in Hypothetical #6 were for sound recordings of various animals and birds, arranged in such a way as to sound like Bach's *Symphony No. 40*. Ms. Graduate would like to continue webcasting and streaming this content, as well as license these recordings for movie soundtracks and ringtones. What are some of the issues to consider?
>
> *A suggested response to this hypothetical question can be found in Appendix 6.*

ENDNOTES

1. 17 U.S.C. § 801(b) (1) (2006).
2. 17 U.S.C. § 801 (a) (2006).
3. 17 U.S.C. § 801 (e) (2006).
4. 17 U.S.C. § 802 (a) (1) (2006).
5. 17 U.S.C. § 802 (c) (2006).

6. 17 U.S.C. § 802 (f) (2) (A) (2006).
7. 17 U.S.C. § 801 (b) (3) (2006).
8. 17 U.S.C. § 801 (b) (8) (2006).
9. 17 U.S.C. § 802 (g) (2006).
10. 17 U.S.C. § 802 (h) (2006).
11. 17 U.S.C. § 802 (i) (2006).
12. 17 U.S.C. § 803 (a) (2006).
13. 17 U.S.C. § 803 (b) (6) (A) (2006).
14. 17 U.S.C. § 803 (b) (2006).
15. 17 U.S.C. § 804 (b) (2006).
16. 17 U.S.C. § 803 (b) (2) (2006).
17. 17 U.S.C. § 803 (b) (3) (2006).
18. 17 U.S.C. § 803 (b) (4) (2006).
19. 17 U.S.C. § 803 (c) (3) (2006).
20. 17 U.S.C. § 803 (c) (5) (2006).
21. 17 U.S.C. § 803 (c) (6) (2006).
22. 17 U.S.C. § 803 (d) (1) (2006).
23. 17 U.S.C. § 803 (d) (3) (2006).
24. 37 C.F.R. § 251.2.
25. 37 C.F.R. § 251.3.
26. 37 C.F.R. § 251.5.
27. 37 C.F.R. § 251.3.
28. 37 C.F.R. § 251.4.
29. 37 C.F.R. § 251.6.
30. 37 C.F.R. § 251.8.
31. 37 C.F.R. § 251.11.
32. 37 C.F.R. § 251.14.
33. 37 C.F.R. § 251.13.
34. 37 C.F.R. § 251.14.
35. 37 C.F.R. § 251.16.
36. 37 C.F.R. § 251.15.
37. 37 C.F.R. § 251.50.
38. 37 C.F.R. § 251.55.
39. 37 C.F.R. § 251.56.
40. 37 C.F.R. § 251.21.
41. Copyright Clearance Center, *About Us* (2011), http://www.copyright.com/content/cc3/en/toolbar/aboutUs.html.
42. Todd Mattingly and Michael R. Samardzija, *Minimizing Liability for Copyright Infringement*, 21(1) INTELLECTUAL PROPERTY AND TECHNOLOGY LAW JOURNAL (2009), 16–19.
43. Paul Biba, *Copyright Clearance Center Slammed Over Funding Lawsuit Against University Libraries; CCC Uses Specious Defense of Its Actions* (November 22, 2010), http://www.teleread

.com/copy-right/copyright-clearance-center-slammed-over-funding-lawsuit-against-university-libraries-ccc-uses-specious-defense-of-its-actions/.
44. Tracey Armstrong, *Copyright Clearance Center: Providing Compliance Solutions for Content Users*, 42 JOURNAL OF LIBRARY ADMINISTRATION, 3&4 (2005), 55–64.
45. Mattingly and Samardzija, *supra*, note 42.

12
WHAT IS PROPRIETARY AND PRIVATE INFORMATION?

IN THIS CHAPTER

We look at other proprietary information, including proprietary search engines and trademarks, and examine the notion of privacy in digital content:
- Proprietary information
- Proprietary search engines
- Privacy
- Evaluating data providers

PROPRIETARY INFORMATION

In this book, we have focused on copyright protection as the major issue in digital content management. However, as mentioned previously, not all digital management issues revolve around copyrights. In this chapter, we examine other aspects of protection that the digital content manager should pay attention to: proprietary and private information. Proprietary information refers to commercially valuable information over which an owner—generally an employer or a service provider—claims ownership, either because the owner originated the information and has it covered under one of the intellectual property tools of protection or the information derives its value from not being generally known in the field, as in, for example, trade secrets.[1] However, information does not need to be a trade secret for it to be proprietary. Nor does it need to be protected by copyright. Digital content managers often work with content and systems that have proprietary information, much of which is unprotected by copyright.

Trade Secrets versus Proprietary Information

To qualify as a protectable trade secret, the information must be confidential and secret; it derives its value from not being generally known. Courts trying to determine the existence of a trade secret will look at factors such as (1) the

135

> **Notable Points 55: Proprietary Information**
> - Proprietary information is commercially valuable information over which an entity claims ownership.
> - The information does not necessarily need to be protected by copyright but may be protected by other tools, including trade secrets.
> - Digital librarians often work with proprietary information.

extent to which the information is generally known, (2) the security measures taken to ensure it remains confidential, and (3) the resources expended in developing the information and other evidence of the value of the information.[2] Trade secrets are subject to state statutes, such as trade secrets, criminal, and unfair competition statutes. They may also be protected by the common law of torts and unfair competition. Some states have also adopted the Uniform Trade Secrets Act[3] as state law. Other federal laws may also apply, such as the Electronic Communications Privacy Act[4] and the Computer Fraud and Abuse Act.[5] A license for digital content may have a clause that prohibits the digital content manager or any licensee from disclosing trade secrets that may be contained in the content or systems. Disclosure of such information attracts significant penalties. A court may also issue an injunction against the party that has received the information.[6]

Although both types of information derive their value from not being generally known, a trade secret is generally defined as a "formula, pattern, compilation, program, device, method, technique, or process" that is secret and for which the owner has taken steps to protect as a secret,[7] while proprietary information could be any information that the owner keeps confidential and which is not ascertainable by proper means.[8] In most cases, this confidentiality will be maintained by contract under nondisclosure agreements. This type of information is also covered by the doctrine of misappropriation, which penalizes the taking of others' work without authorization.[9]

Items considered trade secrets that might be included in the terms of the license contract are systems technical information and data, testing information tools and cover areas such as restrictions of using the trade secret, copying or modifying documents containing the trade secret, whether improvements or reverse engineering are allowed, as well as confidentiality obligations.[10]

Kristen Osenga notes that many information products derive their value from being used, and thus this could trigger their ineligibility as trade secrets.[11] As well, trade secrets hinder, rather than facilitate, the flow of information that is so essential to the working of the established intellectual property incentive–creativity balancing theories.

Notable Points 56: Trade Secrets and Proprietary Information

- A trade secret derives its value from not being generally known; it must remain confidential and secret.
- To determine whether a trade secret exists, courts look into:
  - the extent to which the information is generally known,
  - the security measures taken to protect its confidentiality,
  - the resources expended in developing the information, and
  - other evidence of the value of the information.
- Licenses for digital content may have clauses prohibiting the digital content manager from disclosing trade secrets, which may be contained in the content or system used to manage content, such as:
  - Systems technical information and data
  - Testing information tools
- Disclosure of trade secrets carries significant penalties.
- Trade secrets have been criticized as restricting the flow of information.
- Proprietary information could be any information which an owner keeps confidential and which is not easily ascertainable by legal means.
- Proprietary information is usually protected by nondisclosure agreements in license agreements.

PROPRIETARY SEARCH ENGINES

The process of a search engine spider crawling the web indexing and updating pages has not generally brought up issues of intellectual property. Where the web search is transactional, however, the result may be a copy of the document reproduced on a viewer's screen. This could potentially bring up the issue of reproduction. However, we are concerned with the larger issue of utilizing, modifying, or optimizing search engines that are proprietary without authorization. When the contract between the Chinese company Sina Corporation and Google expired in March 2011, Sina replaced Google's search engine with a proprietary search engine on its portal.[12] Internet search engines are usually protected by patents as search technologies, which includes such areas as methods of ranking documents based on relevancy and other factors, and identifying duplicate pages. Before incorporating or modifying a search engine into a system, the digital content manager will examine the license to ensure the terms of the license are not violated. Proprietary search engines and content management systems may involve licensing fees and are tied in to the developer, who will most likely charge for maintenance and support.

> **Notable Points 57: Proprietary Search Engines**
>
> ▶ Because search engines are in many cases protected by patents, the following activities may be restricted:
> - Utilizing the search engine
> - Modifying the search engine
> - Optimizing the search engine
>
> ▶ There may be a license fee to conduct any of the above activities.

Meta Tags

Courts have variously described meta tags as "buried code" or "machine readable code."[13] Meta tags allow information about a webpage to be read by a search engine in such a way that the page will be displayed in the manner the designer intended, or they may be used as an index or reference source to identify the content of the page. However, sometimes meta tags contain trademark information that could inadvertently be distributed with content, thus violating trademark law. Other issues for the digital content manager to consider while examining digital webpages include the inadvertent inclusion of information that would violate privacy and the right of publicity, or inclusion of misleading information as to the source of the page. As search technology has advanced, meta tags have diminished in importance for the purposes of web searching.

> **Notable Points 58: Meta Tags**
>
> Meta tags:
>
> ▶ allow a webpage to be displayed the way the designer intended,
>
> ▶ may be used as an index or reference source to identify page content,
>
> ▶ may sometimes contain trademark information,
>
> ▶ may contain private information or violate right of publicity, and
>
> ▶ may include misleading information as to the source of the page.

PRIVACY

Evolving digital technologies that enable the collection of diverse data into digital libraries continue to raise privacy issues. This is no less so in the copyright arena. Although the two might seem at first blush to be unconnected, it often happens that unintended disclosure of information does occur, which goes beyond the niceties of copyright. Yet our legal conception of privacy remains muddled, as the U.S. Constitution does not explicitly refer to privacy as such, except with reference to government intrusion of a person's property. Yet courts have found implied rights of privacy, through other doctrines, for instance, in the decision of *Roe v. Wade*.[14]

In the United States, privacy is grounded on the notion of "expectation."[15] David Bender has noted that this notion of "expectation of privacy" preceded the digital environment, but courts are increasingly applying it in the present context.[16]

In most digital content transactions, whether accessing or providing access, a lot of private information is collected. Some of this collection is by design, while some is by the default processing in the systems involved. This then raises the issue of privacy in the digital content. The concept of privacy is less developed in the United States than it is, for example, in Europe, but more and more questions are being raised about what happens with private data after it has been collected.

The first issue that arises is the security of the data collected. Several states have enacted laws regarding data security breach notifications. They require entities holding private data to notify customers when there is reason to believe a breach has occurred. California, for example, requires any person or business conducting business in the state and has computerized data that contains personal information that is unencrypted and has been accessed by unauthorized persons to notify the individuals affected as expeditiously as possible.[17] The notification may be delayed for law enforcement purposes.[18] The California statute defines personal information as an individual's name in combination with any data element such as social security number; driver's license or identification number; financial account numbers and access codes, medical and health insurance information.[19] In California, personal information does not include information from public records.[20]

At the international e-commerce level, there have been efforts at developing guiding principles for handling personal data which might be of relevance to digital collections that contain personal information. The Electronic Steering Group of the Asia-Pacific Economic Cooperation, for example, developed the privacy framework for what kinds of privacy expectations consumers would have online. The framework includes nine principles:

1. preventing harm—making sure personal information is not misused to harm the individual;
2. notice—requiring the posting of privacy practices and policies, including why information is collected, who keeps it, who accesses it, and option for limiting access;
3. collection limitation—to ensure information is collected lawfully and relevant to purpose of the collection;

4. uses of personal information—collection is limited to the purposes for the information;
5. choice—in appropriate cases, a mechanism for deciding on the information collected;
6. integrity of personal information—a requirement the information is accurate, complete and up-to-date;
7. security safeguards—to safeguard personal data against unauthorized access, disclosure, modification or destruction;
8. access and correction—where appropriate, to disclose existence of personal information and to provide an opportunity for correcting errors in the information;
9. and accountability—to ensure compliance with these principles, even when the information is to be transferred to a third party.

These principles are invoked whenever the information is about an identified or identifiable individual.[21]

In negotiating a license agreement, therefore, the digital content manager will pay attention to the data security and privacy issues and to what extent responsibility lies. This can be a confusing area to navigate, given that there are such a plethora of laws dealing with this area. These laws include various state laws that deal with privacy, as well as industry-specific laws. Federal laws include the Health Insurance Portability and Accountability Act (HIPAA),[22] Electronic Communications Privacy Act,[23] and others.

> **Notable Points 59: Privacy**
>
> ▶ Concept of privacy in the United States is less developed than it is in Europe.
> ▶ In the United States, the concept is grounded on the "expectation" of privacy.
> ▶ Many digital transactions involve the collection of private information.
> ▶ Many states have enacted laws for private data breaches.
> ▶ At a minimum, persons affected must be notified.
> ▶ International efforts are ongoing to address the management and security of private data.
> ▶ A digital content license may have clauses that place certain obligations on the digital librarian in the handling of content that contains personal data.

A related area of privacy has to do with the content of digital collections, where unauthorized data about individuals may sometimes reside, giving rise to claims of the right of publicity or defamation.[24] Social networking spaces and tools is an area that is fraught with not only copyright problems for both content manager posts and third-party posts, but also can give rise to defamation claims.[25]

EVALUATING DATA PROVIDERS

Digital librarians often work with content that has been provided by third parties. While some immunities are provided by the Internet service provider (ISP) safe harbor, not all digital libraries might qualify as ISPs. Content managers therefore need to evaluate their data providers on several aspects.

The first question to look into is whether any of the data provided is copyrightable. For data that is copyrightable, the inquiry would then move to the ownership of copyright and whether the data provider has permission to use or license the data. More specifically, whether the license with the service provider includes an indemnity clause in favor of the digital library in case of infringement claims. Questions along these lines also include an inquiry into whether the data is free from infringement of other work, and whether it is free from libelous and unlawful statements.

Then there are the issues of quality, accuracy, and completeness of the data provided. Is the data provided stable or is it prone to errors; is the data provider itself stable or is it a shaky business? Other questions to pursue include how quickly and consistently the data provider delivers content. If the provider stores some of the client data, whether the data provider has data security systems in place and how well

> ☑ **Checklist 14: Evaluating Data Providers**
>
> ❏ Is the data copyrightable?
> ❏ Does the provider have permission to use and license the data?
> ❏ Is there an indemnity clause in case of copyright infringement claims?
> ❏ Is the data of high quality, accurate, and complete?
> ❏ Is the data provided quickly and consistently?
> ❏ Is the provided data stable or prone to errors?
> ❏ Is the data provider stable or is it likely to go out of business?
> ❏ Is the data secure and how prepared is the system for a breach?
> ❏ Does the data provider have data security systems in place and is it well prepared to deal with breaches and invasions of privacy?
> ❏ Are there any confidentiality obligations between the provider and the digital library?
> ❏ Is the work free from libelous or unlawful statements?
> ❏ If the data is foreign, does it have moral rights claims?
> ❏ If there are moral rights claims, how might they affect any planned customization of the content to meet user needs?

prepared it is to deal with breaches and invasions of privacy. If the data provider is foreign, it might be necessary to determine whether the data carries any moral rights claims and how these might affect any planned customization of the content to meet user needs. Finally, it is also important to examine what kinds of confidentiality obligations exist between the data provider and the digital library.

> HYPOTHETICAL #12
>
> Mr. Digital Librarian has begun to have some misgivings about the ability of his colleagues and others to access the collection in Hypothetical #1. Besides copyright issues, what else should he be thinking about? Also, it turns out that the SISE Company has a data provision service that can provide content to the digital library of New Age Library. What additional issues should concern Mr. Librarian?
>
> A suggested response to this hypothetical question can be found in Appendix 6.

ENDNOTES

1. Chris Montville, *Reforming the Law of Proprietary Information*, 56 DUKE LAW JOURNAL (2007), 1159–1200.
2. Alois Valerian Gross, *Annotation: What Is "Trade Secret" So As to Render Actionable under State Law Its Use or Disclosure by Former Employee*, 59(4th) AMERICAN LAW REVIEW (1988), 641.
3. National Conference of Commissioners on Uniform State Laws, *Uniform Trade Secrets Act* 1(4) (Minneapolis, MN: NCCUSL, 1985).
4. 18 U.S.C. § 2701 et seq. (2006).
5. 18 U.S.C. § 1030 et seq. (2006).
6. Montville, *supra*, note 1.
7. National Conference of Commissioners, *supra*, note 3.
8. Montville, *supra*, note 1.
9. Kristen Osenga, *Information May Want to Be Free, but Information Products Do Not: Protecting and Facilitating Transactions in Information Products*, 30 CARDOZO LAW REVIEW (2009), 2099–2145.
10. Peter J. Kinsella, *Special Issues in Trade Secret Licensing*, 1036 PRACTISING LAW INSTITUTE (2011), PLI/Pat 33.
11. Osenga, *supra*, note 9.
12. Jin Zhang, *Sina Embeds Proprietary Search Engine in Portal, Drops Google*, BUSINESS CHINA (March 29, 2011), http://en.21cbh.com/HTML/2011-3-29/1NMjUyXzIwOTc1NQ.html.
13. *Brookfield Communications v. West Coast Entertainment*, 174 F.3d 1036 (9th Cir. 1999), note 23.
14. 410 U.S. 113 (1973).
15. *United States v. Miller*, 425 U.S. 435 (1976).

16. David Bender, *Privacy/Data Protection Development—2008*, Patents, Copyrights, Trademark, and Literary Property Handbooks Series, 947 PRACTISING LAW INSTITUTE (2008), PLI/Pat 39.
17. Cal. Civ. Code 1798.82 (a).
18. Cal. Civ. Code 1798.82 (c).
19. Cal. Civ. Code 1798.82 (e).
20. Cal. Civ. Code 1798.82 (f).
21. Bender, *supra*, note 16.
22. 42 U.S.C. § 1320 (a) (2006).
23. 18 U.S.C. § 2701 (2006).
24. Paul D. Healey, PROFESSIONAL LIABILITY ISSUES FOR LIBRARIANS AND INFORMATION PROFESSIONALS (New York: Neal-Schuman, 2008).
25. John F. Delaney, *Poking and Tweeting: Social Media Overview*, 1034 PRACTISING LAW INSTITUTE (February–March 2011), PLI/Pat 43.

13

INTERNATIONAL ASPECTS OF COPYRIGHT

IN THIS CHAPTER

We conclude with an examination of the international aspects of copyright, including the various international treaties to which the United States is a party:
- The Berne Convention
- WIPO Copyright Treaty
- Universal Copyright Convention
- Agreement on Trade-Related Aspects of Intellectual Property Rights (TRIPS)

INTRODUCTION

The world has become a global village, and this is true as well in the area of copyright. While there is no such thing as an international copyright law, issues of copyright are part of the international give-and-take in trade and politics. Because of globalization of information technology, even a domestic digital content manager is likely to have to deal with international copyright issues, most notably in the areas of access and data protection issues.

Copyright in the international arena is mainly governed by international agreements and treaties—some multinational, others bilateral. The major treaties governing copyrights are the Berne Convention; the World Intellectual Property Organization (WIPO) Convention, which currently administers 24 treaties; and the General Agreements on Tariffs and Trade/World Trade Organization (GATT/WTO) Trade-Related Aspects of Intellectual Property Rights (TRIPS). The Paris Convention is another major treaty that mainly protects patents and trademarks and addresses unfair competition. By joining a treaty, a country undertakes to follow the requirements established by the treaty. The United States is a signatory to these major treaties.[1] The United States also has other bilateral and multilateral treaties that have an impact on copyright, including the North American Free Trade Agreement (NAFTA), which joins the United States, Mexico, and Canada. NAFTA's provisions are not bound by either the Berne Convention or the WIPO, except inasmuch as the United States has obligations to those two bodies. But NAFTA also incorporates substantive provisions of major conventions, including the Berne and Paris conventions.

> **Notable Points 60: International Treaty**
>
> ▶ Digital content managers are becoming increasingly likely to deal with international copyright issues.
> ▶ Copyright in the international context is mainly governed by international treaties and agreements.
> ▶ Major treaties governing copyright in the international context include the Berne Convention, the WIPO Convention, and the WTO, including TRIPS.
> ▶ The United States is a signatory to the major treaties, as well as a number of other bilateral and multilateral agreements.

THE BERNE CONVENTION

The Berne Convention came into force in 1886 in Berne, Switzerland, and was designed to protect literary and artistic works in all member countries (referred to as the Union)[2] and provides this protection to nationals of any Union member country for published or unpublished work[3] as well as nationals of a nonmember country who published in a member country.[4] Nonnational residents are also covered,[5] especially for "cinematographic" and architectural works.[6] The convention approached copyright protection from an author's rights point of view, including moral rights, rather than from a mainly economic concern. The convention has been revised several times since 1886, most notably in 1971 (and then amended in 1979).

The rights protected in the Berne Convention are roughly parallel to the rights protected by U.S. copyright law. These include the right of reproduction,[7] the right of translation,[8] the rights of public performance and communication of the performance to the public of dramatic and musical works and their translations,[9] the right to authorize broadcasting, wire and wireless communication, to receive royalties from compulsory licensing,[10] and the right to authorize the making of derivative works.[11]

The Berne Convention also gives authors of literary works the exclusive right to authorize public recitation of their work by any means or process, and the communication to the public of such recitals.[12] The convention also bestows on the authors of literary works rights with respect to translations during the term of the copyright protection of the original work.[13] Furthermore, with respect to works of art and manuscripts, the author (or if deceased, persons authorized to exercise the author's rights) shall continue to "enjoy the inalienable right to an interest in any sale of the work subsequent to the first transfer by the author of the work" where the national legislation allows for such a right.[14] This right is referred to as *droit de suite* and would be contrary to the U.S. first-sale doctrine.

The subject matter of protection under the Berne Convention is for "literary and artistic works," but these also include works in the scientific domain.[15] The Convention leaves it to the individual signatory countries to decide whether to require fixation in some tangible form.[16] Translations, adaptations, music arrangements, or other alterations (what we might refer to under U.S. copyright law as derivatives) are "protected as original works without prejudice to the copyright in the original work."[17] The convention also leaves it to individual countries whether they wish to protect government documents, including legislative and judicial material.[18] Generally, many countries consider such material to be in the public domain, but some commonwealth countries claim copyright. The convention also protects collective works as well as the individual contributions in the collective work.[19]

While member countries may under the convention legislate on whether to extend protection to "political speeches and speeches delivered in the course of legal proceedings"[20] as well as whether public lectures may be reproduced and broadcast to the public,[21] the exclusive right to make a collection of such speeches remains with the author.[22]

Authors in a member country enjoy the rights of copyright in their country of origin, as well as the rights under the convention.[23] Nonnationals also enjoy the same rights as nationals of a member country for their works in the country of origin, as defined by the convention.[24] Nonmember countries that do not give adequate copyright protection to nationals from member countries may be sanctioned by having their nonresident nationals receive restricted protection in the member country,[25] but the restrictions shall not affect any rights such persons may have had in the member country, before the sanctions.[26]

As in U.S. copyright law, there are significant limitations on the copyright owner's exclusive right, similar to fair use. Quotations may be made from a protected work, provided such quotations are made in a manner "compatible with fair practice" and do not exceed what would be justified for the purpose.[27] Member countries are free to legislate conditions that permit the utilization of protected works in illustrations for teaching purposes.[28] Such use must attribute the source and author's name, if available.[29] Recording of musical works may also be subject to compulsory licensing, according to the individual member country legislation.[30]

A big difference between copyright protection under the Berne Convention and protection under U.S. copyright law is the former's emphasis on the author's moral rights. These refer to the author's right to continue to claim authorship of a work even after the transfer of the economic rights, and to protect his honor and reputation by being able to object to distortion, mutilation, other modification or derogatory action to the work that would threaten such reputation and honor.[31] These moral rights continue to be exercised by persons or entities entitled to do so even after the author's death. Countries that did not protect such rights after an author's death could continue to extinguish such rights after the author's death.[32]

An author's name or his well-known pseudonym has to appear on a literary or artistic work for that author to be entitled to bring an infringement suit.[33] For cinematographic works, the person or corporate name appearing on the work shall be presumed to be the maker of the work, unless there is contradicting proof.[34] For anonymous and pseudonymous works (where the pseudonym does not identify the author), the publisher of the work is deemed to represent the author in enforcing the author's rights, unless there is proof to the contrary or the author appears to announce his claim.[35] For unpublished material where the author cannot be identified but where it is presumed that the author is a national of a member country, such member country may designate by legislation a competent authority to represent the unknown author.[36]

Similar to U.S. law, the convention provides for seizure of infringing copies in a member country where the work is legally protected, as well as copies imported from countries where such work is not legally protected.[37] Member countries are free to make legislation that gives more rights than those provided for in the convention[38] and to enter into bilateral and multilateral agreements which offer more extensive rights and other rights that are not contrary to the convention.[39] Disputes regarding this convention may be adjudicated before the International Court of Justice where countries have agreed to be bound by the Court's jurisdiction in this matter, or the countries involved may agree on some other form of settlement.[40]

The term of copyright protection provided by the Berne Convention runs for the life of the author plus 50 years following the author's death.[41] In the case of joint authors, the life used to calculate the term of protection is that of the last surviving author.[42] For cinematographic works, however, member countries may legislate the expiration of copyright protection 50 years after the work was made publicly available with the author's consent or 50 years since it was first made.[43] Anonymous and pseudonymous works are also protected for 50 years since being made available to the public, except for where the real identity of the author is determined; then it would be the life of the author plus 50 years. There is no obligation to protect anonymous and pseudonymous works where there is a reasonable assumption that the author has been dead for 50 years.[44] For photographic works and works of applied art protected as artistic works, member countries may legislate the period of protection, which must be at least 25 years after the creation of the work.[45] Member countries are free to provide protection terms in excess of the ones provided by the Berne Treaty.⁴⁶ Some countries with a shorter period of protection at the ratification of the convention were allowed to maintain the shorter period.⁴⁷ As noted earlier, the United States, for example, provides protection for the life of the author plus 70 years. But the term of protection available is determined by the

Notable Points 61: Berne Convention

- The Berne Convention is the bedrock of international copyright law.
- It provides protection for published and unpublished work to nationals of contracting member states, as well as certain nationals of non–contracting member states.
- Rights protected are roughly parallel to those under the U.S. Copyright Act, with major differences:
  - The Berne Convention, unlike U.S. law, has an emphasis on the author's moral rights, i.e., the right to continue to claim authorship even after transferring all economic rights.
  - Thus, the Berne Convention allows an interest in the work subsequent to the first transfer, which would be against the U.S. Copyright Act's doctrine of First Sale.
  - These moral rights survive the author's death.
- A publisher of an anonymous or pseudonymous work is deemed to represent the author in enforcing the author's rights.
- For an anonymous or pseudonymous unpublished work, a member country may by legislation designate a competent authority to represent the unknown author in the enforcement of rights.
- The term of copyright protection under the Berne Convention is the life of the author or the last surviving author plus 50 years.
- Anonymous and pseudonymous works are protected for 50 years since they were made available to the public, unless there is reason to believe the author has been dead for 50 years.
- Member countries may make legislation providing for more rights than those available under the Berne Convention.
- The United States dispensed with the copyright formalities of notice and registration to conform to the Berne Convention.
- The International Court of Justice adjudicates disputes regarding the Berne Convention.
- Member country authors enjoy the rights of copyright in their own countries as well as rights under the Berne Convention.

legislation of the country where the claim is lodged and cannot exceed the term that was made available in the country of origin.[48] In other words, a claimant cannot seek life plus 70 years' protection in the United States for a work that had life plus 50 years when created in the country of origin.

Before signing onto the Berne Convention, the United States required formalities of notice and registration before a work could be protected, and the protection was only for a fixed term, that was renewable. The Berne Convention, on the other hand, does not require the notice and registration formalities before a work can be copyrighted. The provisions of U.S. copyright now largely reflect the provisions of the Berne Convention.

WIPO COPYRIGHT TREATY

To protect computer programs and databases and the rights of authors to authorize transmission online, the WIPO Copyright Treaty (WCT) was adopted in Geneva, Switzerland, on December 20, 1996, its purpose to update the Berne Convention. Recognizing the changing technological, social, cultural, and economic landscape, particularly the convergence of information and communication technologies, the contracting parties (signatory members) wished to give some uniformity to the development and maintenance of protection of rights for authors of literary and artistic works in the digital environment. (A sister treaty, the WIPO Performances and Phonograms Treaty, was also passed at the same time.) The contracting parties also professed to recognize the need to maintain balance between authors' rights and public interest in information access for education and research.[49]

Unlike the Berne Convention, WCT makes explicit that copyright protects expression, not ideas, procedures, methods of operation, or mathematical concepts.[50] It adds computer programs to literary works protected under the Berne Convention[51] and extends protection to compilations of data that have been selected or arranged in such a way as to constitute intellectual creation, without protecting the data itself or prejudicing any existing copyright in the data or material.[52]

WCT specifically mentions three exclusive rights: the right of distribution; the right of rental of computer programs, cinematographic works, and works embodied in phonograms; and the right of communication to the public. Authors of literary and artistic works have the exclusive right to authorize the distribution of original and copies of their works by sale or other transfer. However, the contracting parties can determine the condition of the exhaustion of this right after the author-authorized first sale or other ownership transfer of the original or copy of the work.[53] Although the treaty does not mention the exclusive right of reproduction, this right seems to be implied under article 6.

The exclusive right to authorize commercial rental to the public of computer programs, cinematographic works, or other works embodied in phonograms belongs to the authors of such works. This right does not apply where the computer program is not the essential object of the rental, or where, in the case of cinematographic works, such commercial rental has not led to widespread copying that has materially impaired the author's exclusive right of reproduction. A contracting party that has a compulsory licensing system in place may opt to keep that system, as long as such a system does not lead to the impairment of the author's exclusive right of reproduction.[54]

Authors of literary and artistic works have, in line with the Berne Convention, the exclusive right of authorizing the wired or wireless communication of their works to the public, including in situations where members of the public can individually choose the place and time of accessing such works.[55]

With respect to photographic works, the WCT specifically prohibits contracting parties from using article 7(4) of the Berne Convention, which provided for member countries at least a 25-year term of protection since the creation of a photographic work or a work of applied art that is protected as an artistic work.[56] Contracting parties may also legislate limitations or exceptions to the rights granted to authors under WCT in cases where a conflict with the normal exploitation of the work and the author's legitimate interests are not prejudiced.[57]

Also, similarly to the U.S. Digital Millennium Copyright Act (DCMA) discussed in earlier chapters, WCT contracting parties are obliged to "provide adequate legal protection and effective legal remedies against the circumvention of effective technological measures that are used by authors in connection with the exercise of their rights... and that restrict acts, in respect of their works, which are not authorized by the authors concerned or permitted by law."[58] They are also obliged to provide legal remedies against persons who knowingly interfere with electronic rights management information or distribute, import, or communicate to the public works in which they know the electronic rights management information has been unlawfully removed or altered. The WCT defines rights management information as "information which identifies the work, the author of the work, the owner of any right in the work, or information about the terms and conditions of use of the work, and any numbers or codes that represent such information, when any of

Notable Points 62: WIPO Copyright Treaty

▶ The WIPO Copyright Treaty (WCT) adds computer programs to literary works protected under the Berne Convention and extends protection to compilations of data that contain some originality.

▶ WCT brings the Berne Convention into the digital age.

▶ WCT has similar prohibition to the Digital Millennium Copyright Act against circumventing technological measures.

these items of information is attached to a copy of a work or appears in connection with the communication of a work to the public."[59] There are 88 contracting parties, including the United States and the European Union, that subscribe to the WCT.

UNIVERSAL COPYRIGHT CONVENTION

At the onset of the Berne Convention, some countries felt the intellectual property protection demanded by the convention was too onerous and benefited mainly Western countries. The United Nations Educational, Scientific, and Cultural Organization (UNESCO) came up with an alternative copyright protection scheme for these countries in 1952, in the form of the Universal Copyright Convention (UCC). This was later revised in Paris in 1971. Curiously, the first 12 countries to sign on to the revision included the United States. This was because the Berne Convention required doing away with notice and registration formalities as well as other changes in the U.S. copyright law that the United States was not ready to do.

Essentially, each contracting state (member country) undertook to provide adequate copyright protections and to provide the same protection to works published in other member countries, as well as unpublished works in such countries.[60] The UCC required member countries to legally protect unpublished works of nationals of other member states.[61] It also simplified the formalities for those countries whose laws continued to demand formalities, by allowing authors from other member states to simply have a copyright symbol, the name of the copyright proprietor, and year of first publication affixed to the work in such a way that there was notice of claim of copyright.[62] Countries that wished to continue with full formalities for their nationals were also free to do so under the UCC.[63]

As in the other treaties discussed, UCC allows member countries to legislate the duration of the terms of copyright protection, except that the term should not be less than the life of the author plus 25 years, or at least 25 years if a member state does not use the computation method of author's life plus x years after the death of the author. For photographic works or works of applied art, the period of protection should not be less than ten years.[64]

The author's exclusive rights covered by UCC include the right to authorize reproduction, public performance, and broadcasting.[65] They also include the right to make and publish translations of the work.[66] Member countries may pass domestic legislation restricting such translation rights.[67]

The UCC gave certain developing countries some leeway in making exceptions to protections of works in their countries under a limited set of circumstances for a limited time, including, for instance, a compulsory license to make a translation of the work in a language other than English, French, or Spanish where the original author has denied permission for a translation, or the author could not be located,[68] or a compulsory license to publish and distribute where copies of a work have not been adequately distributed in the developing country at a reasonable price.[69]

With intellectual property issues now an agenda item for international trade agreements under the World Trade Organization, the UCC has slowly been losing its relevance. It is important to know, however, that this convention specifically copy-protects works published by the United Nations and its agencies.

> **Notable Points 63: Universal Copyright Convention**
>
> ▶ UCC was developed by UNESCO and was a response to what some countries considered the onerous demands of the Berne Convention.
>
> ▶ Original signatories to UCC included the United States, partly because the United States was not ready to abandon copyright formalities and other changes that the Berne Convention required.
>
> ▶ UCC puts the minimum term of copyright protection at 25 years.
>
> ▶ UCC maintained some flexibilities in certain developing countries, allowing them, for instance, to issue some compulsory licenses to translate, to publish, and to distribute a work under certain circumstances for a limited time.
>
> ▶ UCC has slowly been losing its relevance as intellectual property issues become an agenda item for international trade agreements.

AGREEMENT ON TRADE-RELATED ASPECTS OF INTELLECTUAL PROPERTY RIGHTS (TRIPS)

TRIPS was a successful attempt to ease the exclusive dominance of WIPO over intellectual property issues by tying such issues to international trade agreements through the World Trade Organization (WTO). This was done as part of the Uruguay Round of trade negotiations in 1994. Thus intellectual property issues became an item of discussion in the General Agreements on Tariffs and Trade (now WTO) negotiations. It is clear right from its preamble that TRIPS was not concerned with maintaining the balance between the public interest and the author's economic rights. It is concerned with intellectual property as private rights.

As is evident from its title, TRIPS covers more than just copyright. But we are here interested in its copyright aspect detailed in article 9 and those that follow. TRIPS does not derogate from members' obligations to the Berne Convention.[70]

TRIPS echoes WCT in that it reiterates that ideas, procedures, methods of operation, or mathematical concepts are not protected by copyright; only expressions are.[71] Similarly, it explicitly extends copyright protection to computer programs and compilations of data.[72] It also closely shadows both Berne and WCT in the areas of rental rights for computer programs and cinematographic works.[73] Where a term of protection is calculated on a basis other than the life of the author, TRIPS requires that the period of protection be no less than 50 years from publication or creation, except in the cases of photographic works or works of applied art.[74]

Members are required to not put limits on or exceptions to the copyright holder's exclusive rights, except in special cases that do not conflict with the normal exploitation of the work or prejudice the legitimate interests of the copyright holder.[75] Performers, phonogram producers, and broadcasting organizations are empowered to prevent unauthorized fixation of their unfixed performance or the unauthorized broadcasting of their live performance.[76] Performers get this protection for 50 years, while broadcasters get it for 20 years.[77] Phonogram producers also have the right to authorize or prohibit reproduction of their phonograms.[78] Broadcasters also enjoy the right to prohibit the unauthorized fixation, reproduction of fixations, and broadcasting of broadcasts by wireless means; this includes television broadcasts. Where broadcasters have no such rights, the member country is required to provide the copyright holder of the broadcast subject matter with the possibility of preventing such fixation or broadcasting.[79]

TRIPS also provides guidance on enforcement of intellectual property rights,[80] including civil and administrative procedures and remedies, as well as criminal procedures for commercial-scale copyright privacy.[81]

Under TRIPS, members are free to require formalities as a condition for acquiring or maintenance of intellectual property rights.[82] Member states are also required to publish laws and regulations pertaining to intellectual property matters and provide these to other members upon request.[83] Also, developing countries were given some breathing space before they had to fully comply with the TRIPS requirements.[84]

Notable Points 64: The Agreement on Trade-Related Aspects of Intellectual Property Rights (TRIPS)

- The Agreement on Trade-Related Aspects of Intellectual Property Rights (TRIPS) ties intellectual property issues into international trade agreements.
- TRIPS is concerned with intellectual property as private rights, not with maintaining balance between public interest and authors' economic rights.
- TRIPs gives member countries the flexibility to require formalities for acquiring and maintaining intellectual property protection.
- TRIPs requires member countries to publish and share intellectual property laws.

CONCLUSION

While it is a truism that copyright laws are territorial, that is, they are applicable within the territory in which they are made, it is equally clear that there is global interdependence on intellectual property matters, particularly copyright. The United States has domesticated many of the international treaties into its intellectual property laws,[85] but new situations will undoubtedly continue to occur that test the limits of the success of such domestication.

HYPOTHETICAL #13

A year later, just when she thought she had the management of Mr. Rich's collection and the *Twilight* series collection under control, Ms. Graduate receives a phone call from Mr. Librarian: "New Age has just acquired sizable digital material from different parts of the world. It is all yours!" What are some of the issues Ms. Graduate should be aware of?

A suggested response to this hypothetical question can be found in Appendix 6.

ENDNOTES

1. See U.S. Copyright Office, *International Copyright Relations of the United States* (2010), http://www.copyright.gov/circs/circ38a.pdf, for a list of treaty countries as of September 2010.
2. Berne Convention for the Protection of Literary and Artistic Works (as variously amended), World Intellectual Property Organization (WIPO), 1161 U.N.T.S. 30, Art. 2 (6) (1971).
3. Berne Convention, 1161 U.N.T.S. 30, Art. 3 (1) (a) (1971).
4. Berne Convention, 1161 U.N.T.S. 30, Art. 3 (1) (b) (1971).
5. Berne Convention, 1161 U.N.T.S. 30, Art. 3 (2) (1971).
6. Berne Convention, 1161 U.N.T.S. 30, Art. 4 (1971).
7. Berne Convention, 1161 U.N.T.S. 30, Art. 9 (1971).
8. Berne Convention, 1161 U.N.T.S. 30, Art. 8 (1971).
9. Berne Convention, 1161 U.N.T.S. 30, Art. 11 (1971).
10. Berne Convention, 1161 U.N.T.S. 30, Art. 11bis (1971).
11. Berne Convention, 1161 U.N.T.S. 30, Art. 12 (1971).
12. Berne Convention, 1161 U.N.T.S. 30, Art. 11ter (1) (1971).
13. Berne Convention, 1161 U.N.T.S. 30, Art. 11ter (2) (1971).
14. Berne Convention, 1161 U.N.T.S. 30, Art. 14ter (1971).
15. Berne Convention, 1161 U.N.T.S. 30, Art. 2 (1) (1971).
16. Berne Convention, 1161 U.N.T.S. 30, Art. 2 (2) (1971).
17. Berne Convention, 1161 U.N.T.S. 30, Art. 2 (3) (1971).

18. Berne Convention, 1161 U.N.T.S. 30, Art. 2 (4) (1971).
19. Berne Convention, 1161 U.N.T.S. 30, Art. 2 (5) (1971).
20. Berne Convention, 1161 U.N.T.S. 30, Art. 2bis (1) (1971).
21. Berne Convention, 1161 U.N.T.S. 30, Art. 2bis (2) (1971).
22. Berne Convention, 1161 U.N.T.S. 30, Art. 2bis (3) (1971).
23. Berne Convention, 1161 U.N.T.S. 30, Art. 5 (1) (1971).
24. Berne Convention, 1161 U.N.T.S. 30, Art. 3 and 4 (1971).
25. Berne Convention, 1161 U.N.T.S. 30, Art. 6 (1) (1971).
26. Berne Convention, 1161 U.N.T.S. 30, Art. 6 (2) (1971).
27. Berne Convention, 1161 U.N.T.S. 30, Art. 10 (1) (1971).
28. Berne Convention, 1161 U.N.T.S. 30, Art. 10 (2) (1971).
29. Berne Convention, 1161 U.N.T.S. 30, Art. 10 (3) (1971).
30. Berne Convention, 1161 U.N.T.S. 30, Art. 13 (1971).
31. Berne Convention, 1161 U.N.T.S. 30, Art. 6bis (1) (1971).
32. Berne Convention, 1161 U.N.T.S. 30, Art. 6bis (2) (1971).
33. Berne Convention, 1161 U.N.T.S. 30, Art. 15 (1) (1971).
34. Berne Convention, 1161 U.N.T.S. 30, Art. 15 (2) (1971).
35. Berne Convention, 1161 U.N.T.S. 30, Art. 15 (3) (1971).
36. Berne Convention, 1161 U.N.T.S. 30, Art. 15 (4) (1971).
37. Berne Convention, 1161 U.N.T.S. 30, Art. 16 (1971).
38. Berne Convention, 1161 U.N.T.S. 30, Art. 19 (1971).
39. Berne Convention, 1161 U.N.T.S. 30, Art. 20 (1971).
40. Berne Convention, 1161 U.N.T.S. 30, Art. 33 (1971).
41. Berne Convention, 1161 U.N.T.S. 30, Art. 7 (1) (1971).
42. Berne Convention, 1161 U.N.T.S. 30, Art. 7bis (1971).
43. Berne Convention, 1161 U.N.T.S. 30, Art. 7 (2) (1971).
44. Berne Convention, 1161 U.N.T.S. 30, Art. 7 (3) (1971).
45. Berne Convention, 1161 U.N.T.S. 30, Art. 7 (4) (1971).
46. Berne Convention, 1161 U.N.T.S. 30, Art. 7 (6) (1971).
47. Berne Convention, 1161 U.N.T.S. 30, Art. 7 (7) (1971).
48. Berne Convention, 1161 U.N.T.S. 30, Art. 7 (8) (1971).
49 WIPO Copyright Treaty (WCT), 1996, Preamble, http://portal.unesco.org/en/ev.php-URL_ID=15241&URL_DO=DO_TOPIC&URL_SECTION=201.html.
50. WCT, Art. 1.
51. WCT, Art. 4.
52. WCT, Art. 5.
53. WCT, Art. 6.
54. WCT, Art. 7.
55. WCT, Art. 8.
56. WCT, Art. 9.
57. WCT, Art. 10.

58. WCT, Art. 11.
59. WCT, Art. 12.
60. Universal Copyright Convention (UCC), Art. I, II.
61. UCC, Art. III (4).
62. UCC, Art. III (1).
63. UCC, Art. III (2).
64. UCC, Art. IV.
65. *Id.*
66. UCC, Art. V (1).
67. UCC, Art. V (2).
68. UCC, Art. Vter.
69. UCC, Art. Quater.
70. Agreement on Trade-Related Aspects of Intellectual Property Rights (TRIPS), Art. 2 (2), http://www.wto.org/english/docs_e/legal_e/legal_e.htm#TRIPs.
71. TRIPS, Art. 10 (2).
72. TRIPS, Art. 10.
73. TRIPS, Art. 11.
74. TRIPS, Art. 12.
75. TRIPS, Art 13.
76. TRIPS, Art. 14 (1).
77. TRIPS, Art. 14 (5).
78. TRIPS, Art. 14 (2).
79. TRIPS, Art. 14 (3).
80. TRIPS, Art 41–49.
81. TRIPS, Art. 61.
82. TRIPS, Art. 62.
83. TRIPS, Art. 63.
84. TRIPS, Art. 66.
85. See, for example, 17 U.S.C. § 902 (2006) and 17 U.S.C. § 914 (2006) on extending protections to foreign nations, the DMCA, the Berne Convention.

APPENDIXES

Appendix 1

NOTICES OF TERMINATION OF TRANSFERS AND LICENSES (CODE OF FEDERAL REGULATIONS)

37 C.F.R. § 201.10 Notices of termination of transfers and licenses.

This section covers notices of termination of transfers and licenses under sections 203, 304(c) and 304(d) of title 17, of the United States Code. A termination under section 304(d) is possible only if no termination was made under section 304(c), and federal copyright was originally secured on or between January 1, 1923, and October 26, 1939.

(a) Form. The Copyright Office does not provide printed forms for the use of persons serving notices of termination.

(b) Contents.

 (1) A notice of termination covering the extended renewal term under sections 304(c) and 304(d) of title 17, U.S.C., must include a clear identification of each of the following:

  (i) Whether the termination is made under section 304(c) or under section 304(d);

  (ii) The name of each grantee whose rights are being terminated, or the grantee's successor in title, and each address at which service of the notice is being made;

  (iii) The title and the name of at least one author of, and the date copyright was originally secured in, each work to which the notice of termination applies; and, if possible and practicable, the original copyright registration number;

  (iv) A brief statement reasonably identifying the grant to which the notice of termination applies;

  (v) The effective date of termination;

  (vi) If termination is made under section 304(d), a statement that termination of renewal term rights under section 304(c) has not been previously exercised; and

  (vii) In the case of a termination of a grant executed by a person or persons other than the author, a listing of the surviving person or persons who executed the grant. In the case of a termination of a grant executed by one or more of the authors of the work where the termination is exercised by the successors of a deceased author, a listing of the names and relationships to that deceased author of all of the following, together with specific indication of the person or persons executing the notice who constitute more than one-half of that author's termination interest: That author's surviving widow or widower; and all of that author's surviving children; and, where any of that author's children are dead, all of the surviving children of any such deceased child of that author; however, instead of the information required by this paragraph (vii), the notice may contain both of the following:

(A) A statement of as much of such information as is currently available to the person or persons signing the notice, with a brief explanation of the reasons why full information is or may be lacking; together with

(B) A statement that, to the best knowledge and belief of the person or persons signing the notice, the notice has been signed by all persons whose signature is necessary to terminate the grant under section 304 of title 17, U.S.C., or by their duly authorized agents.

(2) A notice of termination of an exclusive or nonexclusive grant of a transfer or license of copyright or of any right under a copyright, executed by the author on or after January 1, 1978, under section 203 of title 17, U.S.C., must include a clear identification of each of the following:

(i) A statement that the termination is made under section 203:

(ii) The name of each grantee whose rights are being terminated, or the grantee's successor in title, and each address at which service of the notice is being made;

(iii) The date of execution of the grant being terminated and, if the grant covered the right of publication of a work, the date of publication of the work under the grant;

(iv) For each work to which the notice of termination applies, the title of the work and the name of the author or, in the case of a joint work, the authors who executed the grant being terminated; and, if possible and practicable, the original copyright registration number;

(v) A brief statement reasonably identifying the grant to which the notice of termination applies;

(vi) The effective date of termination; and

(vii) In the case of a termination of a grant executed by one or more of the authors of the work where the termination is exercised by the successors of a deceased author, a listing of the names and relationships to that deceased author of all of the following, together with specific indication of the person or persons executing the notice who constitute more than one-half of that author's termination interest: That author's surviving widow or widower; and all of that author's surviving children; and, where any of that author's children are dead, all of the surviving children of any such deceased child of that author; however, instead of the information required by this paragraph (b)(2)(vii), the notice may contain both of the following:

(A) A statement of as much of such information as is currently available to the person or persons signing the notice, with a brief explanation of the reasons why full information is or may be lacking; together with

(B) A statement that, to the best knowledge and belief of the person or persons signing the notice, the notice has been signed by all persons whose signature is necessary to terminate the grant under section 203 of title 17, U.S.C., or by their duly authorized agents.

(3) Clear identification of the information specified by paragraphs (b)(1) and (b)(2) of this section requires a complete and unambiguous statement of facts in the notice itself, without incorporation by reference of information in other documents or records.

(c) Signature.

(1) In the case of a termination of a grant under section 304(c) or section 304(d) executed by a person or persons other than the author, the notice shall be signed by all of the surviving person or persons who executed the grant, or by their duly authorized agents.

(2) In the case of a termination of a grant under section 304(c) or section 304(d) executed by one or more of the authors of the work, the notice as to any one author's share shall be signed by that author or by his or her duly authorized agent. If that author is dead, the notice shall be signed by the number and proportion of the owners of that author's termination interest required under section 304(c) or section 304(d), whichever applies, of title 17, U.S.C., or by their duly authorized agents, and shall contain a brief statement of their relationship or relationships to that author.

(3) In the case of a termination of a grant under section 203 executed by one or more of the authors of the work, the notice shall be signed by

each author who is terminating the grant or by his or her duly authorized agent. If that author is dead, the notice shall be signed by the number and proportion of the owners of that author's termination interest required under section 203 of title 17, U.S.C., or by their duly authorized agents, and shall contain a brief statement of their relationship or relationships to that author.

(4) Where a signature is by a duly authorized agent, it shall clearly identify the person or persons on whose behalf the agent is acting.

(5) The handwritten signature of each person effecting the termination shall either be accompanied by a statement of the full name and address of that person, typewritten or printed legibly by hand, or shall clearly correspond to such a statement elsewhere in the notice.

(d) Service.

(1) The notice of termination shall be served upon each grantee whose rights are being terminated, or the grantee's successor in title, by personal service, or by first-class mail sent to an address which, after a reasonable investigation, is found to be the last known address of the grantee or successor in title.

(2) The service provision of section 203, section 304(c) or section 304(d) of title 17, U.S.C., whichever applies, will be satisfied if, before the notice of termination is served, a reasonable investigation is made by the person or persons executing the notice as to the current ownership of the rights being terminated, and based on such investigation:

(i) If there is no reason to believe that such rights have been transferred by the grantee to a successor in title, the notice is served on the grantee; or

(ii) If there is reason to believe that such rights have been transferred by the grantee to a particular successor in title, the notice is served on such successor in title.

(3) For purposes of paragraph (d)(2) of this section, a reasonable investigation includes, but is not limited to, a search of the records in the Copyright Office; in the case of a musical composition with respect to which performing rights are licensed by a performing rights society, a "reasonable investigation" also includes a report from that performing rights society identifying the person or persons claiming current ownership of the rights being terminated.

(4) Compliance with the provisions of paragraphs (d)(2) and (d)(3) of this section will satisfy the service requirements of section 203, section 304(c),

or section 304(d) of title 17, U.S.C., whichever applies. However, as long as the statutory requirements have been met, the failure to comply with the regulatory provisions of paragraph (d)(2) or (d)(3) of this section will not affect the validity of the service.

(e) Harmless errors.

 (1) Harmless errors in a notice that do not materially affect the adequacy of the information required to serve the purposes of section 203, section 304(c), or section 304(d) of title 17, U.S.C., whichever applies, shall not render the notice invalid.

 (2) Without prejudice to the general rule provided by paragraph (e)(1) of this section, errors made in giving the date or registration number referred to in paragraph (b)(1)(iii), (b)(2)(iii), or (b)(2)(iv) of this section, or in complying with the provisions of paragraph (b)(1)(vii) or (b)(2)(vii) of this section, or in describing the precise relationships under paragraph (c)(2) or (c)(3) of this section, shall not affect the validity of the notice if the errors were made in good faith and without any intention to deceive, mislead, or conceal relevant information.

(f) Recordation.

 (1) A copy of the notice of termination will be recorded in the Copyright Office upon payment of the fee prescribed by paragraph (2) of this paragraph (f) and upon compliance with the following provisions:

   (i) The copy submitted for recordation shall be a complete and exact duplicate of the notice of termination as served and shall include the actual signature or signatures, or a reproduction of the actual signature or signatures, appearing on the notice; where separate copies of the same notice were served on more than one grantee or successor in title, only one copy need be submitted for recordation; and

   (ii) The copy submitted for recordation shall be accompanied by a statement setting forth the date on which the notice was served and the manner of service, unless such information is contained in the notice. In instances where service is made by first-class mail, the date of service shall be the day the notice of termination was deposited with the United States Postal Service.

   (iii) The copy submitted for recordation must be legible per the requirements of § 201.4(c)(3).

 (2) The fee for recordation of a document is prescribed in § 201.3(c).

 (3) The date of recordation is the date when all of the elements required for recordation, including the prescribed fee and, if required, the statement

referred to in paragraph (f)(1)(ii) of this section, have been received in the Copyright Office. After recordation, the document, including any accompanying statement, is returned to the sender with a certificate of record.

(4) Notwithstanding anything to the contrary in this section, the Copyright Office reserves the right to refuse recordation of a notice of termination if, in the judgment of the Copyright Office, such notice of termination is untimely. If a document is submitted as a notice of termination after the statutory deadline has expired, the Office will offer to record the document as a "document pertaining to copyright" pursuant to § 201.4(c)(3), but the Office will not index the document as a notice of termination. Whether a document so recorded is sufficient in any instance to effect termination as a matter of law shall be determined by a court of competent jurisdiction.

(5) A copy of the notice of termination shall be recorded in the Copyright Office before the effective date of termination, as a condition to its taking effect. However, the fact that the Office has recorded the notice does not mean that it is otherwise sufficient under the law. Recordation of a notice of termination by the Copyright Office is without prejudice to any party claiming that the legal and formal requirements for issuing a valid notice have not been met.

(6) Notices of termination should be submitted to the address specified in § 201.1(b)(2).

Appendix 2

EXEMPTION TO PROHIBITION AGAINST CIRCUMVENTION (CODE OF FEDERAL REGULATIONS)

37 C.F.R. § 201.40 Exemption to prohibition against circumvention.

(a) General. This section prescribes the classes of copyrighted works for which the Librarian of Congress has determined, pursuant to 17 U.S.C. 1201(a)(1)(C) and (D), that noninfringing uses by persons who are users of such works are, or are likely to be, adversely affected. The prohibition against circumvention of technological measures that control access to copyrighted works set forth in 17 U.S.C. 1201(a)(1)(A) shall not apply to such users of the prescribed classes of copyrighted works.

(b) Classes of copyrighted works. Pursuant to the authority set forth in 17 U.S.C. 1201(a)(1)(C) and (D), and upon the recommendation of the Register of Copyrights, the Librarian has determined that the prohibition against circumvention of technological measures that effectively control access to copyrighted works set forth in 17 U.S.C. 1201(a)(1)(A) shall not apply to persons who engage in noninfringing uses of the following classes of copyrighted works:

(1) Motion pictures on DVDs that are lawfully made and acquired and that are protected by the Content Scrambling System when circumvention is accomplished solely in order to accomplish the incorporation of short portions of motion pictures into new works for the purpose of criticism or comment, and where the person engaging in circumvention believes and has reasonable grounds for believing that circumvention is necessary to fulfill the purpose of the use in the following instances:

   (i) Educational uses by college and university professors and by college and university film and media studies students;

   (ii) Documentary filmmaking;

   (iii) Noncommercial videos.

(2) Computer programs that enable wireless telephone handsets to execute software applications, where circumvention is accomplished for the sole purpose of enabling interoperability of such applications, when they have been lawfully obtained, with computer programs on the telephone handset.

(3) Computer programs, in the form of firmware or software, that enable used wireless telephone handsets to connect to a wireless telecommunications network, when circumvention is initiated by the owner of the copy of the computer program solely in order to connect to a wireless telecommunications network and access to the network is authorized by the operator of the network.

(4) Video games accessible on personal computers and protected by technological protection measures that control access to lawfully obtained works, when circumvention is accomplished solely for the purpose of good faith testing for, investigating, or correcting security flaws or vulnerabilities, if:

> (i) The information derived from the security testing is used primarily to promote the security of the owner or operator of a computer, computer system, or computer network; and
>
> (ii) The information derived from the security testing is used or maintained in a manner that does not facilitate copyright infringement or a violation of applicable law.

(5) Computer programs protected by dongles that prevent access due to malfunction or damage and which are obsolete. A dongle shall be considered obsolete if it is no longer manufactured or if a replacement or repair is no longer reasonably available in the commercial marketplace.

(6) Literary works distributed in ebook format when all existing ebook editions of the work (including digital text editions made available by authorized entities) contain access controls that prevent the enabling either of the book's read-aloud function or of screen readers that render the text into a specialized format.

Appendix 3

QUICK-REFERENCE COMPILATION OF NOTABLE POINTS FROM EACH CHAPTER

Notable Points 1: Material Not Subject to Copyright (C.F.R. 202.1)

Following are examples of works not subject to copyright; applications for registration of such works cannot be entertained:

(a) Words and short phrases such as names, titles, and slogans; familiar symbols or designs; mere variations of typographic ornamentation, lettering, or coloring; mere listing of ingredients or contents;

(b) Ideas, plans, methods, systems, or devices, as distinguished from the particular manner in which they are expressed or described in a writing;

(c) Blank forms, such as time cards, graph paper, account books, diaries, bank checks, scorecards, address books, report forms, order forms, and the like, which are designed for recording information and do not in themselves convey information;

(d) Works consisting entirely of information that is common property containing no original authorship, such as, for example, standard calendars, height and weight charts, tape measures and rulers, schedules of sporting events, and lists or tables taken from public documents or other common sources;

(e) Typeface as typeface.

Notable Points 2: Copyright Protection

- Copyright protects original expression that has been fixed in a tangible medium.
- Copyright is covered under federal law, but some states also have copyright laws. State laws are preempted by federal law in this area.
- Copyright protection is automatic; no registration is required.
- Copyright protection has limited duration.
- Copyright does not protect ideas or facts.
- Copyright can be transferred.
- There are some limitations on copyright, such as fair use.
- Duration:

- Individual author: Life of author plus 70 years
- Joint authors: Life of the surviving author plus 70 years
- Corporate work: The earlier of 95 years after publication or 120 years since creation

Notable Points 3: Trademark Protection

▶ No originality requirement is needed for trademark protection.
▶ Trademarks are protected by federal, state, and common law.
▶ A digital content owner can have a trademark in collection even when another party has intellectual property rights in other aspects of the collection.
▶ Degree of trademark protection will depend on the mark's strength, with arbitrary and fanciful marks receiving the strongest protection.
▶ Over time, marks can move from arbitrary to generic.
▶ Check your digital content or system does not violate others' trademark.
▶ Duration: Not limited. A trademark is valid as long as it is commercially used and as long as the mark does not become generic.

Notable Points 4: Patent Protection

▶ Patents protect novel, useful, and nonobvious inventions.
▶ Patents exclude others from using the invention without the patent holder's authorization.
▶ Patents are issued under federal law.
▶ Duration:
  - Utility: 20 years from the date of filing
  - Design: 14 years from the date of issue

Notable Points 5: Trade Secret Protection

▶ Trade secrets are valuable because they are not generally known.
▶ Trade secrets are protected under state law.
▶ Trade secrets derived from reverse engineering are not protected.
▶ Duration: Not limited. Protection may be perpetual, as long as the trade secret remains a secret.

Notable Points 6: Dynamism of Digital Content

▶ Digital content is dynamic.
▶ Technology changes in format, data definition, and metadata content can threaten the accessibility of digital content.

- Migration of data may infringe on the exclusive right of reproduction.
- Structural and data elements rearrangement may infringe on the exclusive right to make derivative copies.

Notable Points 7: E-books as Example of Multimedia Collection

- E-books are a good example of multimedia digital collections.
- Publishers use digital rights management (DRM) technology to control access to e-book content.
- Some non-copyright-protected e-books are available to digital libraries.
- E-book aggregators provide access to digital library content on their servers by negotiating rights with publishers.
- Access to digital content is subject to DRM technology and different pricing models.

Notable Points 8: New Challenges in Digital Content

- Digital versions of familiar formats present new legal challenges.
- Because search engines show thumbnails to users, they may be in violation of the author's exclusive right of display.
- Court cases have, however, found most uses of thumbnails to fall under the fair use exemption.
- The next frontier in legal issues will probably be presented by social networking tools and spaces.

Notable Points 9: The Internet and Digital Content

- Digital collections come in multiple types; they are heterogeneous.
- The Internet can be said to be the biggest digital collection of all.
- Legal issues on the Internet have included linking and framing.
- Courts have found the unauthorized posting of copyrighted material on the web to be copyright infringement.

Notable Points 10: Compilations and Collective Works

- Databases that meet Feist's requirement for originality are protected.
- Compilations are also protected, but underlying preexisting material is not protected.
- Compilations and collective works are not necessarily the same.

- Individual components in a collective work are generally independent copyrighted works.
- Compilations may include material that is not copyrightable.

▶ Separate contributions to a collective work have copyright protection that is distinct from the copyright in the work as a whole.

▶ Copyright in a collective work entitles its owner to reproduce and distribute the contribution as part of that particular collective work and its revisions.

Notable Points 11: Copyright Ownership

▶ Copyright initially vests in the author.

▶ Where there are joint authors, copyright is jointly owned by all the authors.

▶ A co-owner of a copyright is free to independently grant a license for the use of that work.

▶ Authors become joint where there is collaboration and the intent to create a joint work.

▶ Other ways a work may become joint:
- For works subject to renewal terms (pre-1976), the renewal rights for works subject to renewal terms might have vested in more than one person.
- Termination rights may vest in more than one person.
- A copyright may pass by will to two or more persons.
- A copyright owner may make a nonexclusive transfer of the copyright to more than one person, thus creating joint ownership.
- In some states, a work may be subject to community property laws, creating a right of ownership of copyright proceeds for the nonauthor spouse.

Notable Points 12: Derivative Works

▶ A derivative work based on an expired copyright is still copyrightable.

▶ The original copyright owner has derivative rights unless specifically transferred.

▶ The owner of a derivative copyright does not necessarily own copyright in the underlying work.

▶ License agreements for derivatives can be divided up by format of adaptation, such as film.

▶ Originality requirement for derivatives cannot be met simply by reproduction in another medium.

▶ Derivates made without copyright owner's permission belong to the copyright owner.

Notable Points 13: Government Works

- No copyright can be applied to works of the federal government.
- Some works of state governments may be copyrighted.
- The law, whether state or federal, does not have copyright protection.

Notable Points 14: Copyright Ownership and Transfer

- Content authors are not necessarily content owners.
- Only owners have standing to sue.
- A copyright co-owner can grant a license in the copyrighted work without co-owners' consent.
- Generally, a licensee is insulated from an infringement action by nonconsenting owners.
- Operating digital or other equipment that fixes a work in a tangible medium of expression does not automatically confer copyright on the operator.
- Contributors to a collective work hold separate copyright from the holder of the copyright in the collective work.
- Transfer of copyright may be by written agreement or by operation of law.
- Copyright is personal property that can be bequeathed.
- Exclusive rights can be transferred separately.
- There may be other unforeseen claimants in a copyright.

Notable Points 15: Right of Reproduction

- Owner of copyright has the exclusive right to make or authorize the reproductions of the work.
- Authors usually assign the right of reproduction to publishers.
- Right of reproduction is subject to certain limitations, such as fair use.
- Showing an image on a computer screen is not necessarily reproduction.
- Loading a computer program into electronic memory may be reproduction.
- Analog-to-digital conversion by scanning may be reproduction.
- Despite the constraints of reproduction, digitization efforts continue.

Notable Points 16: Right to Make Derivative Works

- The owner of copyright has the exclusive right to make derivative works.
- Examples of derivatives include translations, dramatizations, motion picture versions, and art reproductions.

- A derivative need not be fixed in a tangible medium (e.g., a novel performed as an opera).
- Work must be based on a preexisting copyrighted work.
- Copyright in the derivative is distinct from copyright in the underlying work.
- The digital librarian may need to determine the owner of underlying copyright before exercising rights in the derivative.
- Digital annotations may be derivatives or freestanding copyrightable works.
- An issue in the annotations of an electronic record is to what extent the annotation amounts to creating a derivative work.

Notable Points 17: Right of Distribution and First-Sale Doctrine

- Owner of copyright has exclusive right to distribute work to the public.
- This right of distribution extends to the first copy.
- Under the doctrine of first sale, the new copy owner may distribute that particular copy.
- The new copy owner has no copyright in the copy.
- The doctrine of first sale is unclear in the digital environment.

Notable Points 18: Right of Public Performance

- The copyright owner has the exclusive right to public performance.
- Performance includes reciting, acting, playing, or dancing a work.
- Performance need not be for profit.
- A digital library making a video clip of a musical available on a website may be performing.

Notable Points 19: Right of Public Display

- The copyright owner has the exclusive right to display the work in public.
- Display includes showing the work either directly or by using audiovisual devices.
- Public performance and display does not constitute publication of the work.
- Museums that have digital collections should be particularly aware of this right.

Notable Points 20: Visual Artists Rights

- Authors of visual art have additional rights under the Visual Artists Rights Act (VARA), including:

- right to claim authorship of a work;
- right to disclaim attribution of authorship of a work;
- right to disclaim attribution of authorship of a work that has been distorted or mutilated; and
- if the work is a recognized stature, right to prevent its destruction.

▶ Authors of visual art do not need to own copyright in the work to exercise VARA rights.

▶ Only the author of a work can exercise VARA rights.

▶ VARA does not protect works for hire.

▶ VARA rights generally last for the life of the author or, for joint works, the longest surviving coauthor.

▶ A waiver of rights by a joint author waives rights for all coauthors.

▶ Many countries have similar or expanded rights, which they term *moral rights*.

Notable Points 21: Digital First Sale

▶ First-sale doctrine distinguishes between the physical copy and the expression contained in the copy.

▶ After the sale of the first copy, the rights holder cannot control the further distribution of that copy.

▶ First-sale doctrine seems to have limited application in the digital environment.

▶ In a report to Congress, the Librarian of Congress recommended that the first-sale doctrine does not extend to digital transmissions.

▶ Digital transfers still leave a copy of the transferred copy at the original source.

▶ Law in this area is unsettled.

Notable Points 22: Fair Use (Part 1)

▶ Fair use is a public policy that balances the needs of the public to access information and the need for incentives to create the information.

▶ Fair use is an affirmative defense against infringement claims.

▶ Factors in the determination of fair use:
- Purpose and character of use
- Nature of the copyrighted work
- Amount and substantiality of the portion used
- Effect of use on the potential market or value of the work

Notable Points 23: Summary of Copyright Owner's Rights and Limitations

- A copyright owner can authorize a digital library to reproduce protected work.
- Because of mixed media, there may be multiple copyright owners.
- Conversion from print to digital without the copyright owner's permission may infringe on right of reproduction.
- Derivatives need not be fixed to violate the copyright owner's right of performance.
- The rights under copyright have several limitations, including the fair use exemption to infringement.
- Authors of visual art may have moral rights that continue even after they have parted with the copyright.
- Certain libraries have an exemption from copyright infringement in reproduction under section 108 of the copyright code.

Notable Points 24: Copyright Duration for Single and Multiple Authors

- Single-authored works have copyright protection for the life of the author plus 70 years.
- Multiple-author works are protected for the life of the last surviving author plus 70 years.
- The copyright assignee takes the remainder of the term.
- The copyright in some unpublished or uncopyrighted works created before January 1, 1978, expired on December 31, 2002.
- The copyright in some uncopyrighted works created before January 1, 1978, but published on or before December 21, 2002, will expire December 31, 2047.

Notable Points 25: Copyright Duration for Anonymous Works, Pseudonymous Works, and Works for Hire

- Anonymous works, pseudonymous works, and works for hire are protected for 95 years from publication or 120 years from creation.
- If the author of an anonymous or pseudonymous work is later revealed, the term of protection reverts back to life of the author plus 70 years, or the life of the last surviving author plus 70 years.
- The digital librarian should examine the registration records in the Copyright Office to determine if an author's identity has been ascertained.
- The digital librarian should examine the registration records in the Copyright Office to determine if an author is still living.

▶ Where a work is:
- 95 years old from when it was first published or
- 120 years have passed since it was created and
- there is no indication in the register's record that the author is alive or has been dead for less than 70 years, a certified report creating the assumption that the author has been dead for more than 70 years may be obtained from the Copyright Office.

▶ Good faith reliance on the certified report is a complete defense to infringement.

Notable Points 26: Example of Duration for Work Published in 1925

As an example of duration, we use a work that was first published in 1925:

Is the work in the public domain due to formalities failure?
    Yes. It stays in the public domain.
    No. It has an additional 28 years' protection (until 1953).
        Was the work properly renewed?
            No. Copyright expires December 31, 1953.
            Yes. It has an additional 28 years' protection (to 1981).
                If still protected, in 1976 it has an additional 19 years' protection (to 2000).
                If still protected, in 1998 it has an additional 20 years' protection (to December 31, 2020).

Notable Points 27: Example of Distribution of Termination Rights

The author is married and has no children.

The spouse has full termination rights.

The author is married and has three children: X, Y, and Z.

The author dies:
    The spouse has one-half of the author's interest.
    Children X, Y, and Z have the other half, divided equally among them.
    The spouse dies:
        Children X, Y, and Z own the entire termination interest, divided equally among them.
    If child X dies:
        His interest passes on to his children, divided equally among them (their share in a termination interest can only be exercised by the majority).
The author dies, spouse dies, and there are no surviving children or grandchildren:
    The author's executor, administrator, personal representative, or trustee owns the entire termination interest.

Notable Points 28: Termination of Rights for Pre-1978 Works

- For pre-1978 works, the window for exercising the termination runs during the five years following 56 years since the original copyright, or beginning January 1, 1978, whichever is later. Thus, if a copyright was secured on January 1, 1977, the right could potentially be available during a five-year window beginning 2033.
- Termination right is exercised by notifying the grantee or successor in writing two to ten years before the effective date of termination.
- Notice must be recorded in the U.S. Copyright Office.
- The termination is effected regardless of prior agreement not to terminate.
- Termination right is designed to ameliorate the consequences of unwise grants before the value of a work is known.

Notable Points 29: Reversion of Termination Rights

- The rights of terminated grants revert back to the author or successors.
- Contractual rights grantee had with third parties are not included in the reversionary rights.
- Derivative rights transferred or licensed are allowed to continue following termination, as long as no new derivates are made from the terminated rights.
- Further grants on a terminated grant are not valid unless made after the termination's effective date.

Notable Points 30: Restoration of Rights Lost Due to Formalities Noncompliance

- Beware: Not all pre-1976 works not complying with formalities are in the public domain.
- Copyrights were restored to foreign authors who had lost them because of not complying with U.S. formalities.
- Only authors from the Berne Convention or World Trade Organization member countries are eligible for the restoration.
- If work was still protected in the country of origin, restoration of rights was automatic.
- Rights for most countries were restored with effect from January 1, 1996.
- Protection is for the remainder of the time copyright protection would have been available in the United States if the work had not entered the public domain.

Notable Points 31: Expiration of Copyrights

- Even though most individual works have copyright protection that covers the life of the author plus 20 years, and corporate works have protection between 95 and 120 years, the actual period of protection may vary depending on the particular circumstances of the works.
- Copyrights for works created after 1978 cannot be lost to the public domain because of failure to follow formalities.
- Copyright transfers and licenses subject to renewal can be terminated by the granting author or legally authorized persons during a specific window, which for most works runs until 2034.
- Contractual rights and obligations based on a copyright expire when that copyright expires.

Notable Points 32: Copyright Transfers

- Copyright ownership is property that can be transferred.
- The rights in copyright are divisible and can be separately transferred, thus different rights may belong to different parties.
- Copyright ownership rights cannot involuntarily be transferred from an owner by government.
- Transfer of copyright or an exclusive license must be by a written and signed instrument of conveyance by the copyright owner.
- A court may interpret an agreement to find express or implied transfer.
- A nonexclusive license agreement can be oral or even implied, because it does not involve a transfer of copyright.
- Recording of the copyright transfer conveyance instrument gives constructive notice of the identity of the copyright owner and resolves the priority of conflicting transfers: the first executed and recorded transfer prevails. It also serves to perfect security interests in copyrights.
- A nonexclusive license granted before the execution and recording of a transfer prevails over a conflicting transfer of copyright ownership.
- The courts use principles of contract law to interpret copyright transfers.

Notable Points 33: Termination of Copyright Transfers

- Previously made copyright transfers may be terminated during a specific window of time.
- This right allows copyright owners to enjoy the later success of their works whose rights they transferred before their full value was known.

- For post-1978 works, many termination rights will begin to be exercised in 2013.
- Termination rights can be exercised despite agreements to the contrary.
- Only a living author, or persons entitled to exercise more than one-half of the author's termination interest, may terminate.
- Notice of termination must be served on the transferee not less than two years or more than ten years before the effective date of termination and must be recorded in the Copyright Office before the date the termination is to become effective.

Notable Points 34: Effect of Termination of Copyright Transfers

- Rights to terminated grants revert to the author or successors in interest.
- Previously granted rights to make derivative works survive the termination under the terms of the original grant.
- New derivative works may not be made based upon the terminated work.
- A copyright transfer termination right is not automatic; it has to be exercised.
- Transfers that are not terminated continue to the end of the copyright protection term.

Notable Points 35: Licenses

- Intellectual property license is based on the underlying rights conferred by the copyrighted work.
- Unlike a copyright transfer, a license allows the copyright holder to retain copyright while allowing others to use some of the owner's rights.
- A license can be exclusive or nonexclusive; if exclusive, it must be in writing.
- An owner of an exclusive license has standing to bring suit on infringement of the licensed right.

Notable Points 36: Licenses and Multiple Copyright Owners

- In digital media licensing, there is often need to interact with multiple rights owners.
- The duration of copyright protection varies.
- Authors may not necessarily hold all the exclusive rights.
- It is important to conduct due diligence to ensure no conflict with licenses granted to third parties.

Notable Points 37: Scope of Licenses

- Shrink-wrap licenses are enforceable.
- Instead of obtaining a license, some content may be used by paying a royalty to a royalty collection agency.
- The use of a license cannot exceed the purpose for which it was granted.
- An escrow service can be utilized for software source code.
- Read the small print in licenses:
  - Use of a license may be limited by such restrictions as geography, language, or even platform use.
  - There may also be restrictions on the ability to alter or modify content.
- A license cannot exceed the period of the copyright protection of the underlying work.

Notable Points 38: Compulsory Licenses

- Despite their controversy, compulsory licenses are available to make or distribute phonorecords of nondramatic musical works, if the work has been distributed to the public under the copyright owner's authority.
- Compulsory licenses apply only to those sound recordings that were originally lawfully made.
- The copyright owner must be provided with a Notice of Intent to Use a compulsory license.
- Failure to pay royalty terminates a compulsory license.

Notable Points 39: Prima Facie Infringement

- Elements of prima facie infringement:
  - Existence of a valid copyright
  - Infringement of an exclusive right
- Elements of prima facie copying:
  - Access to the copyrighted work
  - Substantial similarity to the copyrighted work

Notable Points 40: Contributory and Vicarious Infringement

- Inducing, causing, or materially contributing to infringing conduct by third parties can lead to liability for contributory infringement.
- Supplying the instruments for committing the infringement may also lead to contributory infringement.

- No intent is required for a finding of contributory infringement.
- Acts of infringement by a person or entity that you control may lead to liability for vicarious infringement.
- A library is not liable for vicarious infringement liability in cases where unsupervised reproduction equipment is used by third parties, as long as where such equipment displays a copyright notice.

Notable Points 41: Fair Use (Part 2)

- Fair use is a judiciary-derived limitation of the copyright owners' exclusive rights, which has now been codified in the Copyright Act.
- Among the factors considered by a court to determine fair use are:
  - purpose and character of the use,
  - nature of the work,
  - amount and substantiality of the portion used in relation to the work as a whole, and
  - market and economic impact of the use.
- A finding of fair use depends on the specific facts of the case.

Notable Points 42: Fair Use (Part 3)

- For teaching purposes, a work comparable to what would be typically displayed in a live classroom session may be digitally transmitted under section 110(2) of Title 17 in the U.S. Code.
- Works that are produced or marketed primarily for display or performance as part of mediated instructional activities are not covered by this exemption.

Notable Points 43: Remedies for Infringement

- A legal or beneficial owner of a copyright right is entitled to bring suit against an infringer.
- Remedies for injunction may include:
  - injunctions against the infringer and/or
  - impound and disposition of the infringing articles.
- Penalties for infringement may be civil or criminal.
- Civil actions must be brought within three years after the infringement is discovered.
- Criminal infringement action must be brought within five years.

Notable Points 44: Digital Rights Management

▸ Digital rights management systems are software technological measures that assist copyright owners to prevent unauthorized access to content.

▸ The Digital Millennium Copyright Act prohibits the circumvention of technological measures that a copyrighted work's owner has embedded in a work to prevent unauthorized access to the content.

▸ Circumvention is defined as descrambling a scrambled work, decrypting an encrypted work, or otherwise avoiding, bypassing, removing, deactivating, or impairing a technological measure that effectively protects a copyright owner's right, without the copyright owner's permission.

▸ The DMCA prohibits the manufacturing, importation, offering to the public, providing, or otherwise trafficking in certain analog devices that do not conform to automatic gain control copy control technology.

Notable Points 45: Exemptions to the Anticircumvention Prohibition

▸ Exemptions for libraries and similar institutions allow circumventing to gain access for the purposes of determining if they wish to acquire the work.

▸ Reverse engineering allows for identifying and analyzing interoperability of computer programs.

▸ The encryption research exemption allows persons to circumvent a technological measure in a published work in an act of good faith encryption research.

▸ A privacy exemption allows the circumvention of a technological measure that effectively controls access to a protected work that collects or disseminates personally identifying information reflecting online activities without providing the user with a conspicuous notice of such collection or a means of preventing or restricting such collection or dissemination.

▸ A security testing exemption can be made for the purpose of good faith testing, investigating, or correcting a security flaw or vulnerability with the computer system or network owner's authorization.

▸ The Librarian of Congress makes rulings at three-year intervals whether users of copyrighted works are likely to be adversely affected in their ability to make noninfringing uses of copyrighted works in a particular class and publishes this list as being exempt from the prohibition. Factors to consider:
  - Availability of copyrighted works for use
  - Availability for use of works for nonprofit preservation, educational, and archival purposes
  - Impact on news reporting, criticism, and scholarship

- Effect of circumvention of technological measures on value or market for copyrighted works
- Other factors the Librarian may consider appropriate

Notable Points 46: Challenges to DMCA

▶ Most court challenges to the DMCA have been unsuccessful.
▶ Challenges have included:
  - that the DMCA is inconsistent with the intellectual property clause of the Constitution;
  - First Amendment challenges; and
  - that the DMCA is overly broad and prevents access to unprotected material.

Notable Points 47: DMCA and Fair Use

▶ There is tension between the DMCA and the fair use doctrine.
▶ To utilize fair use, one must have gained lawful access to the content.
▶ Circumvention of access control is not lawful access.
▶ It is unclear whether copying for fair use would be lawful after an unlawful access.

Notable Points 48: Infringement and Internet Service Providers

▶ ISPs are generally companies that offer backbone connectivity or provide end users with Internet access.
▶ Depending on circumstances, digital libraries and educational institutions can be viewed as ISPs.
▶ Section 512 of the Copyright Act protects ISPs from liability by infringing action of third parties.
▶ To qualify for this protection, ISPs must designate an agent to receive notices of claimed infringing actions.
▶ Notices of infringement must be in writing and meet requirements of the act.

Notable Points 49: Internet Service Providers Conditions for Infringement Liability Protection (Part 1)

▶ An ISP may be protected from liability for infringing claims based on the ISP's mere transmission or intermediate or transient storage, without modification, of infringing material on its network.
▶ An ISP cannot interfere with information feedback technology provided by the person supplying the content.

- The information feedback technology cannot interfere with the ISP's system or network.
- The ISP must provide access only to those users who meet the content owner's preaccess conditions.
- The ISP must respond to notification of a claimed infringement.

Notable Points 50: Internet Service Providers Conditions for Infringement Liability Protection (Part 2)

- Service providers may be protected from infringing claims based on providing users links to sites with infringing material or activity.
- Service providers are not required to monitor their service or affirmatively seek facts indicating infringing activity.

Notable Points 51: Royalties

- Royalties are the mainstay of the incentive provided by the limited-term monopoly envisioned in the Constitution.
- Royalties allow the copyright holder to permit use of the exclusive rights by others.
- Royalties may be based on contract or set by law.

Notable Points 52: Goals of Royalties

Copyright royalties seek to:

- ensure that the availability of creative works to the public is maximized,
- ensure a fair return for the creative works to the copyright owner, and
- provide the copyright user an opportunity to make a fair income even after paying royalty.

Notable Points 53: Powers of Librarian of Congress to Appoint Judges

- The Librarian of Congress is empowered to appoint copyright royalty judges, including the chief copyright royalty judge.
- Copyright royalty judges:
  - set and adjust royalty rates,
  - authorize distribution of collected royalties, and
  - accept royalty claims and petitions.
- The Librarian of Congress makes the appointments in consultation with the register of copyrights.

- The Librarian of Congress may sanction or remove a judge for violation of standards of conduct for judges, after giving notice and providing the judge an opportunity for a hearing.
- A royalty judge must be an attorney with seven years' legal experience.
- One of the three judges must have knowledge of copyright law.
- Another one of the three judges must have knowledge of economics.
- Judges serve for six-year terms with the possibility of renewal.
- Determinations of the judges must be supported by a written record indicating findings of fact relied on.
- The Librarian of Congress is responsible for the publication of the determinations in the *Federal Register*.
- Appeals to determinations go straight to the U.S. court of appeals for the District of Columbia circuit.

Notable Points 54: Copyright Clearance Center

- The Copyright Clearance Center (CCC) collects copyright clearance fees on behalf of copyright owners.
- Though established in the United States, the CCC is international in scope.
- The CCC provides both pay-per-use and annual copyright use licenses.
- The CCC provides content owners with services that include royalty payment tracking as well as approving permission requests.
- CCC has recently been criticized for joining with a publisher in litigation against an academic library.

Notable Points 55: Proprietary Information

- Proprietary information is commercially valuable information over which an entity claims ownership.
- The information does not necessarily need to be protected by copyright but may be protected by other tools, including trade secrets.
- Digital librarians often work with proprietary information.

Notable Points 56: Trade Secrets and Proprietary Information

- A trade secret derives its value from not being generally known; it must remain confidential and secret.
- To determine whether a trade secret exists, courts look into:
  - the extent to which the information is generally known,

- the security measures taken to protect its confidentiality,
- the resources expended in developing the information, and
- other evidence of the value of the information.

▶ Licenses for digital content may have clauses prohibiting the digital content manager from disclosing trade secrets, which may be contained in the content or system used to manage content, such as:
  - Systems technical information and data
  - Testing information tools

▶ Disclosure of trade secrets carries significant penalties.

▶ Trade secrets have been criticized as restricting the flow of information.

▶ Proprietary information could be any information which an owner keeps confidential and which is not easily ascertainable by legal means.

▶ Proprietary information is usually protected by nondisclosure agreements in license agreements.

Notable Points 57: Proprietary Search Engines

▶ Because search engines are in many cases protected by patents, the following activities may be restricted:
  - Utilizing the search engine
  - Modifying the search engine
  - Optimizing the search engine

▶ There may be a license fee to conduct any of the above activities.

Notable Points 58: Meta Tags

Meta tags:

▶ allow a webpage to be displayed the way the designer intended,

▶ may be used as an index or reference source to identify page content,

▶ may sometimes contain trademark information,

▶ may contain private information or violate right of publicity, and

▶ may include misleading information as to the source of the page.

Notable Points 59: Privacy

▶ Concept of privacy in the United States is less developed than it is in Europe.

▶ In the United States, the concept is grounded on the "expectation" of privacy.

▶ Many digital transactions involve the collection of private information.

▶ Many states have enacted laws for private data breaches.

- At a minimum, persons affected must be notified.
- International efforts are ongoing to address the management and security of private data.
- A digital content license may have clauses that place certain obligations on the digital librarian in the handling of content that contains personal data.

Notable Points 60: International Treaty

- Digital content managers are becoming increasingly likely to deal with international copyright issues.
- Copyright in the international context is mainly governed by international treaties and agreements.
- Major treaties governing copyright in the international context include the Berne Convention, the WIPO Convention, and the WTO, including TRIPS.
- The United States is a signatory to the major treaties, as well as a number of other bilateral and multilateral agreements.

Notable Points 61: Berne Convention

- The Berne Convention is the bedrock of international copyright law.
- It provides protection for published and unpublished work to nationals of contracting member states, as well as certain nationals of non–contracting member states.
- Rights protected are roughly parallel to those under the U.S. Copyright Act, with major differences:
  - The Berne Convention, unlike U.S. law, has an emphasis on the author's moral rights, i.e., the right to continue to claim authorship even after transferring all economic rights.
  - Thus, the Berne Convention allows an interest in the work subsequent to the first transfer, which would be against the U.S. Copyright Act's doctrine of First Sale.
  - These moral rights survive the author's death.
- A publisher of an anonymous or pseudonymous work is deemed to represent the author in enforcing the author's rights.
- For an anonymous or pseudonymous unpublished work, a member country may by legislation designate a competent authority to represent the unknown author in the enforcement of rights.
- The term of copyright protection under the Berne Convention is the life of the author or the last surviving author plus 50 years.

- Anonymous and pseudonymous works are protected for 50 years since they were made available to the public, unless there is reason to believe the author has been dead for 50 years.
- Member countries may make legislation providing for more rights than those available under the Berne Convention.
- The United States dispensed with the copyright formalities of notice and registration to conform to the Berne Convention.
- The International Court of Justice adjudicates disputes regarding the Berne Convention.
- Member country authors enjoy the rights of copyright in their own countries as well as rights under the Berne Convention.

Notable Points 62: WIPO Copyright Treaty

- The WIPO Copyright Treaty (WCT) adds computer programs to literary works protected under the Berne Convention and extends protection to compilations of data that contain some originality.
- WCT brings the Berne Convention into the digital age.
- WCT has similar prohibition to the Digital Millennium Copyright Act against circumventing technological measures.

Notable Points 63: Universal Copyright Convention

- UCC was developed by UNESCO and was a response to what some countries considered the onerous demands of the Berne Convention.
- Original signatories to UCC included the United States, partly because the United States was not ready to abandon copyright formalities and other changes that the Berne Convention required.
- UCC puts the minimum term of copyright protection at 25 years.
- UCC maintained some flexibilities in certain developing countries, allowing them, for instance, to issue some compulsory licenses to translate, to publish, and to distribute a work under certain circumstances for a limited time.
- UCC has slowly been losing its relevance as intellectual property issues become an agenda item for international trade agreements.

Notable Points 64: The Agreement on Trade-Related Aspects of Intellectual Property Rights (TRIPS)

- The Agreement on Trade-Related Aspects of Intellectual Property Rights (TRIPS) ties intellectual property issues into international trade agreements.

- TRIPS is concerned with intellectual property as private rights, not with maintaining balance between public interest and authors' economic rights.
- TRIPs gives member countries the flexibility to require formalities for acquiring and maintaining intellectual property protection.
- TRIPs requires member countries to publish and share intellectual property laws.

Appendix 4

QUICK-REFERENCE COMPILATION OF COMPLIANCE CHECKLISTS

Checklist 1: Baseline Questions

- ❏ Is the digital work subject to copyright law?
- ❏ Who "owns" the copyright?
- ❏ What are the available rights?
- ❏ What, if any, are the limitations on these rights?

Checklist 2: Follow-Up Baseline Questions

- ❏ What content is protected by copyright?
- ❏ Does the digital librarian have all the necessary rights?
- ❏ Are there privacy and confidentiality issues?

Checklist 3: Test for Joint Authorship

- ❏ Did each author make an independently copyrightable contribution to the work?
- ❏ Did the authors mutually intend to be coauthors?
- ❏ Do the facts bear out this intention?

Checklist 4: Is It a Work for Hire?

- ❏ Is the work for use as:
    - ❏ a contribution to a collective work?
    - ❏ part of a motion picture or other audiovisual work?
    - ❏ a translation?
    - ❏ a supplementary work?
    - ❏ a compilation?
    - ❏ an instructional text?
    - ❏ a test?
    - ❏ answer material for a test?
    - ❏ an atlas?

- ❏ Did the parties expressly agree to have the work considered a work for hire in a written and signed instrument?

Checklist 5: Section 108 Eligibility

- ❏ Is there no direct or indirect commercial advantage in the reproduction or distribution of such copy?
- ❏ Is the library or archival collections open to members of the public or available to other persons doing research in a specialized field?
- ❏ Is a notice of copyright or statement that the work may be copyright-protected included on the reproduced or distributed copy?
- ❏ Does the work to be copied belong to a class to which the right does not apply?

Checklist 6: Replacement of Works Under Section 108

- ❏ Is the work lost, stolen, damaged, or deteriorated?
- ❏ Is the work in an obsolete format?
- ❏ Is the machine necessary to use the work no longer available in the marketplace or no longer being manufactured?
- ❏ Has the library or archive made an unsuccessful reasonable effort to find an unused replacement at a fair market value?
- ❏ Will the reproduction in digital format be made unavailable to the public in digital format outside the library's premises?

Checklist 7: Reproduction and Distribution of Unpublished Works

- ❏ Is it solely for preservation and security, or for deposit in another eligible library or archive?
- ❏ Is the work currently in the reproducing or distributing library's collection?
- ❏ Are copies reproduced in a digital format withheld from distribution in that format or not made available to the public outside the library or archive premises?

Checklist 8: Copying or Modifying Computer Program Copies by Owners

- ❏ Is the copying or modification done as an essential part of utilizing the program in a machine?
- ❏ Is the copy made for archival purposes?
- ❏ Is the copy destroyed when possession of the copy is no longer rightful?

Checklist 9: Ineligibility to Use Section 108

- ❑ Is the reproduction and distribution of copyrighted work systematic, as opposed to sporadic?
- ❑ Is the library or archives aware it is engaging in related or concerted reproduction of single or multiple copies of the same material?
- ❑ Is the material intended for aggregate or separate use by individuals or members of a group?

Checklist 10: Copying a Work within the Last 20 Years of Its Copyright Term

- ❑ The library or archive has, after a reasonable investigation, found that work is not subject to commercial exploitation,
- ❑ the work cannot be obtained at a reasonable price, or
- ❑ the copyright owner has not provided notice that the work is subject to commercial exploitation.

Checklist 11: Lost Copyrights Due to Noncompliance with Formalities

- ❑ Was the copyright lost in the United States due to noncompliance with formalities?
- ❑ Was the copyright owner from a country that is a Berne Convention or World Trade Organization member?
- ❑ Is the work still protected in its country of origin?
- ❑ Have you been served with a notice of intent to enforce copyright or an exclusive right, or has the owner filed such a notice with the U.S. Copyright Office, or are you aware of any such service of notice on another party?

Checklist 12: TEACH Act Exemptions

- ❑ Is the performance or display:
  - ❑ made by, at the direction of, or under the actual supervision of an instructor?
  - ❑ an integral part of a class session offered as a regular part of the systematic mediated instructional activities of a government body or an accredited nonprofit educational institution?
  - ❑ directly related and of material assistance to the teaching content?
- ❑ Is the transmission, to the extent technology will allow, made solely for the students enrolled in the course or government body officials as part of their official duties or employment?
- ❑ Does the transmitting body have copyright policies and copyright information that it relates to its users?

- ❏ Does it provide notice to the users that the course material may be subject to copyright protection?
- ❏ Has the transmitting body applied technological measures to prevent retention of the work that is in an accessible form by recipients beyond the end of the class session?
  - ❏ If so, do these measures prevent further dissemination of the work to others by the recipients?
- ❏ Has the transmitting body refrained from engaging in conduct that would interfere with technological measures put into place by copyright owners to prevent such retention or further unauthorized dissemination?

Checklist 13: Innocent Service Provider

- ❏ The ISP had no actual knowledge material or activity of network was infringing.
- ❏ The ISP had no awareness of facts or circumstances indicating infringing activity.
- ❏ The ISP acted expeditiously to remove or disable access to material upon knowledge or awareness of infringing activity.
- ❏ No financial benefit to the ISP was directly attributable to the infringing activity.

Checklist 14: Evaluating Data Providers

- ❏ Is the data copyrightable?
- ❏ Does the provider have permission to use and license the data?
- ❏ Is there an indemnity clause in case of copyright infringement claims?
- ❏ Is the data of high quality, accurate, and complete?
- ❏ Is the data provided quickly and consistently?
- ❏ Is the provided data stable or prone to errors?
- ❏ Is the data provider stable or is it likely to go out of business?
- ❏ Is the data secure and how prepared is the system for a breach?
- ❏ Does the data provider have data security systems in place and is it well prepared to deal with breaches and invasions of privacy?
- ❏ Are there any confidentiality obligations between the provider and the digital library?
- ❏ Is the work free from libelous or unlawful statements?
- ❏ If the data is foreign, does it have moral rights claims?
- ❏ If there are moral rights claims, how might they affect any planned customization of the content to meet user needs?

Appendix 5
RESOURCES FOR FINDING COPYRIGHT OWNERS AND CLEARANCES

American Federation of Musicians
http://afm.org

American Society of Composers, Authors, and Publishers (ASCAP)
http://ascap.com

American Society of Media Photographers (for photos)
http://asmp.org

American Society of Picture Professionals (for photos)
http://aspp.com

Art Museum Image Consortium
http://amico.org

Artists Rights Society
http://arsny.com

Association of American Publishers
http://publishers.org

Association of Authors' Representatives
http://aaronline.org

The Authors Guild
http://authorsguild.org

Authors Registry
http://www.authorsregistry.org

Broadcast Music, Inc. (BMI)
http://www.bmi.com

Copyright Clearance Center
http://www.copyright.com

The Copyright Licensing Agency (United Kingdom)
http://www.cla.co.uk

Copyright Renewal Database (1923–1963)
http://collections.stanford.edu/copyrightrenewals/bin/page?forward=home

iCopyright (for web content)
http://icopyright.com

Internet Movie Database
http://www.imdb.com

Motion Picture Licensing Corporation
http://mplc.org

National Music Publishers Association (Harry Fox Agency)
http://nmpa.org

Notices of Restored Copyrights
http://copyright.gov/gatt.html

Search Copyright Information
http://copyright.gov/records/

SESAC
http://sesac.com

United States Patent and Trademark Office
http://www.uspto.gov

The WATCH File: Writers, Artists, and Their Copyright Holders (United Kingdom)
http://tyler.hrc.utexas.edu/

Appendix 6

SUGGESTED ANALYSES FOR HYPOTHETICAL QUESTIONS FROM EACH CHAPTER

Hypothetical #1

Mr. Digital Librarian has just signed a license to embed the Super Intelligent Search Engine (SISE) into the library website. It is touted as so intelligent that it anticipates the direction of the research as the user types in a search. Mr. Librarian is so excited about his new toy that he makes a presentation before 500 of his colleagues at a conference and invites them to check it out for one week, providing a password that will allow them to look at the technical insides of the search engine as well as make copies of the technical specifications and user-guide documents. What issues should Mr. Digital Librarian have taken into account?

Suggested response: Search engines may involve the whole range of intellectual property (IP) tools. While usually protected by patents, search engines may also involve trademarks, trade secrets, confidentiality, privacy, and copyright. The ultimate question would be the scope of the license: to what extent it allows Mr. Librarian to engage in these activities. Assuming that the license does not cover these activities, then several IP areas come into play.

Copyright—the presentation itself could implicate the copyright owner's exclusive right of public performance and display. However, because of the setting and the use, a fair use defense would probably be successful. What might not be as easily defensible is making of copies of the technical specifications and guide documents, assuming they are copyrightable. Mr. Librarian could be liable for contributory copyright infringement for assisting the copying to take place; 500 copies of a multipage document can quickly add up. Section 108 discussed in Chapter 4 would not apply since it is not the library making a copy, even if it were an eligible library.

Trademarks—SISE probably has a trademark on the engine. Even though unlikely, some of the users might be confused as to the source of the engine, since they will be seeing the trademark in the context of the New Age Library website.

Patents—Users looking at the technical insides of the search engine might be infringing the SISE patent on the engine, as they might be practicing the patented work without a license.

Trade Secrets—Because they are allowed to look at the technical insides of the search engine, expert users might be able to find trade secrets embedded in the search engine. The license Mr. Librarian signed with SASE most likely included a clause obligating New Age to protect SASE's trade secrets.

Confidentiality—By allowing users to look at the technical insides of the search engine, Mr. Librarian is most likely violating confidentiality obligations included in the SASE license.

Privacy—Allowing the colleagues to access the technical insides of the search engine may expose data about user searches that would violate those users' privacy.

Hypothetical #2

The New Age Library has just acquired the digital collection of the *Twilight* series, newly reformatted into 3D video. The collection also includes scholarly commentary in different digital media, some of it from Europe. New Age Library patrons are able to electronically access all of the digital collection, including the *Twilight* series, and can friend the commentators on Facebook. What are the issues to consider?

Suggested response: "Acquired" may mean two different things here, which may affect the issues New Age may have to consider. If the collection was "acquired" by a license, then the terms of the license would prevail and there may not be a need to determine copyright ownership. This is of course assuming there is an indemnity clause regarding infringement in the license. If, on the other hand, the series came in a physical copy, for example, a DVD, then the library can use the doctrine of first sale to lend the collection. But here the patrons are able to electronically access the collection. If the library mounted the DVD so it could be accessed electronically, then the library, in migrating the data, may have violated the exclusive right of reproduction because it made an electronically accessible copy, may have violated the exclusive right to distribute, and may also have violated the exclusive right to make derivative copies because the copyright owner retains the right to convert the DVD into an electronically accessible copy.

New Age may have section 108 privileges (discussed in Chapter 4), if it meets the eligibility requirement. Assuming it is not covered by section 108, then it may want to seek permission from the copyright owner to use the collection in the manner it contemplates. This would mean determining the ownership of the various components of the *Twilight* collection, which could include separate owners for video, sound, embedded commentary, and so on. Even if the producing studio has a copyright in the collection as a whole, the separate contributions to a collective work have protection distinct from protection of the work as a whole. Also, there could be separate copyrights and different copyright owners in the various components of the commentary. The commentators would likely own copyright in the comments by Facebook friends.

Depending on how the collection is made available for electronic access, there may be violations of the anticircumvention prohibitions of the Digital Millennium

Copyright Act. If the material is protected by digital rights management technology, then there may be issues of access limitations, which may include who and how many people can access the work, and what they can do with the results of the access.

Because some of the material is from Europe, there may be an issue with moral rights that preserve certain rights to authors, even after they have died. New Age may also want to determine to what extent the *Twilight* copyright owner will still be in business and whether there will be changes in technology that will make 3D obsolete. Other issues to think of may include right of publicity, if users are able to extract and reuse material that contains the actors in the series. Think of any other issues that are suggested to you by the reading here or other sources.

Hypothetical #3

Mr. Rich, a prominent writer, scholar, and thinker, died in an accident when his little plane came down during a heavy thunderstorm. At the reading of his will it was discovered that he left a huge collection of digitized material from his personal library to the New Age Library. The library has given Ms. New Graduate the responsibility "to manage" this new collection. What issues should Ms. Graduate consider?

Suggested response: The first task for Ms. Graduate is to determine copyright ownership of different pieces in the collection. Even though copyright ownership initially vests in the author, authors are free to assign their copyright by transfer or license. So even after determining the initial authorship, Ms. Graduate will have to determine if there have been any transfers of the copyright in the piece. Also, it is important in the case of jointly authored pieces to determine if any of the authors has granted a nonexclusive license in the piece, which might conflict with New Age's interests. Ms. Graduate also should determine if any of the pieces is subject to termination rights (discussed in Chapter 5) and when those rights are likely to be exercised. Also, if any of the authors is from a community property state, Ms. Graduate may want to determine whether there are any issues in the ownership of the marital property. Also, if any of the work is a work for hire, then the copyright belongs to the entity doing the hiring. If there are any derivative works, Ms. Graduate may want to find out who owns the copyright in the underlying work. Also, for any government works in the collection, Ms. Graduate needs to determine whether the work is by federal or state government. If it is federal government, there is no copyright. But a federal employee who created a work acting out of his or her own volition and outside the scope of employment may have a copyright in the work. States generally have copyright in their works, except for judicial opinions, legislation, or regulations. Think of any other issues that are suggested to you by the reading here or other sources.

Hypothetical #4

Ms. New Graduate from Hypothetical #3 has determined who owns the copyrights in Mr. Rich's collection and is now planning to have the collection available to the public. She wants to further redigitize the collection in the new Everlasting Format that has just been introduced, and she wants to create an archive of the collection. What additional issues should she now address?

Suggested response: The first determination is whether New Age is an eligible section 108 library. There are certain privileges granted to libraries and archives by this section. Ms. Graduate should determine exactly what rights Mr. Rich owned. New Age can exercise all the copyrights Mr. Rich had, as copyright is property that can be bequeathed. For the other pieces not owned by Mr. Rich, Ms. Graduate will have to determine each author's exclusive rights, as some authors may have transferred some of the exclusive rights. Making the collection available to the public, redigitizing, and archiving the collection all involve one or more of the exclusive rights of the copyright holder. For each right, Ms. Graduate will determine what, if any, limitations exist. Because Ms. Graduate wants to redigitize the collection, she will have to consider whether she will be exercising the copyright owner's exclusive right to make derivative copies. Think of any other issues that are suggested to you by the reading here or other sources.

Hypothetical #5

Refer back to Hypothetical #3 for situation background. However, in this instance, a significant portion of the collection is by anonymous and pseudonymous authors, and some of it is previously unpublished. Also, a small portion of the collection might be in the public domain, because the authors were foreigners who had not complied with the former copyright registration formalities. Some pieces were published in 1921, others in 1925. In addition, some authors transferred their copyrights to Mr. Rich in 1977, and some licensed to him the right to create derivative works. What additional issues should Ms. Graduate be concerned with?

Suggested response: There are several issues Ms. Graduate should be concerned with here. The first is to determine when a particular work was first published or created: this will determine the period of protection for the pieces in which Mr. Rich did not own the copyright. Copyright protection for anonymous and pseudonymous works is 95 years from the date of first publication, and 120 years from the creation of the work. Ms. Graduate should also check the records of the Copyright Office to find out if the identity of an author was later revealed. If the author was later revealed, the term of protection would revert to the life of the author or last surviving author plus 70 years. Ms. Graduate would then need to know if the author is still living. There is a presumption of death if work is 95 years since publication or 120 years since creation and no indication whether the author is alive or dead. The fact that some of the work is unpublished is immaterial, as there is no distinction between published or unpublished works as far as copyright protection is concerned.

For the material that Ms. Graduate believes is in the public domain because of lost rights, she will need to make sure those rights were not restored later and the work is no longer in the public domain. For other public domain material, pre-1922 works are generally in the public domain. For the works published in 1925, whether there is still protection will depend on whether the copyright in a work was renewed. If copyright was not renewed, then the work is in the public domain. If it was renewed, copyright will expire in 2020 (see Notable Points 26).

For the copyrights transferred to Mr. Rich, Ms. Graduate may want to remember the right of an author or lawful beneficiary to terminate a transfer. She may want to check in the Copyright Office to see if any notice of termination is recorded. If not, she still might want to find out if the transfer window is still open; if, for example, a copyright was secured the same year it was transferred, the window could begin 2033. If any of the grants to Mr. Rich was terminated, then Ms. Graduate will have to deal with the author or successors. However, even if there has been termination, the right to create derivative works belongs to Mr. Rich, but no new derivative works can now be created. Think of any other issues that are suggested to you by the reading here or other sources.

Hypothetical #6

Imagine the same situation as Hypothetical #4. In this instance, Ms. Graduate is interested in the New Digital Library acquiring rights from some of the copyright owners. What *additional* issues should Ms. Graduate be concerned with?

Suggested response: The assumption here is that Ms. Graduate has identified the rightful copyright owners and that she wishes to acquire the copyright. This can be accomplished through a transfer. The transfer has to be in writing and must be signed by copyright owner or authorized agent. It is important that the language effecting the transfer be unambiguous. Ms. Graduate will recall that copyrights are divisible, and so she will want to determine exactly what rights are being transferred. Is it all rights, or just some? If some, which ones? While it is not necessary to notarize the transfer document, it might be a good idea to do so, as a notarized document may be evidence of the transfer. Ms. Graduate will also want to determine that there had been no earlier transfer recorded because, in the case of conflicting transfers, the first recorded one prevails. Ms. Graduate should also check to see if there any outstanding termination rights, as these may affect the value of the copyright transferred. For example, many termination rights will begin to be exercised in 2013 for post-1978 works. Works authored by Mr. Rich are exempt from the termination right concern, because they were passed by will. Finally, Ms. Graduate should make sure to record the transfer of copyright ownership with the Copyright Office. Think of any other issues that are suggested to you by the reading here or other sources.

Hypothetical #7

In working on Hypothetical #6, Ms. Graduate discovers that she has to obtain a license for the use of some of the content in Mr. Rich's collection. What *additional* issues should Ms. Graduate be concerned with?

Suggested response: Initially, Ms. Graduate must ascertain who the parties to the license contract are. There should be no surprise parties in the contract. Then she would determine exactly what rights the license provides. She also needs to know whether the license is exclusive or nonexclusive. If it is exclusive, it needs to be in writing so it may be recorded in the Copyright Office. Also, if exclusive, the contract needs to be signed by the owner of the right being licensed. Ms. Graduate also needs to determine if the work is jointly authored; each joint author has the right to separately grant nonexclusive licenses without consent from the other authors. Ms. Graduate needs to conduct due diligence to make sure therefore that there are no conflicting nonexclusive licenses in existence. For multimedia content, Ms. Graduate may need to obtain multiple licenses from multiple parties. In addition, she needs to make sure she understands what the limitations to the license, if any, are. She needs to determine the duration of the license and make sure she understands what the termination and renewal conditions are. The support that comes with the license is a major factor, as are the various obligations of the parties. Finally, Ms. Graduate needs to determine if there is a choice of law in the license: if it came down to litigation, where would this take place? Think of any other issues that are suggested to you by the reading here or other sources.

Hypothetical #8

Ten months into managing Mr. Rich's collection, New Age Library recognizes Ms. Graduate's high quality of work and gives her the additional responsibilities of managing the works in Hypothetical #2. Despite her best efforts to comply with copyright law, Ms. Graduate begins to worry that she may be infringing some copyrights on some of the works in the collection. What are some of the issues she would need to address?

Suggested response: Ms. Graduate needs to keep in mind that violation of any of the copyright owner's exclusive rights may constitute infringement. As an employee acting in an official capacity, she may be considered an infringer. So it is imperative to examine whether New Age is exercising any of the rights of reproduction, distribution, creating derivative works, public performance, or display. If she was successful in obtaining the copyrights in Hypothetical #6 and licenses under Hypothetical #7, then she does not have much to worry about. For material to which she does not have the rights, some of the likely violations are discussed in Hypothetical #2. Ms. Graduate will do well to remember that copyright infringement is a strict liability offense, which means she does need not have had an intention to infringe. She will need to consider whether by making the material electronically accessible she is not subject to contributory infringement, or, from New Age's point of view, vicarious infringement. Not all acts exercising any of the copyright holder's rights constitute infringement. Some acts may be privileged as, for example, by fair use. Also, New Age Library may qualify for section 108 exemptions from infringement liability if it is not copying for commercial purposes and the library is open to the public or other researchers and provides notice that reproduced works may be protected by copyright. Ms. Graduate should be aware at all times of the significant penalties exacted for copyright infringement. Think of any other issues that are suggested to you by the reading here or other sources.

Hypothetical #9

While worrying about Hypothetical #8, Ms. Graduate discovers that some of the items are protected by DRM systems. What *additional* issues should Ms. Graduate now address?

Suggested response: The strongest tool for the enforcement of DRM systems is the anticircumvention prohibitions of the Digital Millennium Copyright Act (DMCA). The first determination that Ms. Graduate should make is whether any of these DRM-protected works are in the Librarian of Congress's class of copyrighted works whose use would be adversely affected by the circumvention prohibition of the DMCA. Inclusion in this list exempts the work from the anticircumvention prohibition. This list is published as part of the Code of Federal Regulations (see Appendix 2) and is valid for three years following publication. For works not exempted, Ms. Graduate will need to make sure that she and the library are not engaged in any of the activities prohibited by the DMCA. Finally, she will need to determine if any of New Age's activities are covered by any of the exemptions provided under the DMCA, especially the exemptions for libraries and similar institutions. The library exemptions, for example, allow for circumvention to gain access to evaluate whether the library wishes to acquire the work, provided the access is not retained for longer than necessary to make a good faith evaluation, the access is not used for any other purpose, and an identical copy of a work is not available in another format. Think of any other issues that are suggested to you by the reading here or other sources.

Hypothetical #10

Consider the same scenario as in Hypothetical #1, but in addition, Mr. Digital Librarian has developed a webpage within the library website that allows his colleagues and other users to post comments about the search engine, as well as share their own experiences with other proprietary search engines. Mr. Librarian does not edit or modify the material posted in any way. What *additional* issues should Mr. Librarian be concerned with?

Suggested response: The library should be concerned about the possibility of infringing material being uploaded on the special New Age webpage, or DRM systems circumvention activities by the users. In addition to the issues discussed in Hypothetical #1, Mr. Librarian may want to determine whether New Age would be considered a service provider. In providing the webpage for posting by users, New Age can be said to be providing online services or network access and operating the facility to provide these services, which, by the statutory definition, makes it a service provider. Section 512 of the Copyright Act provides a safe harbor against infringement liability and circumvention activities to service providers who qualify. The library would need to take proactive steps if it wanted to qualify for the limitations on liability provided by section 512. Mr. Librarian would need to make sure that there was a designated agent to receive notifications of claimed infringements and provide this information to the Copyright Office, as well as on its website. He must be prepared to act on valid infringement notifications and take down or remove infringing material. Because Mr. Librarian is not modifying the posted content but is merely transmitting the posted material, he may be protected from liability for infringing claims. Also, if there is a showing that New Age had no actual or implied knowledge of infringing material or activity, the library may be able to claim Innocent Service Provider status, which would exempt it from monetary relief. If Mr. Librarian has provided links to other sites that contain infringing material, he might escape liability by showing that he had no actual knowledge of the infringing activity or material, that he took steps to disable access to the material, and that New Age has no financial benefit directly attributable to the infringing activity. Mr. Librarian must also be prepared to execute a valid subpoena seeking the identity of an infringing individual or a court injunction against providing access to infringing activity or material. Think of any other issues that are suggested to you by the reading here or other sources.

Hypothetical #11

It turns out that some of the rights New Age Library acquired in Hypothetical #6 were for sound recordings of various animals and birds, arranged in such a way as to sound like Bach's *Symphony No. 40*. Ms. Graduate would like to continue webcasting and streaming this content, as well as license these recordings for movie soundtracks and ringtones. What are some of the issues to consider?

Suggested response: Ms. Graduate can enter into individual licenses for the use of these recordings in movie soundtracks or as ringtones, or she can use a copyright clearance service for New Age to receive royalties. The Copyright Clearance Center collects copyright clearance fees on behalf of copyright owners. However, Ms. Graduate should also be aware of the fact that sound recordings are subject to compulsory licenses, where users would simply use the material without asking and pay the library a royalty amount specified by statute. Compulsory license rates are set by copyright royalty judges, who are appointed by the Librarian of Congress, in consultation with the register of copyrights. New Age may go before the judges to seek an adjustment to the royalty rate or to make a claim or petition for royalty. Think of any other issues that are suggested to you by the reading here or other sources.

Hypothetical #12

Mr. Digital Librarian has begun to have some misgivings about the ability of his colleagues and others to access the collection in Hypothetical #1. Besides copyright issues, what else should he be thinking about? Also, it turns out that the SISE Company has a data provision service that can provide content to the digital library of New Age Library. What additional issues should concern Mr. Librarian?

Suggested response: Besides copyrights issues, Mr. librarian should be concerned about the existence of proprietary and private information contained in SISE. We discussed some of them in Hypothetical #1. SISE may contain proprietary information that the SISE company developed, or which the SISE company considers confidential or a trade secret. The licensing agreement with the SISE company most likely contains clauses obligating New Age to protect such information. Mr. Librarian needs to review the agreement to determine what these obligations are. There are several laws, mostly state and common law, that provide significant penalties for disclosing trade secrets. If sued for divulging a trade secret, New Age will want to show that the information was generally known, that the SISE company took few measures to protect the information's confidentiality, and that it had expended little resources in developing the information. Because SISE is a proprietary search engine, Mr. Librarian may want to review the licensing agreement for restrictions on utilizing, modifying, or optimizing the search engine. He may also want to make sure that users are not able to access or change the information contained in meta tags, as the tags may contain trademark information that might be distributed with content in violation of trademark law. As well, there may be personal data whose disclosure or misuse could violate privacy.

As for evaluating providers, perhaps the most important consideration is whether the service provider's content is free of copyright infringement and that it provides indemnity to the library in case of infringement claims resulting from the content it provides. Also, the content needs to be free from libelous statements. Other general questions to consider include the business health of the content provider and whether it will still be in business when technology to access the data changes. Think of any other issues that are suggested to you by the reading here or other sources.

Hypothetical #13

A year later, just when she thought she had the management of Mr. Rich's collection and the *Twilight* series collection under control, Ms. Graduate receives a phone call from Mr. Librarian: "New Age has just acquired sizable digital material from different parts of the world. It is all yours!" What are some of the issues Ms. Graduate should be aware of?

Suggested response: Ms. Graduate will need to determine if any of the material comes from countries that are signatories to the same international treaties to which the United States is a signatory. The United States would be obligated to provide the same or similar copyright protection as is available in this country. If the material comes from states outside these treaties, she may not have to worry too much about copyright. However, most countries are signatories to the Berne Convention, of which the United States is a member. Berne Convention and U.S. copyright protections are roughly parallel. Ms. Librarian should be aware of the European emphasis on the moral rights of authors, as these allow the author to continue claiming authorship of a work even after transferring economic rights to the work and to protect the work's integrity. These moral rights are exercised even after the author's death, by the author's estate. Ms. Librarian will need to examine the applicability of any of the major international treaties to the material from different parts of the world.

Index

A

ABC, Gilliam v., 82
Abrams, Howard, 85
Abstraction-filtration-comparison analysis, 88
Access
 to digital collection, 22
 DMCA circumvention prohibition, 103–104
 DMCA violations, 104–107
 limitations for e-books, 15
 open access/closed access, 22–24
 preaccess conditions/removal of infringing material, 117–118
 See also Internet service providers
ACTA (Anti-Counterfeiting Trade Agreement), 114
Agent, designated, 114–115
Aggregators, of e-books, 15
Agreement on Trade-Related Aspects of Intellectual Property Rights (TRIPS)
 as major treaty governing copyrights, 145
 notable points, 189–190
 overview of, 153–154
Alexandria Digital Library at the University of California Santa Barbara, 41
Alteration of content, 83
American Federation of Musicians, 195
American Society of Composers, Authors, and Publishers (ASCAP)
 collection of copyright fees, 82, 131
 website, 195
American Society of Media Photographers, 195
American Society of Picture Professionals, 195
Analog devices, compliance with DMCA, 107–109
Annotations, 41–42

Anonymous works
 Berne Convention on, 148
 copyright duration for, 58, 59, 176–177
Anticircumvention prohibition
 of DMCA, 103–104
 DMCA challenges, 109–110
 DMCA violations, 104–107
 Exemption to Prohibition Against Circumvention, 167–168
 exemptions to, 183–184
 notable points, 108
Anti-Counterfeiting Trade Agreement (ACTA), 114
Arbitrary or fanciful trademarks, 7, 8
Arbitration, former copyright arbitration panels, 129–131
Archives
 DMCA exemptions for, 105
 reproduction as noninfringement, 92–93
Armstrong, Tracey, 131
Arriba Soft Corp., Kelly v., 16–17
Art Museum Image Consortium, 195
Artists. *See* Visual artists rights
Artists Rights Society, 195
Association of American Publishers, 195
Association of Authors' Representatives, 195
Attribution, right of, 4–5, 45
Audio clips, 83
Authenticity, of digital collection, 22
Authors
 Berne Convention rights, 146–150
 content owners, determination of, 27
 copyright duration, post-1978 works, 57–59
 copyright ownership, determination of, 3–4
 Creative Commons and, 23
 initial ownership, 28–29
 reacquisition of rights/licenses by reversion, 74–75

▶ 207

Authors *(cont'd.)*
  restoration of lost rights due to
    formalities, 64–66
  rights in copyright, 2, 4–5
  rights with Universal Copyright
    Convention, 152–153
  visual artists rights, 44–46
  WIPO Copyright Treaty, 150–152
  of work for hire, 30
Authors Guild, The, 195
Authors Registry, 195
Authorship, 28
Automatic gain control copy control
    technology
  description of, 108–109
  fair use and DMCA, 110–111

B

Bad faith, 91
Bender, David, 139
Berkeley Digital Library SunSITE, 40
Berne Convention
  formalities, removal of, 64
  as major treaty governing copyrights, 145
  notable points, 188–189
  restoration of rights of foreign authors, 59
  rights protected in, 146–150
  VARA rights and, 45
Besek, June M., 16
Bilateral license, 81
Brabec, Jeffrey, 83
Brabec, Todd, 83
Broadcast Music, Inc., 131, 195
Broadcasters, 154
Bush, George W., 99

C

California
  copyright ruling in, 33
  privacy statute in, 139
CCC. *See* Copyright Clearance Center
Certification marks, 7
Checklists, compliance, 191–194

Cinematographic works
  Berne Convention protections for, 148
  right of rental with TRIPS, 154
  right of rental with WIPO Copyright
    Treaty, 150–151
Circumvention
  definition of, 104
  DMCA anticircumvention prohibition, 103–104
  DMCA violations, 104–107
  Exemption to Prohibition Against
    Circumvention, 167–168
  exemptions to anticircumvention
    prohibition, 108, 183–184
  fair use and DMCA, 110–111
  WIPO Copyright Treaty on, 151
Civil proceedings, 97–98
Clearances, 35–36, 195–196
Closed access, 24
Code of Federal Regulations
  Exemption to Prohibition Against
    Circumvention, 167–168
  Notices of Termination of Transfers and
    Licenses, 161–166
Collective works
  copyright ownership for, 4, 31
  copyright protection for, 20–21
  joint work vs., 29
  notable points, 171–172
Commercial databases, 19–20
Community property laws, 29
Compilations
  copyright protection for, 20–21
  notable points, 171–172
Compliance checklists, 191–194
Compulsory licenses
  for copyrighted music, 84–85
  notable points, 181
  WIPO Copyright Treaty and, 151
Computer Fraud and Abuse Act of 1986
  DMCA exemption for security testing, 107
  trade secrets, proprietary information and, 136
Computer programs
  copyright protection with TRIPS, 153–154

Index ▶ 209

DMCA challenges and, 109
DMCA exemption for security testing, 107
DMCA reverse engineering exemptions, 105–106
noninfringement activities, 95–96
Section 108 on copying/modifying, 51
transfer of copyright, 70
WIPO Copyright Treaty, 150–152
Confidential information
data providers, evaluation of, 142
trade secrets vs. proprietary information, 135–137
Connaway, Lynn S., 3
Content owners
collective works, 31
copyright transfers, 34
derivative works, ownership in, 31–32
determination of, 27
government works, 32–33
hypothetical question, 36
initial ownership, 28–29
notable points, 35
other claimants, 33–34
recovering damages/profits, 34
resources for finding copyright owners/clearances, 35–36
work for hire, 30
See also Copyright ownership
Content owners, rights of
limitations on rights, 46–53
right of distribution, 42–43
right of performance, 43–44
right of reproduction, 39–41
right to display, 44
right to make derivative works, 41–42
visual artists rights, 44–46
Continental Airlines, Shugrue v., 70
Contributory infringement
notable points, 181–182
overview of, 89, 90
Conwell v. Gray Loon Outdoor Marketing Group, 70
Co-owners, 45
See also Multiple copyright owners

Copy
analog devices, compliance with DMCA, 107–109
of computer programs, 95–96
digital first sale and, 47–48
fair use and DMCA, 110–111
in first-sale doctrine, 46
as infringement, 88
library/archives reproduction as noninfringement, 92–93
limitations on rights, 49–53
transfer of ownership of copy, 70
See also Reproduction, right of
Copy control, 108–109
Copyright
access to digital collections and, 22
commercial databases and, 19–20
content owners, determination of, 27
Creative Commons, 23
data providers, evaluation of, 141
definition of, 2
digital media licenses, 79–85
DMCA circumvention prohibition, 103–104
dynamism of digital content and, 14
Exemption to Prohibition Against Circumvention, 167–168
framing as infringement of, 19
infringers, identification of, 121
Internet linking and, 18–19
ISPs, conditions for infringement liability protection, 115–119
ISPs, designated agent requirement for, 114–115
ISPs, takedown or disable liability, 120–121
limitations on rights, 5–6
material subject to, determination of, 2–3
notable points, quick-reference compilation of, 169–190
Notices of Termination of Transfers and Licenses, 161–166
other claimants, 33–34
ownership, 3–4
ownership, initial, 28–29
ownership, transfer of, 4

Copyright *(cont'd.)*
  page thumbnails and, 16–17
  privacy and, 138–139
  reacquisition of rights/licenses by reversion, 74–75
  resources for finding copyright owners/clearances, 35–36, 195–196
  rights in, 4–5
  safe harbor for ISPs, 113–114
  termination of rights in transfers/licenses granted after January 1, 1978, 72–74
  transfer of, 34, 69–72
  See also Infringement
Copyright, duration of
  expiration of copyrights, 66
  formalities, effect of, 63–66
  hypothetical question, 67
  post-1978 works, 57–59
  preexisting works, 59–60
  termination of transfers/licenses for pre-1978 works, 61–63
Copyright, international aspects of
  Berne Convention, 146–150
  hypothetical question, 155
  notable points, 188–190
  overview of, 145–146
  TRIPS, 153–154
  Universal Copyright Convention, 152–153
  WIPO Copyright Treaty, 150–152
Copyright Act
  joint authorship and, 28
  rights granted to authors with, 2
  safe harbor for ISPs, 113–114
  on work for hire, 30
Copyright Act of 1909, 69
Copyright Act of 1976
  copyright duration extension under, 60
  duration of copyright under, 57
  perfection of security interest under, 71
  termination rights with, 72–73
  on transfer of copyright ownership, 69
Copyright arbitration panels, former, 129–131

Copyright Clearance Center (CCC)
  collection of license fees, 82
  notable points, 186
  overview of, 131–132
  website, 195
Copyright divisibility, 70
Copyright Extension Act of 1998 (Sonny Bono Copyright Term Extension Act)
  duration of copyright under, 57, 60
  termination rights, 63
Copyright Licensing Agency, The, 195
Copyright notice, 63–64
Copyright ownership
  in collective works, 31
  in derivative works, 31–32
  determination of, 3–4
  notable points, 172, 173
  recovering damages/profits, 34–35
  resources for finding copyright owners/clearances, 35–36, 195–196
  rights/limitations of owner, 176
  transfer of, 4, 34, 35, 69–72
  work for hire, 30
  See also Content owners
Copyright ownership, rights of
  limitations on rights, 46–53
  right of distribution, 42–43
  right of performance, 43–44
  right of reproduction, 39–41
  right to display, 44
  right to make derivative works, 41–42
  visual artists rights, 44–46
Copyright protection
  for collective works, compilations, 20–21
  for e-books, 15–16
  expiration of, 66
  notable points, 169–170
Copyright registration. *See* Registration, copyright
Copyright Renewal Database, 195
Copyright royalties
  compulsory license royalties, copyright royalty judges, 126–129
  conclusion about, 132
  Copyright Clearance Center, 131–132

Index ▶ 211

definition of, 125
former copyright arbitration panels, 129–131
hypothetical question, 132
notable points, 185
Copyright Royalty and Distribution Reform Act, 129
Copyright Royalty Board, 127–129
Copyright royalty judges, 185–186
Counternotification, 120–121
Creative Commons, 23
Criminal proceedings, 98–99

D

Damages
  for DMCA violations, 105
  for infringement, 97–99
  recovery of, 34
  takedown or disable liability, 120–121
Data providers, evaluating, 141–142
Data sets, 19–20
Database
  legal issues of, 19–20
  WIPO Copyright Treaty, 150–152
Dempsey, Lorcan, 3
Derivative works
  in Berne Convention, 146
  copyright ownership in, 31–32
  notable points, 172, 173–174
  restoration of lost rights due to formalities, 65–66
  right to make, 41–42
  termination of rights, 62–63, 74
Descriptive category of trademark, 7
Designated agent requirement, 114–115
Determinations
  of copyright arbitration panel, 130
  of copyright royalty judges, 128–129
Digital collections
  different goals of, 21–22
  multiple, heterogeneous collections, 18–22
  Section 108, limitations on rights, 49–53
Digital content
  dynamism, problem of nonpermanence, 13–15

first-sale doctrine, 46–48
  notable points, 171
Digital content management, 135
Digital first sale
  notable points, 175
  overview of, 47–48
Digital libraries, legal issues in
  copyright, 2–6
  hypothetical question, 10
  overview of, 1
  patents, 8–9
  publicity/privacy rights, 9
  trade secrets, 9
  trademarks, trademark protection, 6–8
Digital libraries, special features of
  dynamism, problem of nonpermanence, 13–15
  multimedia content, complexity of, 15–18
  multiple, heterogeneous collections, 18–22
  open access/closed access, 22–24
Digital library
  data providers, evaluation of, 141–142
  DMCA exemptions for, 105
  as ISP, 114
  reproduction as noninfringement, 92–93
  right of reproduction, 40
  Section 108, limitations on rights, 49–53
Digital media licenses
  compulsory licenses for copyrighted music, 84–85
  examining the license, 81–84
  hypothetical question, 86
  multiple parties, need to interact with, 80–81
  overview of, 79–80
Digital Millennium Copyright Act (DMCA)
  analog devices compliance with, 107–109
  challenges to, 109–110, 184
  circumvention prohibition, 103–104
  fair use and, 110–111
  linking liability, 18–19
  migration of digital content and, 15
  safe harbor for ISPs, 113–114, 122
  violations of, 104–107

Digital Public Library of America, 41
Digital rights management (DRM) systems
  analog devices compliance, 107–109
  definition of, 103
  Digital Millennium Copyright Act, 103–104
  DMCA challenges, 109–110
  for e-books protection, 15
  exemptions to anticircumvention prohibition, 108
  fair use and DMCA, 110–111
  notable points, 104, 183
  violations of DMCA, 104–107
Digital scanning, 88
Digitization, 40–41
Disable liability, 120–121
Disclosure, right of, 45
Display
  performance/display for teaching/instruction, 93–95
  right of public display, 44, 174
Disposition, 97
Distance education, 93–95
Distribution
  limitations on rights, 49–53
  right of, 42–43, 150
DMCA. *See* Digital Millennium Copyright Act
Doctrine of misappropriation, 136
Document icons, 16–18
Download, 85
DRM systems. *See* Digital rights management (DRM) systems
Duration of copyright rights
  ARA rights, 45
  for digital media licenses, 80
  expiration of copyrights, 66
  formalities, effect on duration of copyright, 63–66
  hypothetical question, 67
  notable points, 176–177
  post-1978 works, 57–59
  preexisting works, 59–60
  provided by Berne Convention, 148–150
  termination of transfers/licenses for pre-1978 works, 61–63
  with TRIPS, 154

  with Universal Copyright Convention, 152
  with WIPO Copyright Treaty, 151
DVD Copy Control Association, Realnetworks v., 110
Dynamism
  of digital libraries, 13–15
  notable points, 170–171

E

E-books
  legal issues of, 15–16
  notable points, 171
Economic right theory, 2
Education
  fair use and, 91
  performance/display for teaching/instruction, 93–95
Educational institutions
  DMCA exemptions for, 105
  as ISPs, 114, 119
Electronic Communications Privacy Act, 136, 140
Electronic Steering Group of the Asia-Pacific Economic Cooperation, 139–140
Electronically Stored Information (ESI), 22
Employee, 30
Employer, 30
Encryption
  DMCA encryption research exemption, 106–107
  DMCA violations, 104
ESI (Electronically Stored Information), 22
Exclusive license, 79–80
Exemption to Prohibition Against Circumvention (Code of Federal Regulations), 167–168
Exemptions
  to anticircumvention prohibition, 183–184
  DMCA exemptions, 105–107
  Exemption to Prohibition Against Circumvention, 167–168
  innocent service provider, 118
  intermediate storage on ISP, 116–117

linking exemption, 118–119
transitory transmissions by ISPs, 115–116
Expectation of privacy, 139
Expiration, of copyrights, 66, 179

F

Fair Copyright in Research Works Act (H.R. 801), 33
Fair use
  Berne Convention on, 147
  copyright protection and, 5–6
  damages for infringement and, 98
  determination of noninfringement, 90–91
  DMCA and, 110–111, 184
  limitations on rights, 48–49
  notable points, 175, 182
  page thumbnails and, 16–17
  trademark protection, 7
Federal government, works of, 32–33
Federal Register
  copyright arbitration panel list in, 129
  copyright arbitration panel meeting information in, 130
  copyright royalty determination in, 128, 129
  copyright royalty hearing notices in, 127
  notice of intent to enforce copyright in, 65
Federal Rules of Civil Procedure, 22, 121
Feedback technology, 117
Feist Publications v. Rural Telephone Service, 96
First Amendment
  DMCA challenges on, 109, 110
  fair use and, 48
First-sale doctrine
  Berne Convention vs., 147
  description of, 43
  digital first sale, 175
  limitations on rights, 46–48
  notable points, 174
Foreign authors, 64–66
Formalities
  effect on duration of copyright, 63–64
  restoration of rights lost due to formalities noncompliance, 178

with TRIPS, 154
with Universal Copyright Convention, 152
Formats. *See* Media formats
Framing, 19
French theory, 45

G

Gain control, 108–109
Generic category of trademark, 7
Geographic restriction, 83
Gilliam v. ABC, 82
Goals
  of digital collections, 21–22
  of royalties, 126
Good faith
  DMCA encryption research exemption, 106–107
  infringement, takedown or disable liability, 120
  ISPs, designated agent requirement for, 115
Google
  digitization projects and right of reproduction, 40
  proprietary search engine, 137
Google, Perfect 10 v., 16–17
Government works
  Berne Convention on, 147
  copyright and, 32–33
  notable points, 173
Grants
  reacquisition of rights/licenses by reversion, 74–75
  termination of, 61, 62–63
Gray Loon Outdoor Marketing Group, Conwell v., 70

H

HarperCollins, 15
Harry Fox Agency, 85, 196
Health Insurance Portability and Accountability Act (HIPAA), 140
Hot News Misappropriation doctrine, 19

Hypothetical question
  on acquisition of copyright, 75
  on content owner rights, 53
  on copyright duration, 67
  copyright royalties, 132
  on digital collection, 24, 36
  on digital media licenses, 86
  on DRM systems, 111
  on infringement, 99
  on international aspects of copyright, 155
  on legal issues in digital libraries, 10
  on proprietary information/privacy, 142
  for service providers, 123
  suggested analyses for, 197–206

I

iCopyright, 196
IFRRO (International Federation of Reproduction Rights Organisations), 132
Importation, 88
Impound, 97
Infringement
  action for, 96
  Berne Convention on, 148
  contributory, 89
  damages for, 97–99
  data providers, evaluation of, 141
  designated agent requirement for ISPs, 114–115
  educational institutions and, 119
  hypothetical question, 99
  identification of infringers, 121
  injunctions to service providers, 122
  innocent service provider, 118
  intermediate storage on ISP, 116–117
  ISPs and, 184–185
  linking exemption, 118–119
  noninfringement, 90–96
  notable points, 181–182
  overview of, 87–89
  preaccess conditions/removal of infringing material, 117–118
  remedies for, 96–97
  safe harbor for ISPs, 113–114
  takedown or disable liability, counternotifications, 120–121
  vicarious, 89–90
Injunctions
  for copyright infringement, 96–97
  to service providers, 122
Innocent service provider, 118
Instruction. *See* Teaching
Integrity, right of, 4–5, 45
Intellectual property
  areas covered by, 1
  copyright, 2–6
  patents, 8–9
  publicity/privacy rights, 9
  trade secrets, 9
  trademarks, trademark protection, 6–8
  TRIPS, 153–154
  Universal Copyright Convention, 152–153
Intellectual Property Clause of U.S. Constitution, 109
Intermediate storage, 116–117
International aspects of copyright
  Berne Convention, 146–150
  hypothetical question, 155
  notable points, 188–190
  overview of, 145–146
  TRIPS, 153–154
  Universal Copyright Convention, 152–153
  WIPO Copyright Treaty, 150–152
International Court of Justice, 148, 149
International Federation of Reproduction Rights Organisations (IFRRO), 132
Internet
  digital content and, 171
  linking/framing legal issues, 18–19
  meta tags, 138
  privacy issues, 138–140
  proprietary search engines, 137–138
Internet Archive, 40
Internet Movie Database, 196
Internet service providers (ISPs)
  definition of, 114
  designated agent requirement, 114–115
  DMCA safe harbor, 113–114
  evaluating data providers, 141–142
  hypothetical question, 123
  infringers, identification of, 121

Index ▶ 215

injunctions to service providers, 122
innocent service provider, 118
intermediate storage, 116–117
linking exemption, 118–119
nonprofit educational institutions, 119
notable points, 184–185
preaccess conditions/removal of
  infringing material, 117–118
takedown or disable liability,
  counternotifications, 120–121
transitory transmissions, 115–116
Interoperability, 105–106

J

Joint work
  copyright duration for, 57, 58
  digital media licenses for, 80–81
  overview of, 28–29
  termination of rights in transfers/
    licenses, 73
  visual artists rights, 45
Judges
  copyright royalty judges, 127–129
  powers of Librarian of Congress to
    appoint, 185–186

K

Kelly v. Arriba Soft Corp., 16–17
Kessler, Scanlon v., 19
Kidsoft, Phillips v., 88

L

Language, 83
Lanham Act of 1946, 6, 7
Lavoie, Brian, 3
Legal action, for infringement, 96–99
Lessig, Lawrence, 23
Liability
  innocent service provider, 118
  ISP infringement liability protection,
    184–185
  ISPs conditions for infringement
    liability protection, 115–117
  linking exemption for ISPs, 118–119

safe harbor for ISPs and, 114
takedown or disable liability, 120–121
Liblicense website, 81
Librarian of Congress
  appointment of copyright arbitration
    panel, 129, 130
  copyright royalty judges appointed by,
    127–129
  judicial powers of, 132
  powers to appoint judges, 185–186
Library
  DMCA exemptions for, 105
  as ISP, 114
  reproduction as noninfringement, 92–93
  See also Digital collections; Digital library
Library of Congress
  anticircumvention prohibition, 103–104,
    108
  copyright royalty judges appointed by,
    127–129
Licenses
  compulsory license royalties, 126–129
  Copyright Clearance Center, 131–132
  notable points, 180–181
  Notices of Termination of Transfers and
    Licenses, 161–166
  privacy issues related to, 140
  for proprietary search engines, 137
  reacquisition of rights/licenses by
    reversion, 74–75
  termination of rights in transfers/
    licenses granted after January 1,
    1978, 72–74
  termination of transfers/licenses for
    pre-1978 works, 61–63
  trade secrets and, 136, 137
  See also Digital media licenses
Limitations on rights
  of copyright ownership, 46–53
  fair use, 48–49
  first-sale doctrine, 46–48
  Section 108 of Title 17 of the U.S.
    Code, 49–53
Lindsay v. RMS Titanic, 28
Linking
  exemption for ISPs, 118–119
  legal issue of Internet, 18–19

Lisby, Gregory C., 19
Litigation, for infringement, 96–99

M

Media formats
    analog devices compliance with DMCA, 107–109
    digital information preservation and, 14
    e-books, legal issues of, 15–16
    library/archives reproduction as noninfringement, 92
    right of reproduction and, 40
Mencher, Brian, 47, 48
Meta tags
    digital content manager and, 138
    notable points, 187
Metadata, 41–42
Microsoft, 18
Microsoft Corp., Ticketmaster Corp. v., 18
Migration of data, 14–15
Modification of content, 83
Moral rights
    in Berne Convention, 147–148
    description of, 2
    VARA rights and, 45
Motion Picture Licensing Corporation (MPLC), 82, 196
Multilateral license, 81
Multimedia collections
    document icons, page thumbnails, 16–18
    e-books, 15–16
Multimedia content, of digital libraries, 15–18
Multiple, heterogeneous collections
    collective works, compilations, 20–21
    commercial databases, data sets, 19–20
    of digital libraries, 18–22
    goals of digital collections, 21–22
    Internet, 18–19
Multiple copyright owners
    licenses and, 180
    need to interact with, 80–81
Museums, copyright issues of, 22
Music
    alteration/modification of content, 83
    compulsory license royalties, 126–129
    compulsory licenses for copyrighted music, 84–85

N

NAFTA (North American Free Trade Agreement), 145–146
National Geographic magazine, 21, 31
National Institutes of Health, 33
National Music Publishers Association, 196
NetLibrary, 15
New York Times, 61
New York Times Co., Inc., v. Tasini, 20–21
Nonexclusive license
    description of, 79
    transfer of, 70, 71
Noninfringement
    computer programs, 95–96
    fair use and, 90–91
    library and archives reproduction, 92–93
    performance/display for teaching/instruction, 93–95
Nonpermanence
    ESI, preservation of, 22
    problem of, 13–15
Nonprofit educational institutions, 119
North American Free Trade Agreement (NAFTA), 145–146
Notable points
    Berne Convention, 149
    compilations/collective works, 21
    compulsory licenses, 85
    copyright, material not subject to, 3
    Copyright Clearance Center, 131
    copyright duration, 60
    copyright duration for anonymous, pseudonymous works, works for hire, 59
    copyright duration for single/multiple authors, 58
    copyright owner's rights/limitations, 53
    copyright ownership, 29
    copyright ownership/transfer, 35
    copyright protection, 5
    copyright transfers, 72
    derivative works, 31
    digital first sale, 47

Index ▶ 217

digital media licenses, 80
digital rights management, 104
DMCA and fair use, 111
dynamism of digital content, 14
e-books as example of multimedia collections, 16
expiration of copyrights, 66
fair use, 49, 91, 94
government works, 33
infringement, remedies for, 99
infringement and ISPs, 115
international treaty, 146
Internet and digital content, 19
ISPs, conditions for infringement liability protection, 117, 119
licenses, scope of, 84
licenses and multiple copyright owners, 81
meta tags, 138
new challenges in digital content, 18
patent protection, 8
powers of Librarian of Congress to appoint judges, 128
privacy, 140
proprietary information, 136
proprietary search engines, 138
quick-reference compilation of, 169–190
restoration of lost rights due to formalities, 65
right of distribution, 43
right of public display, 44
right of public performance, 43
right of reproduction, 40
right to make derivative works, 42
on royalties, 126
termination of copyright transfers, 74, 75
termination of rights for pre-1978 works, 62
termination rights, distribution of, 61
termination rights, reversion of, 63
trade secret protection, 9
trade secrets/proprietary information, 137
trademark protection, 8
TRIPS, 154

Universal Copyright Convention, 153
visual artists rights, 46
WIPO Copyright Treaty, 151
Notarization, 70
Notice
of intent to enforce copyright, 65
of Intent to Use compulsory license, 85
Notices of Termination of Transfers and Licenses, 161–166
of termination, 62
of termination of rights in transfers/licenses, 73
Notices of Restored Copyrights, 196
Notices of Termination of Transfers and Licenses (Code of Federal Regulations), 161–166
Notification
of claimed infringement, 117–118
counternotification, 120–121
of infringement, ISPs and, 119
of infringement to designated agent, 114–115
of security breach for privacy protection, 139
Novel uses, digital media licenses and, 82–83

O

Online distance education, 93–95
Open access, legal issues in, 22–24
Osenga, Kristen, 20, 136
Other claimants, 33–34
Ownership
of collective work, 20
of copyright, determination of, 3–4
copyright, limitations on, 5–6
copyright, transfer of, 4
initial, 28–29
transfer of copyright, 69–72
See also Content owners; Copyright ownership

P

Page thumbnails, 16–18
Paris Convention, 145

Patents
  commercial databases and, 20
  definition of, 8
  notable points, 170
  protection with, 8–9
Perfect 10 v. Google, 16–17
Perfection of security interests, 71
Performance
  performance/display for teaching/
    instruction, 93–95
  right to display, 44
  right to make derivative works and, 41
Performance, right of
  in Berne Convention, 146
  in download, 85
  notable points, 174
  overview of, 43–44
  with TRIPS, 154
Phillips v. Kidsoft, 88
Photographic works
  Berne Convention on, 148
  TRIPS on, 154
  Universal Copyright Convention on, 152
  WIPO Copyright Treaty on, 151
Piracy, 109
Post-1978 works, 57–59
Posthumous publications, 60
Pre-1978 works, 61–63
Preexisting works, 59–60
Preservation
  of digital content, 13–15
  goal of digital collections, 21–22
Prima facie infringement
  elements of, 88, 89
  notable points, 181
Prioritizing Resources and Organization
    for Intellectual Property (PRO-IP)
    Act, 99
Privacy
  content of digital collections, 141
  DMCA privacy exemption, 107, 108
  dynamism of digital content and, 14
  framework, 139–140
  license agreement negotiation and, 140
  notable points, 140, 187–188
  overview of, 138–139
  rights of, 9

ProCD v. Zeidenberg, 81
Profits, recovery of, 34
Programs. *See* Computer programs
Proprietary information
  definition of, 135
  meta tags, 138
  notable points, 186–187
  proprietary search engines, 137–138
  trade secrets vs., 135–137
Proprietary search engines, 137–138, 187
Pseudonymous works
  Berne Convention on, 148
  copyright duration for, 58, 59,
    176–177
Public display, right of, 44, 174
Public domain
  copyright duration and, 57
  copyright formalities and, 64
  expiration of copyrights, 66
  government works in, 32
Publication dates, 2–3
Publicity, rights of, 9

Q

Quaid, Vault v., 81

R

Reacquisition, of rights/licenses, 74–75
Realnetworks v. DVD Copy Control Association,
    110
Record, of transfer of copyright, 69–71
Recording Industry Association of
    America, 99
Registration, copyright
  advantages of, 64
  Berne Convention and, 149, 150
  examination of records, 58
  false copyright application, 98
  infringement claims and, 88
  not required for protection, 5, 59
  as prima facie evidence, 60
Reimerdes, Universal City Studios v., 18–19
Removal
  of infringing material, 117–118
  takedown or disable liability, 120–121

Renewal
  of copyright, 60
  joint work and, 28
Reno-Tahoe Specialty, Tiffany Design v., 88
Reproduction, by library/archives, 92–93
Reproduction, right of
  in Berne Convention, 146
  limitations on rights, 49–50
  notable points, 173
  overview of, 39–41
  See also Copy
Research, DMCA encryption research exemption, 106–107
Resources, for finding copyright owners/clearances, 195–196
Restoration of rights
  of foreign authors, 59
  of lost rights due to formalities, 64–66
Reverse engineering, 105–106, 108
Reversion
  reacquisition of rights/licenses by reversion, 74–75
  of termination rights, 63, 178
Right of attribution, 45
Right of communication to the public, 150, 151
Right of disclosure, 45
Right of distribution
  notable points, 174
  overview of, 42–43
  with WIPO Copyright Treaty, 150
Right of integrity, 45
Right of performance, 43–44, 85, 154
Right of public display, 174
Right of public performance, 146, 174
Right of rental of computer programs, cinematographic works, works embodied in phonograms, 150–151, 154
Right of reproduction
  in Berne Convention, 146
  notable points, 173
  overview of, 39–41
Right of termination, 61–63
Right of translation, 146–147, 152–153
Right of withdrawal, 45

Right to display, 44
Right to make derivative works, 41–42, 173–174
Rights
  with Berne Convention, 146–150
  in copyright, 4–5
  copyright, limitations on, 5–6
  reacquisition of rights/licenses by reversion, 74–75
  restoration of lost rights due to formalities, 64–66, 178
  termination of rights in transfers/licenses granted after January 1, 1978, 72–74
  with Universal Copyright Convention, 152–153
  with WIPO Copyright Treaty, 150–152
Rights, duration of
  expiration of copyrights, 66
  formalities, effect of, 63–66
  hypothetical question, 67
  post-1978 works, 57–59
  preexisting works, 59–60
  termination of transfers/licenses for pre-1978 works, 61–63
Rights management information, 151–152
Rights of content ownership
  limitations on rights, 46–53
  right of distribution, 42–43
  right of performance, 43–44
  right of reproduction, 39–41
  right to display, 44
  right to make derivative works, 41–42
  visual artists rights, 44–46
RMS Titanic, Lindsay v., 28
Roe v. Wade, 139
Royalties
  compulsory license royalties, copyright royalty judges, 126–129
  conclusion about, 132
  Copyright Clearance Center, 131–132
  definition of, 125
  notable points, 126, 185
Rural Telephone Service, Feist Publications v., 96

S

Sableman, Mark, 19
Safe harbor
　innocent service provider, 118
　for Internet service providers, 113–114
　for ISPs with DMCA, 122
Scanlon v. Kessler, 19
Scanning, digital, 88
SCCR (Standing Committee on Copyright and Related Rights), 53
Scope of employment, 30
Search Copyright Information, 196
Search engines
　page thumbnails, legal issues of, 16–17
　proprietary, 137–138, 187
Section 512 of Copyright Act, 113–114
Security
　interest, perfection of, 71
　privacy and, 139–140
　testing, DMCA exemption for, 107, 108
Service providers
　definition of, 114
　innocent service provider, 118
　See also Internet service providers
SESAC, 196
Shrink-wrap licenses, 81
Shugrue v. Continental Airlines, 70
Sina Corporation, 137
Social networking spaces, 141
Software, 82
　See also Computer programs; Digital rights management (DRM) systems
Sonny Bono Copyright Term Extension Act. *See* Copyright Extension Act of 1998
Sound Recording Amendment Act of 1971, 16
Sound recordings, copyright protection for, 16
Speeches, 147
Standing Committee on Copyright and Related Rights (SCRR), 53
States, copyright protection for, 33
Storage
　intermediate storage on ISP, 116–117
　transitory transmissions by ISPs, 115–116
Streaming, of illegal content, 99
Strength, of trademark, 7
Subpoena, 121
Suggestive category of trademark, 7

T

Takedown or disable liability, 120–121
Tasini, New York Times Co., Inc., v., 20–21
Teaching
　nonprofit educational institutions as ISPs, 119
　performance/display for teaching/instruction, 93–95
Technology
　DMCA challenges, 109–110
　DMCA violations, 104–107
　fair use and DMCA, 110–111
　WIPO Copyright Treaty, 150–152
Technology, Education, and Copyright Harmonization (TEACH) Act, 91, 93–95
Temporary injunction, 96–97
Termination
　of copyright transfers, 179–180
　example of distribution of rights, 177
　of ISP service for infringement, 121
　joint work and, 28
　Notices of Termination of Transfers and Licenses, 161–166
　reversion of termination rights, 178
　of rights for pre-1978 works, 178
　of rights in transfers/licenses granted after January 1, 1978, 72–74
　of transfers/licenses for pre-1978 works, 61–63
　work for hire and, 30
Testing, security, 107, 108
Thumbnails, page, 16–18
Ticketmaster Corp. v. Microsoft Corp., 18
Ticketmaster v. Tickets.com, 96
Tickets.com, Ticketmaster v., 96
Tiffany Design v. Reno-Tahoe Specialty, 88
Title 17 of the U.S. Code, section 101
　copyright protection, determination of, 2, 3
　definition of compilation, 20
　definition of derivative work, 41

Index ▶ 221

Title 17 of the U.S. Code, section 106
   copyright rights under, 39
   importation as infringement, 88
Title 17 of the U.S. Code, section 107, 48
Title 17 of the U.S. Code, section 108
   exemption for library/archives reproduction, 92
   limitations on rights, 49–53
   on need for preservation of digital collections, 21–22
Title 17 of the U.S. Code, section 110 (2), 93–94
Title 17 of the U.S. Code, section 201 (e), 34
Title 17 of the U.S. Code, section 301, 59, 66
Title 17 of the U.S. Code, section 502, 122
Title 17 of the U.S. Code, section 512, 113, 114
Total News, 19
Trade names, 7
Trade secrets
   definition of, 9, 136
   notable points, 170, 186–187
   proprietary information vs., 135–137
Trademarks
   definition of, 6
   meta tags and, 138
   metadata and, 41–42
   trademark protection, 7–8, 170
Transfer
   of copyright, overview of, 69–72
   of copyright ownership, 4, 27, 34
   of copyright to U.S. government, 32
   digital first sale and, 47–48
   notable points, 35, 173, 179
   Notices of Termination of Transfers and Licenses, 161–166
   termination of copyright transfers, 179–180
   termination of rights in transfers/licenses granted after January 1, 1978, 72–74
   termination of transfers/licenses for pre-1978 works, 61–63
Transitory transmissions, 115–116
Translation, right of
   in Berne Convention, 146–147
   with Universal Copyright Convention, 152–153
Transmissions, 115–116
TRIPS (Agreement on Trade-Related Aspects of Intellectual Property Rights)
   as major treaty governing copyrights, 145
   notable points, 189–190
   overview of, 153–154

U

Uniform Commercial Code (UCC), 71
Uniform Trade Secrets Act, 136
Unilateral licenses, 81
United Nations Educational, Scientific, and Cultural Organization (UNESCO), 152–153
United States Patent and Trademark Office, 196
Universal City Studios v. Reimerdes, 18–19
Universal Copyright Convention
   notable points, 189
   rights with, 152–153
Unpublished works
   Berne Convention on, 148
   copyright duration for, 59
   Section 108, limitations on rights, 50–51
   Universal Copyright Convention and, 152
Uploading, 88
Uruguay Round Agreements Act, 65, 153–154
U.S. Congress
   Copyright Act, power with, 2
   copyright duration and, 57
   termination of transfers/licenses and, 61
U.S. Constitution
   Intellectual Property Clause of, 109
   privacy and, 139
   on royalties, 125

U.S. Copyright Office
    compulsory licenses for copyrighted music, 84–85
    copyright registration records of, 58
    copyright search by, 27
    designated agent requirement for ISPs, 114–115
    digital first sale and, 48
    notice of intent to enforce copyright, 65
    notice of termination of rights in transfers/licenses, 73
    termination notice, 62
    transfer of copyright, 69–72
U.S. Postal Service, 32

V

Vault v. Quaid, 81
VHS format, 109
Vicarious infringement
    notable points, 181–182
    overview of, 89–90
Video clips, 83
Videocassette recorder (VCR), 109
Violations, of DMCA, 104–107
Visual artists rights
    copyright infringement, 87–88
    notable points, 174–175
    overview of, 44–46
Visual Artists Rights Acts (VARA)
    not applicable to work for hire, 30
    rights of attribution and integrity, 4–5
    visual artists rights under, 44–46

W

Wade, Roe v., 139
Waiver
    rights of attribution and integrity and, 5
    of VARA rights, 45
Ward, Thomas M., 71
Washington Post, 19
WATCH File: Writers, Artists, and Their Copyright Holders, The (United Kingdom), 196
Websites
    linking, legal issues of, 18–19
    noninfringement activities, 96
    resources for finding copyright owners/clearances, 195–196
Will
    termination of rights in transfers/licenses, 73
    transfer of copyright by, 69
WIPO Copyright Treaty
    as major treaty governing copyrights, 145
    notable points, 189
    rights with, 150–152
WIPO Performances and Phonograms Treaty, 150
Withdrawal, right of, 45
Work for hire
    copyright duration for, 58, 59
    overview of, 30
World Trade Organization (WTO), 153–154

Z

Zeidenberg, ProCD v., 81